How to Teach Your Dog to Talk

How to Teach Your Dog to Talk

125 easy-to-learn tricks guaranteed to
entertain both you and your pet

Captain Haggerty

GRAMERCY BOOKS
NEW YORK

This 2003 edition published by Gramercy Books, an imprint of Random
House Value Publishing, a division of Random House, Inc., New York, by
arrangement with Fireside, a division of Simon & Schuster, New York.

Gramercy is a registered trademark and the colophon is a trademark
of Random House, Inc.

Printed in the United States of America

Random House
New York • Toronto • London • Sydney • Auckland
www.randomhouse.com

Library of Congress Cataloging-in-Publication Data

Haggerty, Arthur J.
    How to teach your dog to talk : 125 easy-to-learn tricks guaranteed
to entertain both you and your pet / Captain Haggerty.
        p. cm.
    Originally published: New York : Simon & Schuster, 2000.
    ISBN 0-517-22221-3
        1. Dogs—Training. I. Title.

SF431.H2143 2003
636.7'0887—dc21

                                                2003044808

9 8 7 6 5 4 3 2

ACKNOWLEDGMENTS

There are so many people who generously gave of their time in doing this book that I don't know where to begin. This book has been sitting on a back burner for many years, and if it weren't for my agent, Noah Lukeman, it would not have gotten done. He showed me the money. I was blessed with a great editor, Betsy Radin-Herman, with readable handwriting. You may think that an editor's writing would be clear but the reverse is often true. Not so in Betsy's case, and you still owe me a lunch, Betsy. Betsy has an able assistant, Matt Walker. He did his job in an exemplary manner, but he broke my back doing it.

Some of the others I have to thank are Debbie-Lynn Bowden, Steve Diller, Bob Maida, Kate Weiner, Babette Haggerty-Brennan, Tom Philbin, Gordy Brennan, Norberto Martinez (of Martinez Armador Architects) and his lovely bride Brenda. Patt Healy, Esq., Ricki Lynsky and Jordan Heppner.

To cite the specific help that some people gave me, I'd have to start the list with one who gave me the most help: Betty Haggerty—for divorcing me. Tanya Lawlor, of PupPen PlayCare, West Vancouver, BC, Canada, was helpful in supplying suggestions on whisper, pick up toys, tissue/sneeze and bring messages. Trainer Karla Clinch was particularly helpful with the Paint trick. Georgia dog trainer Leah Spitzer helped with the

Stick Your Tongue Out trick. Paul Goldie, for being a good friend and great trainer, who has done over seventy-five productions of *Annie*. Trainer Jo Ann Hise of Roswell, NM, had some great suggestions for the Hold the Dustpan trick and Get the Cellular Phone When It Rings. Susan Muick, a very imaginative trainer, had a lot of suggestions on the following tricks: Get a Cold One, Bunny Hop, Go to Bed (which only gets her an honorable mention). Kathy Ahearn is the reason Susan only gets an honorable mention. Kathy taught that trick to Mug-Z, the first dog on David Letterman's "Stupid Pet Tricks," many years ago. I owe Kathy a great debt of thanks too. A very special thanks to a great trainer and good friend, Susan Zaretsky. Susan was always helpful, especially at the last minute when the chips were down, and she helped get final photos for the book through a New York blizzard.

The ones that really deserve the thanks—the ones that taught me the most—are Go-Go Burroughs, Chan, Satan, Windy, Mickey, Mambo, Tonto, Lisa, Molly, Muffin, Mr. Dog, Longhaired Duke, Ira, Lancer, Bambi, Sweet Pea and so many others. I miss 'em all. My eyes are clouding up now, so I cut the list short. Guys, you were the greatest teachers in the world!

This Book Is Dedicated

to a Great Team:

Frank Inn,
the Granddaddy of Trick Trainers,
and His Faithful K-9 Companion
Benji;

and to those no longer with us:
Carl Spitz,
who recognized early on the class and style of Frank Inn,

and
the very first dog on David Letterman's "Stupid Pet Tricks,"
Mug-Z—

Great People and Great Dogs.

CONTENTS

Contents

1
HOW TO TEACH YOUR DOG TO TALK

Do you want a dog with whom you can have a light conversa-tion over coffee? Or perhaps, during a quiet evening meal, you'd enjoy an in-depth debate on American foreign policy? Though you can certainly commune with your best friend now, you still lack the exciting give-and-take of a profound discussion of some arcane topic. Without the proper training, it's just not going to happen! Hey, even with the proper training you're not going to get that in-depth conversation. When you converse with your dog in a relaxed fashion, even if you're dead wrong, he'll still look at you with adoring eyes. This unquestioning adoration is the communication you'll receive from him. That's why dogs are better than people.

First of all, you need to understand that there's a difference between speaking and talking. It's easy to teach a dog to speak. You say *"Speak!"* and the dog barks. But I'm here to tell you how to get your dog to talk. To actually form words.

The theory is this: The reason the domestic dog barks—as opposed to wild dogs, which merely whine, whimper and howl—is because the dog is trying to mimic our speech. The Basenji, for instance, is a domesticated breed closer to the wild than most. These dogs are incapable of barking. Basenjis are so close to wild dogs that they, like the wild dog, come into season (estrus) only once a year. (The domestic dog normally comes into heat twice a year.) Interestingly, while this African breed is referred to as the "No-bark dog," I once trained one to speak (not talk) on command. With a little more time I'm sure I could have taught him to talk.

Talk? Why bother? Well, to be honest, it's mainly for *you*. But along the way, it helps you to understand and to bond with your dog. Any time I can assist someone to do that I want to sign up.

In contrast to the Basenji, breeds such as the Rottweiler, for example, are more vocal than others. In general, dogs with a high activity level are better at speaking. When selecting a breed for talking we are interested in three main factors: the dog's activity level, the predisposition to vocalize and the head type. The most important factors for success are your relationship with your dog and your willingness to work with your dog for short periods throughout the day. We're going to give your dog a lot of chances to mimic your speech.

Even if your dog's mimicry is off by a country mile, it's still an attempt to talk! The trick is to encourage any nondoglike sound. You encourage with praise, applause, touching, petting, cheering, clicking, jumping up and down, smiling, grinning and even aroma rewards to tell your prideful pooch how wonderfully he works. Food? What about food? Well, maybe food, but you know what your mother said about talking with your mouth full. We are cautious about stopping the sound, which happens when the dog eats.

The quality of your relationship with your dog depends upon how eager you are to interact with him. Being able to "read" your dog is crucial. Reading means understanding your dog's dog-ness as well as the ability to accurately interpret what he's thinking and trying to communicate to you. This communication, silent though it may be, profoundly helps in bonding and in understanding one another. You are continually communicating with your dog and he with you. Believe me, he will pay more attention to you than you do to him, so the more you pay attention to your dog, the greater your success. Communication is happening all the time. To put it simply, "Robert" reads your mind and you read his. He starts moving around, and you know it is time to take him out. Does your significant other know you as well as Robert? That is communication. Not talking, but communicating.

Dogs with a brachycephalic head (wide head, short muzzle), such as the Bulldog, Pit Bull or Bullmastiff, have a cavernous mouth, which produces rounder sounds. This is the preferred head type for talking dogs. The best brachycephalic choice of all is the Rottweiler. This breed, as I've said, while more inclined to vocalize than other breeds, doesn't have a high energy level.

Trail hounds, such as Foxhounds, Coonhounds and Beagles, have been bred to "give tongue" while they work. For this reason they too are more vocal than many other breeds. The sound they make is vocally different from the previously mentioned breeds' and includes howling. Hounds were originally bred as pack dogs and were not meant for the household. Their propensity to bark and howl presented little problem because they were kenneled so far from their masters. In any event, nobody thought to breed for a quieter hound dog, because a nosier dog was easier to follow on the trail. Even now, hound-dog men cherish the "mountain music" of their dogs hot on a scent.

An indoor dog is the best choice for talk training. As you'll see, once I describe the training program, having your dog with you as frequently as possible helps a great deal.

Northern breeds, such as the Siberian Husky, Malamute and Samoyed, are more inclined to howling, though it's of a different type from the trail hounds'. Howling is difficult to control but relatively easy to start—particularly with the northern breeds and the trail hounds. These tendencies offer a great deal of raw talent with which to work.

Terriers, as a group, have a high activity level and for this reason can make excellent candidates. In the final analysis, there are numerous combinations of factors that enable a dog to talk, and this means that your dog can probably talk too.

Getting Started

Let's start off with the assumption that your dog Robert is never going to carry on a conversation with you regarding the President's foreign policies. Even one word would be an accomplishment. Two or three words would be a major accomplishment. I'll guarantee you that you'll have the only dog on your block who talks. Heck, in your neighborhood! I've done a lot of jawing so far, and it's time I started you on one trick. We'll start slow and begin by teaching Robert to speak; talking will come later.

Put Robert in a harness or nonslip collar and tie his leash to a stationary object. Stand three or four feet away from him with some scrumptious tidbits in your right hand and with your index finger raised. That is the hand signal to speak. Call Robert's name. Excite and frustrate him. He wants to come to you. The split second he makes any sound, toss him a treat, tell him what a great dog he is and go up and ruffle his fur. Move away and repeat—only this time you're going to enthusiastically use the word "speak," calling to him and using his name. The first sound from him gets a treat and the same praise and petting as before. The next time, we want a little bit more of a bark. Repeat these steps until either six minutes has elapsed, or you've gotten eight barks (two barks in quick sequence before a reward count as one). You should have more sessions on successive days and demand a little more each time out (but more on that subject in chapter 8, section 2).

Remember: I'm not promising you a rose garden. Training isn't easy, and if you're interested in teaching Robert to talk, you must be prepared to work at it. Six hours a day, seven days a week? No, better twenty-minute sessions throughout the day, seven days a week. Build up to the twenty minutes in two-minute increments. Really short sessions throughout the day help the dog maintain interest.

Keep in mind that, initially, we're going to take what we can get. Any sound is fodder for the talk trick. Any time you hear Robert make a unique sound, encourage and reward him. *Sem-*

per paratus: always be prepared to reward your dog's mumblings! Should he start to make actual, distinct sounds, read chapters 5, 6 and 7 of this book *immediately!* We want to avoid using a food reward in our speak-training method, because not only is your dog too polite to talk with his mouth full, he *can't* talk with food in his mouth. Reward is crucial to training success; you just have to know how to pair the right kind of reward to the trick.

A down-on-his-luck man and a little terrier walked into a seedy bar. The bartender told the man that dogs were not allowed in the bar. The man explained that Spike was a very special dog because he could talk. When the bartender demanded to see this amazing trick, the man countered with a request for a free drink if Spike actually talked. The bartender agreed, and the following conversation ensued:

"Spike, what is this building covered with?" asked the man.

"Roof!" answered Spike.

"Get out of here!" ordered the burly bartender.

"No, no, give him another chance," said the man. "What is the texture of sandpaper?"

"Rough!" answered Spike

"Out, out!"

"No! No! Give him another chance," pled the man. "Spike, who was the greatest ballplayer of all time?"

"Ruuuth!" was Spike's prompt reply.

The bartender came out from behind the bar, gripping a baseball bat, and chased man and dog out of his establishment.

With his hands in his pockets and his head hung low, the man slowly walked away with Spike by his side.

Spike looked up at him and said, "What's the matter, boss? Should I have said DiMaggio?"

There's a point to this joke. In fact, there are three points. First and foremost, getting the "th" sound in the word Ruth. It's not going to happen. Dogs cannot make the "th" sound. There are virtually no sounds that dogs make in the same way that we do. So we must aim for approximations.

Point two is that your command (question) produces the *in-*

terpretation of the dog's response. There are two ways to handle your talking dog. One is to ask Robert to say something specific, such as "water." The other method is to ask him a question in the way our down-trodden drinker did. The latter is preferred from a presentation point of view; *but* if you merely ask what he wants, and Robert says "wa-wa," it ain't gonna fly. A better question to ask is, "Would you rather have a beer or water?" Believe me, he's never going to answer, "I'd rather have a very dry martini—mixed eight to one—with a twist."

Point three is to remember that a single bark sound can be interpreted to mean more than one thing. This trick requires a lot of flexibility, as you will see when we start working with your dog. Spike's "Ruuuff!" meant three different things because of the various questions posed.

Some Philosophy

I don't want to mislead you. As I announced at the beginning of this chapter, you're not going to be able to carry on a long conversation with your dog. If you're diligent, you'll get a few words. Let's hope they'll be at least two syllables each and not the one-syllable texture of sandpaper.

A word is not a word until it has meaning to both the one who utters it and the one who hears it. This is a good definition, but I'm not going to promise you that the words your dog speaks will have meaning for him. Have you ever heard someone singing the words of a song in a language she doesn't know? It would be better if she spoke the language, but many singers are able to learn the words phonetically. Is she still singing words? Let's not worry too much about my definition of words. You can certainly put together a routine that everyone enjoys without going on a long philosophical journey in attempting to give the words meaning to both parties.

To fulfill my previous definition of words, we have to get the dog to ask for something he wants. Let me give you an example: Your dog goes to the door and barks to be let out. We want to change that "ruff" sound to "out." Though there will be a problem with the *t* on the end of "out," this trick would certainly fit my definition. (Check chapter 2 for the way to approximate the *t*.) "Mama" (ma-ma) is probably the word most frequently "spoken" by dogs. The most common early command for that word is also *"mama!" ("Say Mama!").* When you have Robert going really well, you can gradually change the command to a question: "Who am I?" If you are male and don't want to dress up in drag for Robert's show-business career, a different question might be, "Who do you love more?" It's a question that he'll learn. The two easiest two-syllable "words" for a dog to make are "mama" and "water" (wa-wa), but I wouldn't give water full points.

Now, even if your dog said "I wan owwb" for a piece of food or other reward rather than because he wanted to go out, I would say you'd accomplished a great deal. You have a *complete* sentence, which is much harder to attain than one or two sounds. While it still lacks the intention of wanting to go out, it's a full sentence!

$1,000 Reward

There's a $1,000 reward for the first owner who trains his dog to say an entire sentence after reading this book. The contest will be terminated four months after the claim is first made. During this four-month period, other people can claim the prize. The dog that shows the greatest ability to talk will win the $1,000. The author will have the final say as to which dog and owner win the prize. The author can request a "bark off" to determine the winner. Should the author feel that a bark off is necessary, transportation for dog and owner will be paid for residents of and people departing from North America (U.S., Canada and Mexico). The talk must be in English. (Sorry!) Honorable mention will be awarded to any dog that recites the "nose" speech by Cyrano in French or can read anything by Cervantes in Spanish. Preliminary selection will be made in a fashion to be determined by the author. The cost incurred for the preliminary selection will be borne by the owner of the dog and will probably require a videotape.

Singing ain't talking, but Pavarotti makes more money than a monologist does. Should you get a singing sound, don't discourage your dog. Jump forward to the second chapter of this book, and read "Seize the Opportunity" in chapter 8. Then read chapter 3, "Sing, Sing, Sing," before coming back here. We give you choices and options in this book. We also give you ways to maximize your dog's talent while minimizing your effort.

2
MAKING THOSE SOUNDS

High-frequency sounds will cause a dog to howl, particularly the northern breeds. One way to create those high-pitched sounds is to buy a used fire engine (there is a market in used fire engines) and park it in your backyard. That siren will get most of the dogs in the neighborhood to howl. Put *"Howl!"* on command. Once your dog starts howling it is easy to maintain that howling, particularly when the dog's ears are stimulated by high-pitched sounds. If you have neither the money nor the space for a fire engine, there are all sorts of other possibilities. Keep your eyes and ears open. It might be a certain song, your own high-pitched whining, another dog's whining, or any of a wide assortment of whistles, sirens, bells and chimes. A synthesizer is a good bet to give you a wide range of tones. One of the best is the Synclavier, an excellent product that produces a wide range of sounds to tickle your dog's ear canals. Before you rush out to get a Synclavier, be aware of two things. The manufacturer of this brand went out of business, and the prices of used items start at about $35,000. A simple synthesizer that runs $400 or $500 is in a more practical price range but still too high. This type of equipment will give you control over generating the exact sound needed. That exactness can cause your dog to create a couple of different sounds to match the equipment.

The so-called silent dog whistles normally will not encourage a dog to howl.

Once your dog starts howling, we have to control that howling. Putting it on command helps control when the sound is produced. *Do not* put too much control on the sounds themselves. Better too noisy than too quiet. We can always slow your dog down but not always work him up. We want to get other sounds along with the howling. There's whining, growling and barking. Barking can include a number of different sounds, and this is what we want to concentrate on. Encourage, encourage, encourage. But do not use food to reward a barking dog. He can't bark and eat. His mother told him never to talk with his mouth full. Get as much variety in the barking as possible. Let him know you enjoy his barking. Let him see you flip over any unusual sounds. Even if you feel you can't use them, praise your dog. You may be able to use them later. Truncate the barks after they are flowing freely, but do not do it early on. Better too much jabbering than too little. Start working on changes in sound. Let your dog know when he is doing well, and put a label on each sound. Give it a name or command that will help both you and your dog keep track of what you are doing to produce that sound. Bear in mind that you have the option of changing the command once it is learned. In most cases you will have a single sound to work on. Should you be lucky enough to get two or three sounds at the same time you do not want to lose any of them. Let me give you an example. You start getting Robert excited and he gives a little whine. Reward! The reward further excites Robert and you get another whine, immediately followed by low "woof." Reward! We now have two different sounds given in rapid succession. At this point absolutely no attempt will be made to reduce or eliminate a sound. We're trying to get as much as we can. Perhaps you'll get a sequence of whines followed by woofs. The whine sounds like "why" and the woofs sound like "hoof." Start to put the appropriate label on each of these sounds, but make your pronunciation of the sounds similar to the sound Robert produces. The best sequence to follow is to precede Robert's whine with *"Why!"* but if you are unable to do that, then use the *"Why!"* command *after* his whine. If the whine and woof come close together, that may be difficult. Give it your best shot. As you get to know your dog you will be able to tell what Robert is getting ready to say. His body English is different before the "why" and the "hoof" and it is your job to learn those subtleties. Suddenly Robert surprises you! He adds a "growf" to his sequence. Don't stop him! Encourage him! Let's call this *"Grow!"* Three words. We're on a roll. Don't rush into separating them. Concentrate on teaching the names of these words. When you are rocking and rolling on these words in sequence, then it is time to gently try to separate them. A soft hand on the muzzle will stop the progression to the next word. This is how to isolate the words and have them delivered separately. Remember we still have the ability to rename these words. At this point we don't even know how we are going to use them.

The Sounds

The "easy" letters/sounds are *a, e, g, h, i, l, o, r, u, w, x, y* and *z*—half the alphabet, a barker's dozen, one more than the Hawaiian alphabet's twelve letters. Actually, the "easy" letters aren't that easy; and the hard (to impossible) letters, then, are *b, c, d, f, j, k, m, n, p, q, s, t* and *v*.

Letters by themselves are not sounds, but we generally identify sounds with letters, so we will keep it simple and show you how to get the letter sound. Most sounds will be caught, or captured, sounds. The "alphabet" that follows will explain to you how to create these sounds with your dog if you are unable to capture them. The difference between capturing and creating is that in the former, your dog for some reason makes a sound that you mark, or capture, with a clicker or some other device. Creating a sound calls for some trick you use to get the dog to start to make the sound.

Once your dog *starts* to make the sound you can cut it off by *gently* holding his mouth shut with your hand.

• • •

A can be long or short. Always go for the longer sound because it is easier to cut back on a longer sound than extend a shorter one. The *a* can be created from the start of a bark, when the dog is getting up his energy to bark.

E can also be long or short and develops from the beginning or end of a bark.

G can either be a soft *g* as in Gerard, or a hard *g* as in garden. We can duplicate the hard *g* working from the Giggle Gaggle trick in chapter 9. Positioning in the Giggle Gaggle trick is with the back of the dog's head flat on the ground. Look down the dog's throat, which should be open, permitting you to see down the opening of the esophagus, or food passage. (If the head is tilted too far back, the esophagus is covered by the rolled-over tongue. Use that for the letter *l.)* Keep positioning the dog so he repeats the *g* after you give "G!" as a command, over and over again. The reward is vigorous tummy tickling. Breeds such as Boston Terriers, French Bulldogs and Pekingese work well on learning the difficult hard *g* sound through the Giggle Gaggle trick. Get the dog on his back and tickle his tummy to produce more *g*s than a supersonic jet fighter. Over a period of weeks you will have the dog produce the *g* in a number of different body positions, moving from the Giggle Gaggle position to the Dead Dog position on through the sitting position.

H can be started when the dog gets ready to bark. Cut him off before he puts out a full bark. You can cut him off by moving swiftly (but not forcefully) forward and *gently* grasping his muzzle shut as mentioned previously. Do not start doing this refinement until after the dog has a Ph.D. in barking.

I, like *e,* can be long or short, and produced at the beginning or the end of a bark. There is a difference in the sounds, and although they are close enough to be used interchangeably, you should at least attempt to differentiate the *e* from the *i.*

L can also be started from the On Your Back position (chapter 22). You have to look down into the dog's mouth to see if the dog's tongue is touching the roof of his mouth. Use a lot of praise and say *"L!"* when that tongue is up there. The position of the head has to be farther back than in teaching him to make the *g* sound. You can accomplish this with a small pillow or a rolled up sweater placed under the back of the dog's neck. As the dog successfully makes the *l* sound on his back, keep practicing. Slowly attempt to move him to the Dead Dog position as he continues to make the *l* sound. As you are moving the dog around, he may "lose" the *l*. In other words the changing of the body position causes the gravity advantage to shift, thus requiring the dog to use his tongue to do more of the work. Simply go back to the previous position. Have him duplicate the *l* sound and *slowly* change the body position. This is going to take many weeks, if not months, of constant work. It cannot be done in days. The progression from the Dead Dog position is to the Down, and to the Sit positions. Needless to say, as you are moving your dog into the various positions, have him make the *l* sound and use *"L!"* as the command.

O can be done very nicely at the beginning of a howl. The end of a howl also works, but the sound is not as accurate. Foxhounds, Harriers, Petits Bassets Griffons Vendeens and Basset Hounds excel at this.

R can be created at the beginning of a growl. If the growl starts low enough, the *g* will hardly be noticed. Get as much roll on the *r* as a Scot would. We can always cut it back.

U is quite a bit the same as *o* and can grow out of a howl. Coonhounds, Bloodhounds and Beagles excel at this.

W may seem incongruous, but it is actually a common sound produced by some dogs. "Wa-wa" is generally their first word, if you're lucky, for water. They will look at you with their muzzle elevated twenty to twenty-five degrees from the horizontal. The breeds that are best for this are the Field Spaniels, the Sussex Spaniels and older English Springer Spaniels.

X is a rarely used letter that can be taught at the beginning of a bark, particularly if the dog has just eaten or had a snack. A particle of food in the dog's throat can cause a slight hacking.

Y takes on a few different sounds similar to *e, i* and *w.* Your choice!

Z could be taught while the dog is sleeping. He, of course, would never learn when he is sleeping. He's busy chasing rabbits. The dog's snoring originates in the lungs. This sound can be created at the end of some barks, especially if he has just completed a vigorous barking session and is calming down.

Now for some of those difficult (impossible) sounds.

B, d, p, t and the "th" sound can be approximated with the same truncated popping sound. Attempt to cut off any sound swift as lightning and you should have that approximation. C, s and v can very roughly sound correct if you follow the remarks for the letter z. You can come up with a poor approximation of the letters k and q if you read the notes on letter x.

A slightly undershot bite, as found in Affenpinschers, Boxers and Brussels Griffons, is great for the difficult to duplicate "f" sound.

3

SING, SING, SING:
THE SOUND OF MUSIC AND OTHER SOUNDS

Some dogs are musically inclined. Someone out there will have the singingest dog in the world, and we want to foster that dog's career. Give your dog a chance to sing along with you. Different sounds in music can also push your dog to talk. You have to test your canine. Expose him to the classics. Expose him to the greats. The King: Elvis. The Duke: Ellington. Old Blue Eyes: Frank.

What we are looking for is a dog that howls and/or barks when he hears certain music. The main purpose is to teach your dog to say words. In the first chapter we gave a quick introduction to getting your dog to bark. That was to get him started. You can get him to bark by telling him to *"Speak!"* In the second chapter we covered the way to get him to form certain sounds and letters. These two techniques are at either end of the continuum of getting your dog to verbalize. This will work from the simple barking that gets him started, to the more complex and drawn-out technique of forming letters. A better approach lies somewhere in between. That "in between" can very well be music. It cues the dog to bark and has him form a wider variety of sounds with less work on your part. A number of high-pitched sound sources have been mentioned to start your dog barking, and some music carries the appropriate (to your dog) sounds.

Howling is one way to start your dog vocalizing. If you want your dog to sing, it is an even better approach. Here the Shetland Sheepdog Puddleduck is pursing lips in response to the *"Howl!"* command.

Music soothes the savage beast, and high-pitched sound starts him barking and howling. Let's get music that doesn't soothe him, but gets him up and ready to rock and roll. Most

Puddleduck Zaretsky moves her head upward as she approaches the howling position.

Puddleduck emits a full howl. The Sheltie was trained by Susan Zaretsky of Newburgh, NY.

owners discover this by accident. Make note of the type of music and the title, along with the artist and the recording. You *must* find out the *actual* recording. Call the radio station in pursuit of that information if necessary. They will give that info if you call promptly. Three weeks later you are not going to get the answer. Work on that one song with a great deal of praise and rewards for your dog. Make sure you do not overwork your dog. If he starts to flag, tire or lose interest, stop playing the music. You want him fresh. Experiment with different music. Our main purpose is to get him to use different sounds. We have over 150 tricks in this book, why shouldn't your dog learn to sing too?

The better your sound system the more likely your dog is to respond to various sounds. You cannot carry a ninety-eight-piece orchestra with you. Go for a high-end sound system, which you will attempt to downgrade. A ghetto blaster is not as easy to carry as a small pocket tape player. As you downgrade, make sure your dog shows the same enthusiasm, or move back to the upscale equipment.

4
MOTIVATING YOUR DOG

Ahhh! Motivating your dog. That is what it is all about. In the following chapters there are different pointers for motivating your dog. Trick training is highly motivational, and an understanding of motivation will enable you to not only enjoy the work (it's not really work) but to help your dog to enjoy training and performing. Some techniques may seem contradictory, but as you read on it will all come together.

Food reward, praise, petting, scratching and other positive methods are in the back of everyone's mind. They are all good. There are some other, less well known techniques that motivate your dog to the max.

Training books do not address the self-rewarding aspects of dog training. Different things motivate different dogs. Old-time trainers have often said that you can't "make" a dog do nose (scent) work. Teach a dog to use his nose and he is overjoyed. Once started, you can't stop him. U.S. Army scout dogs spend every waking hour using their noses. How is that possible? Dogs enjoy using their noses. Yet to some, it seems revolutionary that dogs can work for the sheer enjoyment of work.

You must let your dog know when he is doing things right. You also have to let him know when he is doing something wrong. A simple soft correction is the cautionary No! delivered in a calm tone of voice. It may be used when he is merely *thinking* about doing something wrong. Trick training is generally correction-free training, but you do need knowledge of corrections to use them properly, on the outside chance that you have to use one. You will probably use few or none at all. Generally, a verbal correction will suffice. The intensity of the correction is important. A perfect correction is neither too soft nor too hard. Animal behaviorists say that a single correction can solve a problem forever. This is not as important in trick training because you are always going to be standing by to guide your dog in doing the right thing and stop him from doing the wrong thing.

An excellent performance deserves an excellent reward. A *good* final exercise merits a reward. A *great* final exercise warrants a jackpot. A jackpot is an exceptional reward, such as more treats, more pats or more applause. Jackpots routinely given at the end of training sessions merely teach the dog that the session is over. A jackpot should not be automatically awarded at the end of a session. Motivate your dog to excel, not merely to finish the training session.

Caught, or captured, behavior is a behavior of opportunity. Your dog does something by surprise, and you immediately decide that here is a trick. Immediately reward your dog and give the behavior a name or command. Is that the way to teach tricks? Seizing the opportunity is not the single best approach, but it is up there. I hope this book gets you thinking so that you will be looking for those behaviors of opportunity and then seize that opportunity. I have even higher hopes for you: I hope that you will see your dog doing something you immediately realize you can make into a trick, put the behavior on command and develop it into a new trick that no one has thought about before. When you and your dog invent that great new trick, please write me about it for the sequel to this book.

The scientist Ivan Pavlov made a name for himself with the conditioned reflex. I contend there is a difference between the conditioned reflex and training. Pavlov rang the bell and fed the dogs. After a period of time he would ring the bell, and the dogs would salivate, a result for which he became famous. That is a conditioned reflex. I practice dog training as an art, not a science. The conditioned reflex is something the dog has no control over. He can't choose not to salivate. In training, the dog has a couple of options. He can do it, or he can refuse to do it. While the conditioned reflex is not pure training, it certainly can be used in training, especially if used by the artistic trainer. Incidentally, Pavlov didn't learn anything that dairy farmers, with cows letting down milk prior to milking, hadn't known for generations.

Frustration is an excellent device to motivate and build up your dog's enthusiasm. Should his performance be a bit slower than you prefer, but he enjoys doing the trick, simply give the command and hold him back, restrain him so that he is eager to perform. The minute you release him he will burst forward to do the job. The dog's struggle with self-control is another form of frustration that improves training on a number of levels. Simply give your dog a *"Sit-Stay!"* command and put a piece of food in front of him. He becomes frustrated as you repeat the stay, but as soon as you say *"Release!"* he explodes forward to grab his food reward. Not only does this frustration increase the dog's desire, but it also increases his self-control. Do this a few times and it will increase the speed of obedience to the preceding command to sit. It makes for more rapid performance.

Much invisible training is accomplished by having your dog hang out with you all the time (see chapter 8). If you can pay a little bit of attention to him, you can turn him into a Lassie, a Benji or a Rin-Tin-Tin. You integrate the training into your lifestyle—invisibly.

In the following chapters you will read about various techniques for teaching a dog tricks. They are all good and valid. Some happen to be better than others for teaching specific tricks. The techniques listed here for each trick are the ones that will get the idea across to the greater number of dogs, and their owners too. Occasionally more than one approach may be listed.

5
THE REWARDS

In trick training, positive reinforcement is, well, very positive.
If your dog does something right, you want to reward him. The
flip side of that is if he does something wrong, you want to correct him.

Reward good behavior. Do not reward bad behavior. That is
not a particularly profound rule, but there are those who are
unaware of it.

Do not be stingy with your rewards. Be generous.

Timing is everything! You must give the reward at that mil-
lisecond in time when it is most appropriate. No, not millisec-
ond, in the right nanosecond. No matter what the reward—the
correct timing increases its efficiency. Reading your dog and
knowing what is passing through his mind will make your timing even better, because you anticipate his actions. You deliver
the reward *as* the dog does the trick. The best way to develop
timing is by working with your dog.

Lure and reward, food reward and baiting may seem all the
same, but there are subtle differences. Lure and reward is leading a dog into performing an exercise. Raise food over your
dog's head, and as he elevates his head to watch the food, you
move it ever so slightly backward. In his attempt to keep his
eyes on the food, he sits, and you give him the food. Lure and

reward! Simple food reward is a bit different picture. We physically manipulate the dog into position (modeling), and as we guide his rump to the ground and say "*Sit!*" we pop a tidbit into his mouth. Food reward! Now we *don't* want the dog to sit. We have a show dog and we want him to remain poised in the stand position. The dog stares at the food with his ears up, looking every bit the Best in Show winner the owner feels he is. That rock-solid stance and alert look are because he is fixated on the bait. For instance a Black-and-Tan Coonhound is in hot pursuit at a water-dog race. He chases the caged raccoon into the water and up the tree and has the pleasure of barking at his tree-bound coon. Lure and reward! A Sealyham Terrier is doing a sit-stay as his owner places a cookie on the ground directly in front of him and repeats the "*Stay!*" command. The owner says "*Release!*" and the Sealy gobbles the cookie up. Food reward! A trainer with the need to get a Jack Russell Terrier's attention on a movie set whips out a crated mouse, and the dog's attention is riveted on the mouse. Baiting! We certainly are not going to feed the dog the bait. We'll save the mouse for another day! Food is not the answer to everything, although it is the most frequently used reward because it is easy to handle and easy to deliver to the dog's mouth.

You will be using secondary reinforcers, even if you are not aware of it. Secondary reinforcement is an additional "thing" that you do when training a dog. For example, if you are teaching your dog to Hold the Dustpan, you must have the dustpan handy, and you probably are in a room without a rug. It's also probably the room where you always practice holding the dustpan. When you actually use the exercise in everyday life, you will have a broom handy. The room, broom and dustpan are secondary reinforcers. In addition, always using the same room creates an area-specific trick. Usually when we are talking about secondary reinforcers we are talking about something planned, such as the use of a clicker. Just because a reinforcer is secondary doesn't mean that it is given after the command. It can be given before, after or during. Are secondary reinforcers good or bad? They are "bad" if you are not aware of them. They are "bad" if you insist that all these reinforcers be present simultaneously. Actually, it is not a matter of good or bad. They are just there, so be aware of them.

When your dog has performed so well that he deserves an added reward, a "jackpot" may be given. The jackpot should be given when the dog does one repetition better than his previous performances. If you have some food left over at the end of a training session and you give it to the dog, that is using the jackpot improperly. Giving a dog a cookie or a singular reward at the end of a training session doesn't teach the dog anything. It is merely a secondary reinforcement for terminating the session. It doesn't teach the dog that he did a good job over the whole training period. The timing is off. It may make you feel good, and of course the dog loves treats anyway, but he learns nothing.

You can use many and varied rewards. Do not fall into the trap of thinking that a brief success with one type of reward marries you to that reward for life. You also must bear in mind that your dog is an individual, and what is a great reward for him may be boring to another. Similarly, specific rewards work best with specific tricks. For example, the Food Refusal trick should not be immediately followed by a food reward. Rather, it should be followed by vigorous verbal praise or clicker, which is followed by energetic rubbing and *then* the food reward. The food should be different (and better) than the food he's refused. This is an example of multiple and varied rewards.

Speed, distance and time should all be taken into consideration in administering rewards. Your distance from your dog and the time it takes to deliver the reward influences the speed of your delivery of the reward. Using a verbal reward, or a sound reward, such as applause, can solve these problems.

As I said before, a caught behavior is behavior that occurs unexpectedly. At this point it is called a behavior because it hasn't been "taught" to the dog. Once he repeats the behavior on command it is a trick. Now, circumstances can be set up that will encourage the dog to perform a behavior. If you can identify these circumstances, you can set yourself up to teach your dog the trick. Catch behaviors whenever you can. An unusual behavior pattern can be made into an unusual trick. Use your imagination and let me know what tricks you and your dog "invent."

In the case of food reward, the one thing that many people fail to do is to wean the dog off the food reward. What? Never reward my dog again? No, but reduce the reward and throw in an occasional "Good boy!" When you were receiving on-the-job training you were told when you did a good job. But there is no one standing at your elbow now saying, "You did a great job addressing that envelope. I really thought that your speed in folding and putting that letter in the envelope was outstanding. Then when you tossed it in the out box without getting up from your seat, I was almost bowled over." Your dog doesn't need that either, although you are standing at his elbow. The pattern has been set for both you and your dog. Setting the pattern is simply doing it over and over again. Now, as mentioned previously, from the dog's point of view, the work itself is the reward. I would hope that you too enjoy your job.

6
THE FIVE SENSES, PLUS ONE

Rewards can take many forms, and you should try to use what your dog likes best. The need for rapid delivery of a reward may preclude you from delivering your dog's favorite reward. For these reasons you need to open yourself up to the variety of rewards that are out there. To discuss rewards intelligently let's review the five ways, plus one, you can reward your dog through the five senses:

TASTE: Food is a time-tested reward that has been used for dog work over the last seventeen millennia. A piece of cheese, a cookie, a dog biscuit or whatever your dog enjoys most. Please keep these treats small so that you do not satiate the dog. As great as food reward is, bear in mind that there are dogs that don't care much about food. I do not want you to starve the dog to get him interested in the food. That is a little bit mean. How would you feel if I forced you to skip a meal? (Of course, skipping a meal might do you some good! I know it would do a great deal for me.) Anyway, the sense of taste is more important than the actual food reward. There is a delay between the taste and that nice warm feeling as the food enters the dog's system. Next time you have dinner at a good restaurant I want you to review what is happening as you eat. First comes the *aroma* (which is tied in to your taste buds), then the *appearance,* the ambient *sounds,* the *texture,* the *taste,* and, last but not least, the food entering your digestive tract and journeying to your stomach. That is the "plus one" in the chapter title. That delayed warm glow preceded by other pleasurable events. The actual great feeling (and dogs and people do get a warm feeling when eating) doesn't occur immediately. I could even make a case that the waiter initiates the whole sequence of visual and auditory cues when he says, "Enjoy your trout, ma'am."

TOUCH: This is one of the most underrated of all rewards. Dogs will go to great lengths in order to be rubbed, scratched, petted and stroked. We all know what petting is, but we are going to teach you Petting 101. Many people forego petting, thinking that their dog prefers other methods of reward. Dogs are tactile animals, and there is more to petting than merely stroking the dog on the head. Dogs *love* to be touched, and I am going to tell you *how* to pet your dog.

As the sun rises in the morning, the "Pleasurable Touch" is there. What is the Pleasurable Touch? Let me give you a couple of examples so that you get a feel for it. Put your arm around your significant other. Just stand there and relax. You are both "leaning" into one another (unless you have just had a fight). No, not leaning, touching. Just barely touching. Enjoying one another's presence. You never think about the contact. It feels good. A dog-oriented example would be when a dog comes up and lays his head on your knee. It is a touch, a caress. It lacks the full weight of his head on your lap. I really love that! Should your dog doze off, the full weight of his head is on you. The full weight of the head isn't as pleasurable as that light touch but still wonderful. It is still pleasant but not quite as pleasurable as the gently touching head. I love that gently touching head!

Molding or modeling a dog into position is a standard training technique. It can be used for minor adjustments or teaching an entire exercise (although I would generally suggest that it not be used exclusively). It involves the slight pressure that is used to guide a dog's body into the desired position without feeling any resistance. The less experienced will feel resistance and back off, then attempt to recover by using more pressure. "Yo-yoing" ensues and the entire attempt collapses. The correct gradual pressure delivered rapidly produces compliance in a relaxed, happy manner. It is a flowing, seamless motion much like a Ginger Rogers–Fred Astaire dance routine. (Just remember this: Ginger Rogers did everything that Fred Astaire did, but backward and in heels.)

Not only must you know how to pet, but where to pet. I would also include scratching and massaging under this heading. One of the advantages of scratching is that you can more precisely deliver the pleasurable touch to an exact location. Interestingly, the spots that "Spot" has trouble reaching are generally the best pleasure points. Massaging can be done with your thumb and the middle and index fingers at the point of the dog's breastbone (prosternum). The "stop" (that position between the eyes) and the root of the tail are two places hard for the dog to reach, but great for you to scratch. Scratching is very relaxing and useful in calming down a dog and reducing stress. A pleasure point is not the same thing as a tickle point. Tickle points are the spots on the dog's body that, when scratched, cause a reflex action of moving one or both hindquarters. It is similar to the reflex action that occurs when the doctor hits your knee with a small rubber hammer, or to the Babinski reflex in babies, in which the big toe curls upward when the sole of the foot is tickled.

Remember, optimal pressure varies from breed to breed. We do not pet an Italian Greyhound in the same way we pet a Bull Terrier: two gentle strokes on the side of the Greyhound's muzzle as compared to the loud, thumping pats we give to the Terrier, between the shoulder and the rib cage. The pressure for each is breed appropriate and specific.

May the Force be with you!

HEARING: A simple "Goood boy!" can be helpful, but applause is one of my favorite rewards. I'd suggest that you use applause early in training, because once "Clarence" starts performing, and especially saying words, you will find his "conversation" punctuated by appreciative audience applause. The applause sound reward has two advantages: (a) rewarding your dog from a distance and (b) excellent timing of the reward. Perhaps the audience as a group is better than you in its timing. The jackpot payoff is there when Clarence does a great job.

Verbal praise is easily controlled and varied to express emotion. A good trick is to carry on a conversation with Clarence. That puts the element of truth into your reward. You will be elated with his performance success, and it will be revealed in your tone of voice. You will feel it and so will Clarence. The tone of voice can't lie.

The clicker is an excellent example of a sound reward. One of the advantages of the clicker seems to contradict the advantage of the previously mentioned verbal praise: It gives a uniform *mark* of correct behavior. As a marker it is great, but we are talking (and I mean talking) about a *reward*. Still, the clicker's unique, characteristic sound is attractive to a dog, and with a bit of effort it can be delivered in a timely fashion. The advantage of voice over the clicker is that it can deliver a longer and nondistracting reward. More on clickers later!

SIGHT: Your joy at Clarence's performance lights up your face, and he will react to that. Jumping up and down and clapping your hands are other visual signals that demonstrate your pleasure and encourage Clarence. An interesting aspect of sight rewards is that your movement also becomes a secondary reward, delivered when Clarence sees your body motion and facial expression. These are subliminal sensory cues, which are great for a mind-reading act. Showing Clarence a food reward is a sight reward. Movement of your body into a preparatory petting position is another sight reward.

SMELL: This is at the bottom of the list because it is the least desirable. It is so because of the problem with delivering a smell reward rapidly enough. It can and should be used as a secondary reward. For example, as you deliver a food reward, there will be a secondary smell reward. The dog's sense of smell, in comparison to humans', is most highly developed. Now, this is different from the reward the dog receives from doing scent work. As pointed out in the previous chapter, dogs *love* to work. They also love to use their noses. The work is the reward. Most dogs do not have the opportunity to be trained to do scent work.

A word about squalene. Squa . . . what? It is an odorless, colorless liquid that dogs go bonkers over. They can smell it even if we can't, and they love the smell and taste. But what is it? It is taken from the livers of deep-sea sharks, which live six thousand feet under the ocean. The livers of these sharks comprise over 25 percent of their body weight. Squalene, incidentally, is said to be a miraculous cure-all for all sorts of maladies. We are not interested in its cure-all abilities but in getting your dog to use his nose. Use this for the rare laggard who doesn't want to use his proboscis.

You can also use it for cheating a little bit. Start using the squalene to get the dog motivated to use his nose. Take an item such as an odd piece of plastic or an empty small plastic pop bottle. Put a dab of squalene on the plastic and throw the object on the floor. Let your dog smell and taste it as you click. This presents a combination of smell, sound and taste—but mostly smell. Here is the proof that rewards are not separate and apart from one another. That does not mean that you can't use one without the other. *All* of the rewards can be used interchangeably, separate, together and in as many combinations as possible.

Wrapped up in any training program is communication. In this book you will get all sorts of "languages" in which to communicate with your dog. You are twelve feet away from Clarence when he performs well. You jump up and down with glee (sight); you applaud (sight and sound). Laugh and cheer (sound and sight), move toward Clarence (sight) and use both hands to vigorously rub and scratch his sides (touch). You show a tidbit to him (sight). You are continually carrying on a conversation with Clarence, telling him how wonderful and brilliant he is (hearing). As you slip the food into his mouth (taste), he receives a secondary cue of smelling the food (smell) and another secondary reward (the plus one, the eating, consuming). A really great reward! There is also touch in the texture of the food. Do not forget food texture. When you sit down for a good meal you subliminally revel in the texture of the food that you are munching on. Most of the time dogs simply gobble food down, but the texture is important to them also. Is your dog a gourmet or a gourmand?

The food reward is a flowing, continuous reward that pleasures Clarence. If you wonder whether the plus one—the actual consuming and the warm feeling it generates within the dog's body—is too late in coming, I want to thank you. Thank you for thinking. Yes, it is true the period of time elapsed is too long for good timing. The delay, however, was *bridged* by all the previous rewards.

7
CLICKER TRAINING

A clicker is a little toy that clicks. You've seen them. You've played with them. You've clicked them. Often they had a frog or cricket punch-pressed on the top. Circle your thumb and forefinger. They are about that size. The old-fashioned clicker, or cricket, is still useful but it is not as substantial as the ones that are being used for training dogs. Clickers are great! Their versatility is made for trick training. The clicker has a unique sound that interests the dog. Its uniqueness means that your dog is not going to come in contact with the sound under normal circumstances. With all the hoopla about the revolutionary changes in dog training there is only one revolutionary area. Clicker training! Though the clicker itself is not new there are continually developing new and improved methods for cashing in on the clicker revolution. The beauty of the clicker revolution is that people are continually losing them. Invest in a clicker factory! Clicker manufacturing is a growth industry. There is a growing mass of people out there adding to variations in the use of clickers. These people are "learning theory" oriented, and that is good. The learning theory, terms and explanation used in this chapter are not confined to clicker training. They apply to all areas of training. For this reason alone I would suggest everyone read this chapter twice. Read it even if you want to use the more traditional methods. It will help broaden your dog's repertoire of tricks and your understanding of dog training.

The explanation in this chapter will be of "pure" clicker training. The explanation of the use of the clicker in various tricks later in this book will not be pure. You'll be shown the shortcuts.

There is a growing mountain of information on clicker training. Once you start working with the clicker, if you find it turns you on, I suggest that you pursue it further. The seminal works of Karen Pryor or Gary Wilkes are highly recommended as further reading. Their writings are designed to explain, rather than an attempt to impress the reader with their erudition.

Now to the fun part. Sit on the floor with your dog with a bunch of small treats in one hand and the clicker in the other. You want to tie the click in with the food reward. You're now going to simply click and treat. One click for one treat. At this point the dog doesn't have to do anything. We are conditioning the dog and, more important, training you. Pay attention to your dog. That is your job. Get those treats out there as fast as possible but only after a response to the clicker. Let him mosey around. Let him sniff. When he starts to get distracted, click and treat to his response. There should not be massive distractions in the room when you are teaching the clicker. Not fourteen kids opening Christmas presents under the tree. Click and treat for five minutes and knock off for the day. The next day take him into a different room in the house. Once you start, you are going to find that he becomes focused on the food in hand. Your training is as important as his. While you have the food in one hand and the clicker in the other, move toward learning to hold both in the same hand. Select a convenient pocket or pouch to put the food in. Do not let your dog see where you are getting the food. He'll figure it out because his nose is smarter than you are, but do not let him sniff or get any food directly from your pocket or pouch. He can sniff the clicker. He can sniff your hand, but when he sniffs your pocket, ignore him and walk away. That break in being focused on the food in your pocket may cause him to wander off. Click and treat. As far as your training goes, you are learning how to sneak the treats out of your pocket and hold two or three treats in your hand. If the dog is investigating your hand without you having clicked, get up and move away. If you have no treats in your hand, let your dog sniff but do not praise or encourage him in any way. Do this for about seven minutes and again knock off for the day.

At this point we have accomplished a number of things. (1) You, hopefully, are paying more attention to your dog's reactions and have learned to quickly give the treat after clicking. (2) You are learning to handle, manipulate and give the food. (3) Your response time to your dog's actions has accelerated. (4) Your dog immediately comes over to you every time he hears the clicker.

The third day's training can be accomplished outdoors if you have a safe, secure training area. Outdoor distractions are different from indoor distractions. Do not gratuitously give a treat this time. Now your dog has to work for it. At this point the work is simple. Respond to the clicker. We are not in a "training" mode yet. We are teaching the dog to respond to the clicker. If your dog comes up to you and paws you, do not give a treat unless you want to teach the pawing trick. The click should always precede the reward at this point in training.

Now let's do invisible clicker training. When you prepare to feed your dog dinner you can click. A better approach would be to tell him to sit. Click as he sits and immediately put the food down.

The rapid putting down of the food is done in the beginning stages, but a delay should be added (and increased) as the training progresses. The best rule of thumb is not to give a food reward unless your dog has done something right. Make him work for it. Hold the food over his head and say *"Sit!"* As he sits, click and treat. Tell him *"Stay!"* which he already knows, and put the food down. In less than a second, you tell him *"Release!"* as you snap your fingers and click, and the food is the treat. Don't worry about only having two hands. We'll work on that later.

There are many reasons to use the clicker. Sometimes the reasons seem contradictory, but with a bit of reflection you'll see that they are not. The uses and advantages of a clicker are:

1. To mark good behavior.
2. To advise your dog that a reward is coming shortly.
3. As a reward for good behavior.
4. To reward at a distance.
5. To aid in shaping.
6. Because it becomes a secondary reinforcer.
7. Because it becomes a reward.
8. Because it works well with a "target stick."
9. Because it improves *your* timing.

How Much Food Reward to Use?

You will find constant reference to food reward in this chapter. As I mentioned earlier, some dogs are just not interested in food. What do you do, starve them? Of course not! You can try more delectable treats *or* another reward. A ball, a toy, a good rubbing are all alternative rewards. But food is the most frequently used and just about the easiest to use, so we will use it throughout this chapter.

What Is Shaping?

Shaping is developing a behavior pattern via the immediate reward of the slightest of movements in the correct direction. "Successful approximations" is another term that is thrown around. In other words, if I can get you moving in the right direction and keep you moving in the right direction, I can get you to reach your goal. The standards are raised as "Jimminy" progresses toward completing the trick. Shaping can be related to the child's game of Hot and Cold. As you get closer to the goal you are told "hot" and if you move farther away, "cold." The slightest movement in the correct direction is rewarded (clicked). Shaping requires preplanning and forethought. You want to break the behavior down to its smallest increment and build on that. Determining that smallest increment and planning it is a problem that people have. This is not a caught behavior. It is developed. (Always keep caught behaviors in the back of your mind.) I digress! And I want you to digress if, instead of permitting you to shape the behavior, Jimminy takes charge and says, "I'd rather do this!" If you want a versatile dog, see where Jimminy is going.

Let's say we want to teach Jimminy to back up. Incidentally, the best place to teach this command is in a hallway, restricting Jimminy's side movement. He is standing facing you and you tell him "*Back!*" Jimminy moves his right forequarter ever so slightly back, and you click and treat. You take half a step forward, give the hand signal for back. (The hand signal for "*Back!*" is the hands at waist height with your wrists bent and the hands hanging down with their backs facing the dog. A shooing motion is made.) We are giving a lot of information to Jimminy. We are giving him a verbal signal, two hand signals and a body signal (which forces him backward). Tell him "*Back!*" again, and the split second he moves one of his feet back, click and toss a food reward. Throw in the command "*Catch!*" You are shaping the behavior one step at a time, but you are not using pure clicker training. By constantly giving him additional information as well as encouragement and rewards, we will accomplish your mission more rapidly. Excellent timing with a clicker is extremely important for maximum results.

The click as an additional reinforcer can be delivered more quickly than the food. Step by step we move Jimminy backward and click. That is shaping the trick. Now raise your standards. A slight movement receives no click. You want more backward movement. As the dog learns, he will automatically give you a greater backward movement. You will "demand" a better movement by withholding the click. An interesting facet of clicker training is that Jimminy is often in charge. If on a roll, Jimminy will offer you off-the-wall behaviors. He is trying to persuade you to click the clicker. He is asking, "What about this?" "Do you like that?" "Please click this, that and the other thing!" Traditional trainers will tell you that is a bad thing. You have to be in charge at all times, they say. There is truth in these claims, but not absolute truth. Keep your eyes open for that unusual movement on Jimminy's part and catch the behavior. Don't worry about Jimminy controlling the situation. Once the behavior is caught, begin to shape it into a new trick. If you are working with a dog that has a fair amount of free-flowing clicker training, you will find a dog that will offer "strange" behaviors. The more you frustrate the dog, the better he gets. "Hey, boss whadda ya want?" He is trying to help you solve the problem by offering different behaviors. "Hey, do you want this? Or this? Whaddabout this? Ya like this?" Your dog keeps offering you behaviors "you can't refuse." Click them! You never can tell where it will lead.

Note: Behaviorists will tell you to teach the exercise before clicking. This is "operant conditioning." Clicker people prefer that you just treat and click at the same time, thus keeping the clicker training pure. Neither is correct. As you can see in the above example, you gave the dog a maximum amount of information while incorporating additional techniques. Be generous with your rewards. Be generous in giving him signals too. Some dogs respond better to one type of signal than to another. That is one of the beauties of clicker training. It is a distinct and additional signal. If you learn nothing else from this book than to use many and varied techniques, I will have done my job.

Chaining

Chaining is similar to shaping, but with one important difference. Chaining is the act of taking completed tricks and attaching them to one another in a proper sequence. In chapter 11, you will find individual tricks chained together: taking the outgoing mail, carrying it to the mailbox, paws up, opening the mailbox door, picking up and inserting the letters in the mailbox, dropping the mail, shutting the mailbox door and putting the flag or arm up. Each one of the smaller individual tricks could be shown off. Chained together they make one great, big, impressive trick.

With shaping it is a slight movement that is developed into a completed trick. Rather than attaching it to a completed trick, it *grows* into a different completed movement. The High Five requires the dog to raise his paw quite high. In shaping, we reward gradual improvement (elevation) in raising the paw. Our goal is to get it higher and higher.

Let's use a human parallel to describe shaping. A photographer tells his model, "Turn your head to the left. That's it. Now elevate your eyes, not your head, just move your eyes up. Good. Just a little bit more. That's right! That's good! Don't move your head, but bring your open right hand just below your throat. Perfect. Don't move!" A flash lets the model know the picture has been taken. That is the idea. Minor adjustments approaching your ideal. Of course, the above example is designed for a single picture and not to train the model to assume that position. You can't talk to your dog the way a photographer does, but you can *communicate* what you want. The photographer shaped the model into the correct position. Our job is to shape the *behavior.*

Chaining tricks together takes a good trick and turns it into a better one. This book wants to get you showing off as soon as possible. At the same time, you can be working on other tricks that you will eventually chain to that first trick. Before you know it, you have a routine!

Back Chaining

Back chaining is a rule of thumb, not a rule of law. It is a good idea, and it certainly works. Here's how it works: You start with the last component of the trick first and move backward to the front of the trick. In the previously mentioned Post the Mail trick, following this dictum would have us teaching raising the mailbox arm first. No way! Teach the retrieve trick first. That is a basic trick you can use in countless other tricks. Is back chaining learning theory? Sure! It applies to humans too. A good actor will often memorize lines by breaking them down into the components and learning the last component first. Try that on any memorizing task you have. Was the above-mentioned Post the Mail trick back chained? No, it was built upon. Putting the arm up was the last trick worked on. It was the frosting on the cake, and everyone knows you bake the cake and let it sit before putting the frosting on it. If you back chained a cake, you would wind up with a colorful glob on the plate. A sweet-tasting glob, but a glob nonetheless. Remember the rule of thumb, but know it is not set in stone. In the Post the Mail trick, we started to build on tricks that could be presented as they stood and then added to them.

In Recap

Shaping is encouraging a dog to move in the direction that will complete a trick. In other words it is a first baby step. In order to have the baby walk, you step back and encourage her forward for one step. Then two steps. And before you know it she is a marathon runner—and winner. Chaining is putting tricks together. Teach your dog to retrieve, and teach your dog to go to family members. *"Take It!"* the command to hold an object, is one of the commands in training a good retrieving dog. *"Go to Daddy!"* is the command to go to Pop. These two commands, when chained together, can become *"Take the Paper to Daddy!"* for a new trick. Back chaining is something that is mentioned for your edification. It is not something that we will do here, because we want you showing off your dog ASAP. It is training the last part of the trick first and working back to the beginning.

What Is a Target or Cue Stick?

This great tool is any "stick" similar to a magician's wand, and it enables you to teach a *wide* variety of tricks—tricks that would be extremely difficult if taught through conventional methods. As the dog moves toward the tip of the target stick, you click. The purpose of the stick is to attract the dog's attention. You want your dog to touch it with his paw, or bump it with his nose. Then it can be used to cue your dog to go to a given spot. If you wanted your dog to open a French door, for example, simply put the target stick's tip on the handle and say *"Touch!"* The stick can be used without clicking, but it works much better when you click. The tip should be of a contrasting color to the rest of the stick. Black stick and white tip is as good a combination as any.

Teaching *"Bump!"* and *"Touch!"* as two different commands widens your dog's performance. Touching is using his paw, while bumping is using his nose. See chapter 9 for a more complete explanation of teaching both tricks.

What Is Targeting?

It is easier to explain how to use the stick than to explain targeting. The idea is to get your dog to zone in on a particular target. Hold the stick in your hand, and as the dog approaches the end of the stick—he is "targeting" the tip of the stick. Using the stick to guide Jimminy to different items or places helps in a wide range of tricks.

What Is Variable Reinforcement?

Variable reinforcement means not giving a treat each time your dog performs, but always giving the click. Now, in every type of training, you want to wean the dog away from the reward. In other words, have the dog perform without the constant petting, praising, feeding, clapping or other rewards. Are we mean? No. We are merely training the dog to do what we want him to do. Your dog will enjoy work, and that enjoyment will become the "reward." In dog training, we want to start weaning the dog away early on, but not too soon. It will not be the end of the world if you keep clicking. Who is going to tell on you? Your dog? Remember that the clicker has become a reward unto itself. Instead of treating each time, treat every other time. This is where the true artistry in clicker training comes in.

You know what is going on in your dog's mind and adjust the reward to get the best results. As soon as you can get away with a treat every other time, then make it every third time. If you are not careful, you will develop a pattern that you are unaware of, but Jimminy will pick up that pattern. We could say that he is smarter than you, but the truth is, he has less on his mind than you do.

A Different Point of View

Trainers generally agree that a dog is trained when the dog will obey a command without the presence of different enticers. Bob and Marion Bailey, the most experienced couple in the field of animal behavior, with over one hundred years between them, feel that it is not necessary to go into variable reinforcement. You can always keep the treats present. After all, why not? This is a fun book designed for the pleasure of both you and your dog. Do not worry about impressing trainers. Impress your friends, neighbors and other audiences.

General Procedure

In using the clicker, you want to shape the dog's actions in the direction of the completed trick. If I want a dog to ring a hotel desk bell, I would put the dog in proximity to the bell. As the dog moved its paw closer to the bell, I would click and treat until by chance he hit the bell, then I would click and give him a jackpot. Back to square one again, and the dog will ring the bell that much sooner. A variation on this procedure would be to take the target stick (assuming the dog is trained to touch it) and guide the dog's paw to the top of the bell. Guiding the paw to the bell eliminates the drawn-out rewarding of approximations on the way to success. This training is not confined to paw guiding. You can use it for any type of body motion.

In training a dog to vocalize, it is better to replace the food reward with a click. As I mentioned earlier, feeding the dog when he is talking just doesn't work.

8
DOG TRAINING TECHNIQUES

Before we move on to specific tricks, let me take a moment to quickly cover miscellaneous points that you can incorporate into the concepts we've already discussed.

Building on Tricks and Picking the Commands

Throughout this book I encourage you to build on tricks. Sitting High is the dog with his hindquarters on the ground and his head and chest directly over those hindquarters. It is sometimes referred to as the beg position. With your dog in this position, you can then teach him to balance something on his nose while sitting high. Of course, you could also teach these actions as two separate tricks and then put them together. Another example of building on tricks and changing commands is when your dog limps, crawls and plays dead. Simply put all three tricks together and change the command for all tricks to *"Bang!"* Make your hand into a gun, point at your dog and give the first command of *"Bang!"* and the dog limps! On the second bang, the dog crawls, and on the third, he dies. Poor dog!

Setting the Pattern

Dogs are creatures of habit. If you always have your dog jump up on the right side of the table, he will always jump up on the right side of the table. Once constant repetition sets the pattern, the dog will follow it. If you have the dog sit before you put his collar on, he will always sit without command until you put the collar on. This is a good, sound practice. Habituate the dog to sitting, and the sit becomes the "default" position. To many dogs the sit is the default position because the pattern has been set. If you tell your dog "No!" he'll stop and sit. It is invisible training, that training that you have done without even realizing it. Do it over and over again and the pattern has been set and the dog will follow that pattern. You are best off having the dog do each trick on command. That way you can control the speed of the presentation and can rearrange the tricks anytime you want. The downside is that if you really start teaching your dog a lot of tricks from this book, you may forget one or two of them. Your dog won't!

Table Work

Training a dog on a table is a great method for a number of reasons, particularly for smaller dogs. It saves your back and teaches the dog to perform everywhere. The edge of the table controls creeping and helps in teaching the stay. The dog that has been worked on a table will work better on makeshift stages.

Hand Signals

Train for as many hand signals as possible—these are very expressive. A conversation between two people in a very noisy restaurant requires both to watch each other's body language in order to "hear" what each is saying. Read about touch control to see some of the advantages. If you use up all your hand signals, then go with foot, leg, body and head signals. Tie your signals into the body language you use when teaching the trick.

Touch Control

Touch control is a subtle touch signal you give that the dog picks up. Quite often, a person training a dog is not even aware that they are giving these signals. For example, in teaching the down position, you use your left hand in a downward motion to signal the down. Without thinking you gently touch the dog's collar as your left hand moves in a downward motion. You can recognize the hand signal for the down. What you are unaware of is that slightly downward touch on the collar. That is touch control. You have given the dog a verbal, visual *and* tactile signal. Touch control! This is all part of the communication between you and your dog. The more information you give a dog, the faster he will respond.

Loss of Interest

There are two approaches to use when you find the dog losing interest. Ending the training session is one way, but I don't especially like it. I prefer to end the training on a high note. Good trainers can sense when a dog is going to lose interest. They end the session on a "better" level, shortly before this point.

The other method is to switch to another command, preferably one that the dog enjoys. Put him through it two or three times *maximum* and then knock off. If you can't think of an exercise that he will do, have him sit-stay and scatter food on the floor. Give him a release so that he can eat the food.

Subliminal Sensory Cues

Touch control (see above) is a subliminal sensory cue that we all give off to our wise dogs. (The best example I can give of a subliminal sensory cue between humans is that if you come home at night and your significant other is in a bad mood, you know it without words.) Such cues can be used to create a mind-reading act between you and your dog. How do you know how to spot subliminal sensory cues? Your dog will tell you. When he starts doing a trick before you tell him, analyze exactly what you have done. Make it into a trick. Ask a spectator, "Do you want him to sit-high or bark? He can read my mind." In competition training "extra" commands are verboten. Don't worry about it. Your dog is going to be so well trained there will be absolutely no dog that can compete with him.

Get Away from Your Dog

As you teach these tricks you want to get farther and farther away from your dog. Should your wonderful dog ever get a photographic assignment, they will probably not want you in the picture. Your dog is the star. When you and your dog have the big chance to appear in Las Vegas, opening for Siegfried and Roy, you want to be ready. To really be ready, read my book *How to Get Your Pet Into Show Business*.

Seize the Opportunity

When an opportunity appears for a "new" trick, do not ignore it. Grab that trick. Sometimes when you are teaching the down position, a dog will start to creep forward. Rather than stopping the dog from creeping, start teaching the crawl. See the next item for further explanation.

Catch the Behavior

If your dog performs a behavior, why not catch that behavior and turn it into a trick? Your dog yawns, and you say *"Yawn!"* Incidentally, this mantra was repeated in Henry East's classic *Dog Tricks* book, written in the thirties. As easy as it sounds. you have to initiate some of the behavior in order to teach tricks. Caught behavior is a perfect opportunity to use the clicker on a clicker-trained dog. The clicker is especially handy if you have it available and the dog's action occurs at a distance. If the clicker is not handy, use your voice to give that instantaneous reward. A clicker-trained dog has a tendency to offer or volunteer behavior. In other words, if he wants a food reward he will start doing all sorts of gyrations to elicit a click. It is your job to be aware of this and catch him in a desirable behavior that you can turn into a trick. Time can be better spent doing other things besides just standing there waiting for your dog to do something, but always be ready for anything that happens spontaneously that can be turned into a trick.

The thought has been advanced that you can reduce undesirable behavior by putting it on command. Barking can be undesirable behavior. Don't permit your dog to bark incessantly; only permit him to bark on command and make it a trick. This is a good and true idea that is a slight variation on catching the behavior.

Length of Training Sessions

How long is each session? I would say short sessions are better, and short sessions on one particular trick during which you can shift to *other* tricks. Be alert to boredom with one trick and change pace (tricks) to maintain enjoyment. If your dog is having a good time, let him continue. It is your job to make sure that he doesn't overtax himself. Dogs will work to exhaustion. You must be aware of the weather and heat conditions. If he is getting bored, switch over to another trick. If you are switching tricks, use a different reward. Do not let the dog determine when the training is over. You must anticipate his boredom and have him successfully complete a session before *you* decide it's over.

Relax Your Dog

An excitable dog with a high energy level is an excellent candidate for trick training. Relaxing your dog is important too.

When you are teaching the dog to play dead, he must be calm and relaxed, not up and excited. Pay attention to the references to calming your dog in this book.

Replacement Commands

An example of a replacement command is telling a dog to stay and then calling him to you. That would be a replacement command. Counterconditioning is telling a jumping dog to sit every time he jumps. You want to avoid giving the dog conflicting commands, because it is unfair. An example of conflicting commands is patting your chest and calling your dog up and then telling him *"No!"* and correcting him for doing something you told him to do. Do not do this, it is confusing, unfair and downright mean.

Invisible Training

More dogs are trained through invisible training than you can imagine. Who taught your dog his name, and when? That is invisible training. I will point out invisible training throughout this book. Use it. Take advantage of it.

Corrections

Corrections are seldom needed in trick training. It is very positive training. Dogs must be shown when they are doing things right. Occasionally a dog will do something wrong. That has to be pointed out to the dog too. A correction's intensity varies with what was done wrong. As Gilbert and Sullivan said in *The Mikado,* "Let the punishment fit the crime." Do not confuse the term "correction" with a term people throw around freely—and improperly: An aversive is not *necessarily* a correction. A beanbag, as mentioned in chapter 13 under the Raus! trick, is an aversive. The dog avoids the beanbag. The word "no" is a correction. A cautionary no is a softly delivered no as a reminder to your dog to not even *think* about doing some-

thing wrong. A quick jerk on the leash is about the hardest correction you will have to use, and you may not even have to use
that.

Context

Commands are delivered in different contexts, helping the
dog to realize what he is supposed to be doing. For example, if
you take your city-dwelling dog to the area where you normally
practice sheep herding, he would know what is expected of
him. You probably won't even have to use a command to start
him working. He realizes that this is not the time when you
want him to jump rope. Back to the sheep herding. In this setting, should you decide to use the terms "right" and "left"
rather than the normally used herding commands, your dog
would understand that you wanted him to go to the left rather
than give you his left paw. Different context, different meaning.
Do not concern yourself with confusing your dog. I'm more
concerned about confusing you.

9

LIGHT AND FLUFFY

Light and fluffy tricks are simply that. For example:

I'm Gonna Catch Ya!

One of a dog's favorite games is Come Chase Me! It consists of your dog enticing you into chasing after him. From the dog's point of view, it's a great game; but there are a number of drawbacks from a behavior/training point of view:

1. Your dog is controlling the situation.
2. It encourages him to stay away from you.
3. It discourages him from coming when called.
4. It encourages him to steal things.

The simple solution to all these problems is to put the game on command so you can control the situation. A number of positive things occur when you do this.

1. It gives you a pleasant exercise for your dog with a minimum effort on your part.
2. Properly administered, it encourages your dog to come when called.

3. It's an excellent assist in getting your dog to retrieve objects.
4. It teaches your dog to give up objects, puts you in control rather than your dog, and helps your dog develop a more rapid performance in a number of tricks and obedience exercises.

By now, your dog "Huck" has introduced you to his Come Chase Me game. Why not play? But play on *your* terms, not his. Start by making the command *"I'm Gonna Catch Ya!"* You never will, but this is the name of the game. You don't even want to try to catch him, just *convince* him that you're trying. I'm assuming that Huck is clicker trained.

When he gets into one of those moods where he's encouraging you to chase him, squat with your arms and legs spread wide apart and say, *"I'm Gonna Catch Ya!"* Lunging and feinting will encourage Huck to run off. Chase him for a short distance. Turn away and click. If he comes up to you, treat. If he doesn't, continue to ignore him. Huck is going to attempt to get you to chase him again. At this point, be satisfied with him coming up for a treat, but if he doesn't, forget about it. What do you do if he comes up three minutes later and wants to play Come Chase Me? Go with the flow (on *your* terms, with *your* command). If he wanders up to you a minute or two later, you can say *"Sit!"* and click and treat. If he wants you to chase him, pop into your I'm Gonna Catch Ya stance, give the command and lunge at him. Should Huck go into a Come-Chase-Me mode, you'll chase him. Each chase is different, but always involves Huck turning to check the progress of your pursuit. At this point, the game is still his game—you want to make it yours.

In the second training session, let Huck check on you twice. If he goes into his "play bow" (see chapter 18) while checking on you, jump into your I'm Gonna Catch Ya pose and give the command. (If he hasn't already learned it, seize the opportunity to teach Huck the Take a Bow trick at this point.) Both times, when he turns around, go through the pose and command. As Huck runs off for the third time, chase him a few feet, then turn away from him and click. Should he come up to you, immediately treat. Keep raising your standards for each click. As he comes in regularly, add the *"Sit!"* command before treating. This increases control and speed of response.

Somewhere along the line, Huck may grab a toy or other item you don't want him to have. Let him have it, because if you focus on getting that toy away from him, you're playing his game. Remember, it's *your* game. The toy is a sidebar of the I'm Gonna Catch Ya trick. Later on, the command can be added to have him return the toy.

Remember to continually raise the criteria. Huck has to do it better each time to be clicked and treated. Your goal is to give the command, along with your body language, and have him spring immediately into action. If you get him in his run-around-the-house mood, you have accomplished another mission: maximum exercise with minimum effort (see chapter 14).

PRESENTATION: Sure, you can show Huck off, but most of the time the two of you will be doing this on your own for Huck's enjoyment and exercise.

Wipe Your Feet

**"WIPE YOUR FEET!" "RIGHT!" "LEFT!" "TURN!"
"LEFT REAR!" "RIGHT REAR!"**

This routine is particularly important for the city dog living in the colder states where there's snow on the ground and salt is used to melt it. Salt between a dog's toes can cause all sorts of irritation.

The following tricks are various versions of the same trick. You'll start with the easiest one first. Place a mat or large towel on the floor at the door Huck comes through. Have another towel, for drying his feet, hanging nearby. When he comes in, tell him *"Stand-Stay!"* on the mat. Your dog's obedience trainer didn't teach him to stand-stay? Go back to that trainer and tell him I said he didn't do his job.

Huck is to stand-stay on the mat/towel while you dry each

one of his cute little feet. (Even Irish Wolfhounds have cute little feet.) Set this ritual up, and it really is invisible training.

1. Reach for his right paw and say *"Right!"*
2. After you wipe the right paw off, tell him *"Left!"* and wipe that one.
3. You are going from right to left so Huck will spin in a counterclockwise direction when you tell him *"Turn!"*
4. Give him a little nudge in the appropriate direction. (See chapter 14 for more information on spinning and turning, but it isn't necessary to read that in order to teach these exercises.)
5. Then say *"Left Rear!"* and go for the left rear foot. Keep that counterclockwise spin as you ask for the last foot. Remain calm throughout the trick.

This is how Huck will learn:

1. He knows the *"Stand-Stay!"* command and will learn that he's going to be handled gently by you and will stand to have his paws petted.
2. He will learn the routine and give the appearance of being trained when for the most part all he is doing is responding to the pattern.
3. He will start to learn the new commands as they are repeated.
4. Eventually he will respond to the individual commands rather than the routine.

The secret is habituating him to the routine as he is taught the commands. You may even have an opportunity to exploit a caught behavior. When dogs are wet or damp, they're in a good, playful mood and love to run around. If that mood strikes Huck, keep him on the towel or mat. Let him run around in a circle on the mat. Remember, the clicker is good for all sorts of caught behaviors. Click and treat the new behavior. When Huck runs around in a circle on the mat, click and command

"Wipe Your Feet!" You may feel that you don't have to go through the laborious bending to wipe his feet individually if you catch that behavior. Not true! Running around on a towel is not going to do as good a job as your careful wiping of each paw. Teach *both* tricks. First presenting each individual foot and then *"Wipe Your Feet!"* (If Huck is still in an up mood, seize the opportunity and add on the I'm Gonna Catch Ya trick.)

PRESENTATION: You can do this presentation before Huck is trained. He already is doing a stand-stay. Manipulate him into position as you teach the other commands. People will think Huck is responding to your voice rather than to the routine. Needless to say, if he does it on the *"Wipe Your Feet!"* command, it's more impressive. After he finishes wiping his feet, tell him, "They aren't clean enough. Wipe your feet again."

Giggle Gaggle

Giggle Gaggle is an easy trick to teach, enjoyed right after a series of other tricks (Down, Dead Dog and On Your Back) or you can go straight into the trick, especially if your dog is in a playful, rambunctious mood. While roughhousing with your dog, get him on his back. With a larger dog it can be rather difficult to flip him over. When I say flip him over, I want to caution you on *how* you flip him over. *Do not* toss him over. Do it gently and lightly. When he is close to the ground, it is easier and safer to get him on his back. Have a hand available to gently lower him. If Huck is a small dog, flipping is easiest when you cup your right hand (if you are right-handed) under his chest and guard the spine by cupping your left hand on his back. Dogs under forty pounds, such as Miniature Bull Terriers, are easier to flip than a larger breed, such as a Bullmastiff, which will require more strength. Playfully get Huck with his back as close to the ground as possible. In his joyful mood he will be twisting and turning on his side. That is an ideal time to flip him. Even this flip should be controlled and broken by your hands. As soon as he gets on his back, you scratch and tickle his chest and tummy and say *"Giggle Gaggle!"* If you are doing this vigorously enough, you'll hear Huck making a cheerful, happy gurgling sound. You will be teaching not only the verbal command, but the hand signal as well. The hand signal is this: Shape your hand like a claw moving toward Huck. Not only do we want Huck writhing on the ground, but we also want to have that gurgling sound. This is the way we will produce the *g* and *l* sounds in getting Huck to verbalize (see chapter 2). Some of the breeds that do well with this trick are the Bullmastiff, Bull Terrier, Lhasa Apso and Staffordshire Bull Terrier.

PRESENTATION: This is a cute trick that can be presented anywhere. Presentation is not the main reason for this trick. The simple use of this trick is a game you and Huck play. The complex application is in developing the *g* and *l* sounds in teaching Huck to talk.

Bump

This can be taught easily, starting from a caught behavior.

1. You are sitting in your armchair relaxing and watching TV.
2. Huck wants to be petted, and he is going to come over and do one of two things: nudge your hand or arm with his muzzle, or use his paw to paw your hand. It doesn't matter which Huck does. In either case have that clicker ready.
3. If he paws you, say *"Touch!"* and read the next trick.
4. If he nudges your arm with his nose, say *"Bump!"* Click and treat. Do that twice. Next time he bumps your arm, click and pet. Most dogs prefer to nudge rather than paw. This is usually not regarded as a trick. It is generally regarded as an annoyance. Dogs generally teach themselves to bump your arm for attention. When they bump your arm, you reward them by petting them. It is a simple training procedure but *you* are supposed to do the training. Your dog is not supposed to train you! I remember renting a guard dog, Chan,

to a motel in the Bronx, New York. During one of my trips to check Chan's training, a clerk asked me about the dog's nudging his arm late at night. I immediately knew what he was talking about. I jokingly said that the motel owner asked me to teach Chan to do that when the clerk dozed off. The clerk, in amazement, commented that you "must be able to teach a dog anything." Well, almost anything.

5. Once you have Huck bumping your arm you want to transfer the bumping over to inanimate objects.

6. Place the object to be bumped, with a small piece of masking tape on it, alongside your arm. Tell Huck to *"Bump!"* and move your arm away so that he bumps the tape.

7. Rather than simply transferring this bump to another object, change it to another trick. Doing two things at the same time doubles your output. Here's an example of a new trick. Make the inanimate object a plastic glass. Do I have to explain why it is plastic? Put the plastic glass on the edge of a low chair or table. Show Huck the glass with the tape on it. Put your arm in front of the glass and say *"Bump!"* Remove your arm so Huck hits the glass. Click and treat. Later you will change that command over to *"Knock the Glass Over!"*

ALTERNATE METHOD: Using a target stick makes the teaching of bumping inanimate objects easier. The secret is to use the clicker to shape Huck's bumping behavior. If he bumps the stick rather than touching it, click and treat. I hesitate mentioning this, but both the bump and touch can be taught at the same time. The reason that I hesitate mentioning it is that it requires a high level-of skill, excellent timing, a lot of dog-training knowledge and a thorough knowledge of your dog. I would assume that you have at least that last piece of knowledge. Teaching both at the same time requires you to adjust to and accept whatever Huck offers you.

PRESENTATION: Rather than a presentation, this is more of a tool for teaching other tricks, such as *"Knock the Glass Over!"*

Let your imagination run wild on the bump as a tool for teaching tricks.

Touch

The Bump trick is certainly tied into this trick. The behavior we want to capture is Huck pawing rather than bumping. The command is *"Touch!"* You then have to expand Huck's pawing to inanimate objects. Distinguishing when to use bumping and when touching is important. The rule of thumb: a downward motion is better as a touch, while an upward motion is better as a bump. For example, a touch is used to press down a French-door handle, opening the door, while a bump is used to elevate a mailbox's arm or flag. By the same token, lowering that arm is best done by a touch.

PRESENTATION: Again, the purpose of the touch is as a tool for teaching other tricks, rather than being a trick on its own.

Kiss My Ass!

Trainer J. C. Shilling deserves credit (or is it blame?) for this suggestion. It's a caught behavior and similar to the Take a Bow trick in chapter 18, but with a different *attitude* and positioning of the head. Huck's head, rather than looking straight on, lies flat, with his cheek resting on the ground. In other words, his tail end is up in the air and his head is on the ground looking up at you, as if to say, "Kiss my ass." The attitude makes the trick hilarious. To catch this behavior, you have to be ready with that clicker when your dog assumes the position. You also have to be ready with a treat. If Huck is in a playful mood, you can run a number of click-and-treat sessions with him. That added playful touch of the head on the ground, looking up, is important.

TWO ALTERNATE APPROACHES. If you didn't catch this behavior, go to chapter 18 and read the Take a Bow trick. Once

Huck knows the bow, use either a lure-and-reward or a modeling trick to get his head into the correct position. In the lure-and-reward technique, you lead his bowed head into the appropriate position with a tidbit of food. The food is *not* the ultimate reward. The ultimate reward is the release from control. This is the type of training that will help you develop a feel and empathy for Huck. If he gets antsy (as in "ants in the pants"), it's time to not only pop the treat in his mouth, but also to give him a *"Release!"* Explode! Applaud! Praise! Clap your hands! You've given him a break, but that doesn't mean you can't go back to training again. As you lure Huck's bowed head into position, work for gradual improvement before giving the reward. The luring motion is flowing and goes widely and gracefully directly toward the ground, then moves the tidbit *along* the ground for five or six inches. You must lure Huck's head across the ground to obtain the correct positioning.

When you are using the modeling technique, Huck's head is moved in an arc similar to the one used in the lure method. Use your right hand to gently cradle his cheek, with your fingers cupped under the left side of his jawbone. Your left hand reaches behind Huck's neck directly below his right ear. Your thumb is parallel to the right rear portion of his jawbone. Move his nose down, and gently start to curve his head to rest cheek on the ground. This is the time to use that release-from-control reward.

PRESENTATION: This position can be used in many fun ways. Say you're in the midst of a heated discussion with a friend. When you want to lighten up the atmosphere, spring the Kiss My Ass trick! Make sure you have a smile on your face, and you can precede the command with, "Well, you can . . . !!"

10
TRICKS FOR THE URBAN DOG
(TRICKS I HOPE YOU'LL NEVER HAVE TO USE)

Cover

You can take this as a joke, or you can take it seriously. It's all up to you. *"Cover!"* and *"Crawl!"* are two commands for the urban dog and owner who are in an area plagued by drive-by shootings. They are taken from a military exercise that, I'm sorry to say, has civilian applications.

The command *"Cover!"* or *"Take Cover!"* is given to military personnel when there are incoming rounds or small-arms fire, because it's a lot safer to be on the ground when there is incoming fire. Incoming small-arms fire has now become a fact of life in some neighborhoods—but no incoming "mail" (mortar or artillery rounds) yet! Your dog "Wayne" must get used to having you crash down on the ground alongside of him. (This exercise will get you in shape too.)

When you hear gunfire, immediately drop to the ground, facedown, breaking your fall with your hands. The command for Wayne is *"Cover!"* but don't start by falling down alongside him immediately. Start by slowly kneeling down on your left knee. (Remember we said your dog should be obedience trained before embarking on trick work.) Wayne must learn two things: not to shy away when you hit the ground, and to get down *fast*.

Accelerate your *"Cover!"* command, and if Wayne is lagging, grasp the leash near the collar as you start to hit the ground. This is a life-threatening situation! Once you're on the ground, stroke Wayne and slide your left arm over his shoulders to comfort him and protect him from incoming fire. It is your job then to raise your head slightly, assess the situation and figure how to crawl the hell out of there.

PRESENTATION: Playing a cassette tape recorder with gunfire on it will add a nice mix of drama and humor to this trick. Milk it for laughs by overacting your panic. Try to stay in decent shape. When you first hear the gunfire, shout *"Cover!"* good and loud.

Crawl

This is considered a tough exercise to teach a dog, but if you follow my guidelines, it's easy. If you own a Golden Retriever, it can be a piece of cake. The "Golden Crawl" is what makes it easy. It's the dog's (very often a Golden) loving attempt to try to get close to you. It's when you're teaching the *"Down!"* command that the Golden crawl usually occurs. Your dog is in the down position and he wants to sit in your lap (which is kind of difficult if you are not sitting). That doesn't seem to bother him.

1. If he starts to crawl, go for it! Your dog may try to get up rather than crawl, and it's your job to make him stay down by applying a downward pressure on his collar.
2. Move away from him as he attempts to get close to you. Make him "reach out and touch someone" (you). This desire for closeness is his motivation.

Standard dog-training dictum states that if a dog does something that he shouldn't, correct him, but this is not a standard book on dog training. As we said in chapter 2, we're going to take anything our dog gives us—just about. There is only one hard and fast rule in dog training: There are no hard and fast rules in dog training. Where is the reward? You are giving it concurrently with his crawling by telling him that he's wonderful. Say it with feeling. Give the hand signal, which is the left hand, palm down, moving back and forth, in a three-inch arc.

Keep the sessions short. You should do three or four sessions of about eight seconds each of actual crawling time. (This can be broken up with other exercises, one of which is *"Down!"*) Do not pet your dog until after he has completed the eight-second session. The petting is your signal to him to stop crawling. Wayne is not to get up, but remain in the down position after he stops crawling. We do *not* want your dog *too* happy with the reward, because he will pop up. How do you stop your dog from being *too* happy? Control the enthusiasm by meting out the petting. Not too exuberant! Slow left-handed stroking across the shoulders, with downward pressure, will reduce Wayne's tendency to pop up. He must stay there until you give him a *"Release!"* command. Gradually increase the length of crawling time.

1. If you don't see a serendipitous Golden Crawl, we have some hard work cut out for us. Well, not that hard, as long as you again work your dog in short increments.
2. You and your dog are lying on your stomachs alongside one another. Now, with a forward *and* downward pressure (with your left hand on the leash), edge your dog forward.
3. Move your hand in the previously described arc while saying, *"Crawl!"* Use voice and hand signals simultaneously. Don't be afraid of giving Wayne too much information. Praise as before.

PRESENTATION: The trick requires you to look around in feigned panic. Milk it for laughs by overacting your panic as you try to escape. (It can be a lot tougher on you than Wayne, so stay in shape.)

Bomb/Explosive Detection

"SEARCH!"

Before embarking upon this trick I want you to understand that locating bombs or explosives *is not a game*. This trick is not for the purpose of doing the real-life work that bomb-sniffing dogs actually do. This should be properly left up to police and military personnel trained to handle this dangerous and life-threatening work. Stop! Realize that when a terrorist or other wrongdoer leaves a bomb, it may be booby-trapped. Even if it's not booby-trapped, it has to be deactivated and moved, or detonated on site. You have neither the training nor experience for this.

"Sherlock" can be trained to locate the source of any odor. For our purposes here we'll teach him to identify two odors: fertilizer and black powder. The fertilizer odor is present in virtually all military and commercial explosives. Some low-level criminals and terrorists use black powder (which lacks the punch and power of the higher quality explosives). In fact, it's been estimated that as many as 60 percent of terrorists use black powder, which says very little for our terrorists. Black powder is preferred by some sportsmen as a crude form of propellant for bullets. It is readily available in one-pound boxes. There is also a product called SOKKS, which contains low levels of explosives and can be used for this training and doesn't require all the special handling, paperwork and ammunition lockers. If you're not connected with law enforcement, SOKKS may be difficult to get your hands on. But this is a trick, and you don't have to be as proficient as the police. Teaching this trick doesn't mean you're able to do the real-life job. Save that work for government, police and military. It is very risky business.

If you decide that you want to teach the bomb-detection trick, please read the section on the Drug-Detection trick, which follows it, and the descriptions of scent work found later in this chapter and chapter 17, "The Knowing Nose," before starting. You'll note that in drug detection, an active alert is normally taught. Active alert means the dog retrieves the source of the desired odor. In detecting explosives, we use a passive alert. Believe me, you *do not* want your dog retrieving bombs.

1. Sherlock is alert, showing you that an explosive device has been scented. He sits at your side and looks up at you. *"Search!"* is your command.
2. Start with the odor inside a small burlap bag. (The burlap is sturdy and gives the odor a chance to circulate.) Use a generous quantity of the odor, especially in the initial phases of training. Use a food reward here.
3. Whenever Sherlock picks up the odor, he should be told to *"Sit!"* The odor thus becomes his command to sit, and his reward is a tidbit, along with petting and praise. This will cause him to look up at you silently, as if to say, "Hey, boss, I found it. Where's my reward?"
4. The food reward should be reduced and switched to petting as training progresses. The reason for this is we don't want Sherlock to fill his tummy up too much, and thus be less eager to work. This was a problem faced by the British trainers of mine-detection dogs during World War II.

PRESENTATION: Demonstrations of bomb detection can be performed on three different levels: as straight entertainment, education and to deliver a warning. In each case, explain to the audience that this is not your job: There are professional bomb squads and dogs that can handle these matters. Even in a presentation as entertainment, you should also be educating the audience about how the dog works. In a presentation your main thrust as education should be to explain the fine work that governmental agencies do in protecting us from these dangers. The warning will let younger people know that if they are going to become involved in bomb making, there are dogs out there that are going to catch them, and they will suffer the consequences. Always use a legitimate odor in putting on these demonstrations. Inert hand grenades are available and inexpensive, and I would suggest that the odor be put inside one of the "pineapple" grenades, which though no longer used (they have been replaced by grenades with a smoother exterior), do have the conventional appearance of a hand grenade.

Small-Arms/Gun Detection

"SEARCH!"

Now, here is an excellent opportunity for building on tricks. Once you teach bomb or explosive detection, you can almost walk into teaching a dog to locate small arms (handguns, rifles, etc.), which generally contain bullets. Dogs sometimes find small arms incidental to a search for explosives: small-arms ammunition contains an explosive. This is not to say that if you teach bomb detection, small-arms detection will be learned simultaneously. No, you do have to actively teach the dog to locate the weapons, as there is no guarantee that a weapon will contain bullets. Of course, a used weapon does have the odor of previously fired rounds, but in such minuscule quantities that your dog must be taught to detect it.

PRESENTATION: If you're restricted from using small arms in your act, explain this to your audience. Ammunition can be used instead of a weapon, but it lacks dramatic punch. Having Sherlock find a pistol with an active alert is quite dramatic, but I advise against it, as there is always the remote possibility of his grabbing the trigger and accidentally firing the weapon. Another consideration is your local weapons laws. It's your job to be aware of these.

Drug Detection

"SEARCH!"

The most difficult part of this trick is finding the substance with which to train your dog. There are many drugs whose scent a true drug dog can pick up. The properly trained drug dog can pick up the following drugs:

1. Amphetamines and amphetamine-based drugs, such as LSD and ecstasy
2. Cocaine
3. Crack-cocaine
4. Hashish and marijuana
5. Heroin
6. Meth and Crystalmeth
7. Morphine and opium derivatives

You'd have a hard time getting your hands on this stuff, and even if you did, legitimately, you'd go crazy filling out the DEA paperwork and managing their requirements for storage, handling, security, etc. Ersatz drugs are easier to get, but not that easy. They're designed for, used by and sold to law enforcement personnel. A helpful, well-connected police officer may be able to help you. The pseudodrugs are not illegal, but if you train with them, prepare yourself for questioning on their source. In any event, do not use illegal drugs in training Sherlock. The penalties for this are very high.

Once involved in controlled-substance searches, the civilian is faced with a great mass of government controls. The DEA is the organization that enforces drug laws, and it is very finicky, so make sure that you stay within the law. A good source for drug odor is SOKKS. The use of SOKKS by civilians seems to be legal. It contains traces or very small amounts of the particular odors of all the previously mentioned drugs.

For a good natural retriever, the retrieve itself is a great motivator. The odor becomes the toy. Encourage Sherlock to look for and play with a SOKKS-scented toy. This same approach can be used with a nonnatural retriever, but somehow there will not be that same built-in drive and motivation. The drug dog works faster than the more deliberate bomb dog. Rather than sitting and turning his head toward you, Sherlock dramatically seizes the drugs. In fact, drug dogs have so much drive and interest in the drugs, some people falsely think they're addicted.

PRESENTATION: Tell your kids that Sherlock is trained to find drugs, and not only are you going to search the house periodically, but you will turn over any wrongdoers, even family members, to the police. Occasionally, have Sherlock search in front of your kids. Tell them he is going to check out their friends too.

Food Refusal

Food refusal consists of the dog turning his head when he is offered food by strangers. Not only is this a useful trick but it can be lifesaving. It precludes someone giving your dog something that will upset his stomach or even poison him. In order to train for this trick, you need to enlist the assistance of a *total* stranger. (Pick someone who will never have to interact with your dog in the future.) There is no command for this trick because it will normally be performed when no one is around (except for the bad guy).

1. With Sherlock in the heel position, the stranger approaches and offers a tidbit.
2. If Sherlock shows even the slightest interest, give him a cautionary *"No!"* If absolutely necessary use a mild leash correction.
3. The stranger again approaches with hand extended.
4. Repeat the leash correction if Sherlock shows interest in the food. It is important that he never succeed in getting the food. Five trials the first time out is sufficient.
5. The next time out, our stranger will encourage Sherlock to take the food.
6. By the end of this second session, each time the stranger offers food he should give Sherlock a small slap in the face with the hand containing the food; this will teach him to turn his head when someone entices him with food. Don't feel sorry for Sherlock. This can save his life.
7. The third phase of this exercise is to tie Sherlock out by himself and have your assistant approach and entice him with an

even better food treat. At this point, Sherlock should automatically turn his head away. He is now fully trained, but this work must be brushed up on periodically.

8. Introduce different assistants.

PRESENTATION: This trick can be done anywhere, for a crowd of one or one hundred. It also affords an excellent opportunity to brush up Sherlock on his training with various assistants and food treats. This is a win-win training/demonstrating situation.

A Word of Caution on the Watch 'Em and Guarding Tricks

The following tricks are *not* presented as a guide to training a police service dog or a military working dog. They're just tricks and are taught as such. The guarding tricks will present your dog as a formidable opponent, even if he is the biggest sissy in town. If you feel you want your dog to be able to actually do any of these things in the real world, then seek the assistance of a dog trainer qualified in this area. All three tricks should be taught together because they work well together.

Guarding You

"WATCH 'EM!"

A simple and handy exercise to teach, especially if you live on the mean streets of an urban community. The impression portrayed to the "bad guys" is that your dog will rip their throats out. If you have read chapters 1 and 2 of this book, you know the difference between talking and speaking. *"Watch 'Em!"* is different from both those commands.

1. With "Cutie Pie" sitting in the heel position at your left side, enlist the help of a friend to come up and make erratic movements in front of her. Erratic movement can be, for example, bending over and sidling in a crablike fashion. Limping,

staggering and weaving will raise Cutie Pie's suspicions. Halloween masks or a paper bag over the head are also suspicious. Make the eyeholes large enough so that your friend will have the good peripheral vision so necessary in judging the distance to Cutie Pie.

2. Cutie Pie, having been clicker-trained (see chapter 7), is going to be rewarded with the sound of the clicker. In addition to holding the clicker in one hand, your friend also will have small pieces of food in the other.

3. He will say *"Speak!"* and as Cutie Pie barks, he will click, tossing a piece of food while clicking. (The best time to toss the food is when Cutie Pie starts to get distracted, is paying less attention, is taking a breath, clearing her throat or otherwise unable to bark.) Remember, dogs can't bark and eat at the same time. This is why the clicker is so helpful in teaching this trick. It leaves the mouth free for barking. Timing is extremely difficult and important here. Your friend has to be attuned to your dog's moods and temperament. That clicker should click every time your dog barks.

4. When the tidbit is tossed, the assistant says *"Catch!"* (Hey, we don't just teach one trick at a time!)

5. Now you point at your assistant as you command, in a stern tone of voice, *"Watch 'Em!"* You say *"Watch 'Em!"* and your assistant says *"Speak!"* (You will rapidly phase out giving the *"Speak!"* command. The difference between *"Speak!"* and *"Watch 'Em!"* is that the dog simply barks on *"Speak!"* while with *"Watch 'Em!"* the dog barks at a person. It is a completely different attitude.)

PRESENTATION: You may feel there is no need for presentation with this trick but there is if you want to convey the impression that your dog is trained to protect. The first thing you should do is change Cutie Pie's name to Killer. Then continually brag about how your dog is protection trained.

Guarding Objects

"GUARD!"

As we're building on the tricks, a word of caution: We are not actually teaching your dog to guard objects but merely to convey this impression. If your dog's a Pit Bull or a Rottweiler, no problem, if it's a Chihuahua or a Maltese, no one will be convinced.

Many years ago I went on television with an attack-trained Chihuahua. People always remind me of that dog, completely forgetting the many German Shepherds and Dobermans with which I appeared on the tube. The point is, you can teach this to any dog.

Protection and attack work can be very dangerous if not done properly. Should you decide to go this route, do it only under the tutelage of a qualified professional. The difference between the trick and the real thing is that if the dog is *really* guarding an object, she is supposed to bite and snap at anyone who gets near the object. For the trick you merely have her sitting and barking at the person who approaches the object.

1. Draw a circle with a diameter of ten feet. This can be done with a sack of flour in an open field, but we must remember that, for the purposes of this chapter, we are training the urban dog, so we'll replace open field with basketball court. (Don't ask me when a basketball court is free in the inner city.)

2 Start with the dog in the sit-stay position in the middle of the circle. Put a handbag, wallet or other object in front of the dog.

3. Put your hand on the object, look your dog squarely in the eye and say *"Guard!"* Step away and have that able assistant approach the circle. He will not tell Killer to speak.

4. At this point *you* will tell Killer, *"Watch 'em!"* Same command, different exercise. As the dog barks, your friend will run off a few feet. It is then up to you to reinforce the *"Stay!"* command. An integral part of object guarding is

that the dog does not stray from the object. Watch Killer; if she drifts away from the object, repeat *"Stay!* or *"Sit-Stay!"* Keep her interest up. Killer should begin barking shortly before your assistant hits the edge of the circle.

Now we get to the hard part: stopping. You must stop training before Killer gets bored, not only before she gets bored, but also on a high point, when she has successfully completed the exercise. We do not want Killer to bite, just bark. Remember, this is a trick. You always have the option of staking Killer out, tying her up so that she remains in the same general area as the object to be guarded. (You can later let her loose. At this point in Killer's training you should have enough control over her so that the tying is unnecessary.) Sitting by herself and playing the part is all we're looking for Killer to do. We are not looking for a lawsuit.

The downside of this exercise is that it takes a bit more work to set up than other tricks. In addition, you need a variety of assistants and can't work the dog for long periods. Tire Killer out and you will have a very unhappy camper on your hands, one who may quit the job.

PRESENTATION: Once your dog is trained, you can present this trick just about anywhere. Tell your audience that Killer is trained to guard objects and have someone volunteer an object to be guarded. Though setting up the training for this trick is a bit difficult, the presentation is easy: You always have everything you need on hand, including new assistants.

Guarding Themselves

"WATCH 'EM!"

In the final phase of *"Watch 'Em!"* Killer is tied up and, when approached, springs into action, barking and threatening anyone who approaches. This is a risky area of training as you do not want your dog to be suspicious of everyone—which is why this exercise is on command only, i.e., Killer only performs when given the command, not when she chooses.

As a trick, when properly done, this can cause a great deal of amusement to those you are trying to impress. As someone approaches, Killer barks and threatens, except she's not really threatening him, just barking, but barking *at* him.

All dogs have the instinct to pursue; chasing someone is reward in itself. Still, we are going to layer a couple of other rewards on top of the chase (to the end of the leash), such as an occasional tidbit tossed at Killer by your assistant when he clicks. The click is the preferred reward, because, as noted before, a dog cannot eat and bark at the same time.

Now, a bad guy feeding the dog is antithetical to *actual* guarding, but we use the food reward precisely because we *do not* want animosity toward the assistant. This is a trick, not real life. It's the appearance of aggression, not actual aggression. Nevertheless, *do not* let the bad guy pet your dog, *ever*. This will cause the dog to fawningly seek out people who could be dangerous, rather than bark.

1. This training is initially accomplished with Killer at your side. Get her to bark at anyone approaching. The command is *"Watch 'Em!"*
2. The food reward should be tossed at the dog and *not* put in her mouth. Again the command *"Catch!"* will be given.
3. Once Killer starts barking ferociously, stop the food.
4. When Killer barks, your assistant will start to run away a few steps, which will encourage Killer to pull and lean into the leash. (After all the trouble you had teaching Killer to stop pulling on the leash, now you're encouraging her to pull!)

You can run into a problem if you put Killer on an alert mode twenty-four hours a day, so don't do it! It's too stressful for both you and her. Ultimately, you will be able to leave Killer "alone" in this trick in much the same manner as in the object-guarding trick. Watch 'em, Guarding Objects and Guarding Themselves are an excellent example of building on tricks.

PRESENTATION: Make a big to-do about Killer guarding herself and offer to demonstrate. Each time you do this you are maintaining Killer's training. People are going to want to know if she really will bite. Don't lie, but here are the top five answers to give when this question is asked: In fifth place, "I wouldn't take a chance." Fourth, "Is your health insurance paid?" Third, "I'd rather not answer that question. Insurance, you know." Second, "What do you think?" And in first place, the winner is (drumroll, please), "Only when she's hungry."

11
TRICKS FOR THE SUBURBAN DOG

It's such a relief to get away from the tumult of the city that training in the suburbs is a treat. Of course, these tricks can be used anywhere, but are more applicable to the suburban dog. You have my permission to teach urban tricks to your dog. You do not have my permission, however, to teach all the tricks in the next chapter: Zoning laws won't permit you to keep a flock of sheep.

Get the Paper

"FETCH!" OR "TAKE IT!"

Chapter 16 deals with retrieving, and if you really want your dog to retrieve first time, every time, I suggest reading that chapter first, because you'll need a deeper understanding of retrieving to get your dog working 100 percent. If you're not that dedicated, don't worry about it. Here, we'll show you how to get him to do it 90 percent of the time. If you're just having fun—especially if you have a natural retriever—this is as much scholarship and information as is necessary. We have so many tricks in this book, we can give you choices.

THE PLAY RETRIEVE

Encourage "Jack" to retrieve different objects, such as balls and sticks. It's fairly straightforward, and most dogs enjoy retrieving—it's a self-rewarding trick, and in many cases it's half a trick; he'll retrieve but not return.

Once you have him retrieving sticks with a certain degree of success it's time to substitute a newspaper.

1. Roll up a newspaper and put either a rubber band or masking tape around it. Masking tape is preferred because it will not break in your dog's mouth and frighten him. If he'll retrieve the stick, he'll retrieve the newspaper. The newspaper, by the way, should not be the size of the Sunday *New York Times*. A skinny, lightweight tabloid will do.

2. After Jack has retrieved the stick a number of times, toss the paper in front of him. Encourage him with praise and applause as he goes out, picks up the paper and brings it back. Punctuate each one of these three steps with a click (see chapter 7 for clicker training).

3. If the dog refuses to give you the paper, simply walk away. He will follow, and if you go into the house, he will ultimately put the paper down. Remember, Jack has learned the first half of the trick: We must now shape his behavior so that he not only gets the paper but returns it to your hand. Making it fun and games by briskly walking away will encourage him to come toward you. Get him to trade the paper for a treat: Jack can't eat and hold the paper at the same time. Once he has mastered the paper retrieval, it's time to start on a variety of other items. Buy a box of Cracker Jack. Jack will love to retrieve the box because of its exciting rattle and enchanting odor. And it's a new and odd shape, but not impossible to carry, unless he is a Chihuahua.

PRESENTATION: Now you just have to make sure that the darn newspaper boy tosses the paper in an accessible location, with a rubber band around it. You won't get him to use masking tape, sadly. Jack will probably tell you when the newsboy arrives, and then you should encourage the dog even more. You can "frustrate" him by not immediately letting him go out the door and retrieve the paper. Hold him by the collar, or let him look out the window as he barks and shouts for a chance to perform his assigned task. Somewhere along the way you'll want to introduce control over the dog, but in the initial phase, cash in on the energizing frustration factor.

The next phase of the trick will present a better-controlled dog, but it will not be as "impressive" as the dog exploding into action, charging out the door and seizing his prize. Should you want to go to that added control step, have the dog sit at the door after the paper is tossed. *Do not* introduce control until after you have developed his enthusiasm to the highest level possible. Slowly open the door with Jack sitting there, and make him wait for the command to *"Take It!"* Then he can charge forward. (For additional clarification, see Doorway Safety trick in chapter 13.)

Get the Mail

"PAWS UP!" "TAKE IT!" OR "FETCH!" "GET THE MAIL!"

You'll need some cooperation from the mailman when starting to teach this trick. (The postal employee's cooperation will be in direct proportion to the proximity of Christmas.) We'll assume you have the standard suburban mailbox, with an arm or flag and a flop-down door. You have to get the mailman to keep that mailbox door down and leave the mail sticking out, with the envelopes bundled together. (At this point, see the previous trick and the following three or four tricks. One flows into the other. They are all different but with similarities; teach one, and the rest readily follow.)

You shouldn't begin to teach this trick using real mail. Save some old envelopes. (Or you might use old bills that you haven't paid; they deserve to get ripped up and slobbered over.) The envelopes won't unbundle if you bind them with masking tape. You can use this same packet over and over again. For added realism, use three different packets of varying sizes.

Yorkshire Terrier fanciers, I'm sorry but your dog cannot do this. Yorkies just can't carry all the junk mail you and I receive. (Even a hermit might get an oversized envelope on occasion.) More important, the Yorkie can't reach the mailbox. A Corgi will not be able to reach the mailbox either, but is large enough to carry the mail. You can put a large box or step in front of the mailbox to enable the Corgi to reach. Make sure the box or step is stationary, not wobbly.

1. Start off with Jack sitting on the ground, in front of the mailbox. Use a lure-and-reward or modeling method to get the dog to reach up to the mailbox. Don't worry about the dog not doing more than that at first.

2. Tell him *"Paws Up!"* (see chapter 18, "Tricks for the Showbiz Dog"). You only have to do this once or twice a day, don't worry about him taking mail out of the box at this point. Make sure that the door to the mailbox is hanging down and the mailbox is good and solid. Should the mailbox or step collapse on Jack, the training will be set way, way back.

3. Get Jack to enthusiastically retrieve the mail from the ground in front of the box. The command is *"Take It!"* or *"Fetch!"* replaced later by *"Get the Mail!"* If he really gets worked up when the mailman comes, send him out to take the mail out of the mailman's hand. This is a great presentation by itself. Most mailmen will enjoy cooperating with you. Postal employees don't have to be anywhere in particular and have time to spare. (Don't tell the postmaster general I said that. They're so sensitive.)

4. Do not have the mailman give the mail to the dog every day. Ultimately, we want him to take it out of the mailbox. Once the dog learns to get the mail, it's a simple matter to have him retrieve it from the box.

PRESENTATION: Having Jack actually retrieve the mail is the best presentation. If you want to put on some demonstrations with your dog, buy an extra mailbox and have either your dog's name or some celebrity's name stenciled onto it. That extra mailbox is a good investment, as you will see in our next trick. Don't use a mailbox mounted on a post if you are traveling to put on a demonstration. It will be too heavy and cumbersome to transport by the time you fit it with a suitable base to keep it from being knocked over.

Post the Mail

"DROP IT!" "MAIL IT!"

It was easy to get Jack to pick up the mail. Now you want to reverse the procedure. One problem is getting him to put the mail into the box: He'll try to put it in with his head, which is impossible. If you bought that spare mailbox, it will be easier to teach Jack to deposit the mail. Tell him *"Drop It!"* (later replaced by *"Mail It!"*) and position the movable box to catch the mail. Jack's normal reaction will be to put the mail straight into the box. However the width of the letters will require him to turn his head in order to do this. Ultimately, Jack will position himself to slide the mail into the box. To keep the loose mailbox door from getting in Jack's way, use duct tape to secure it to the bottom of the box.

Put the Arm Up

"BUMP!" "ARM UP!"

This is the frosting on the cake. Not only will Jack pick up and deposit the mail, he'll also take care of the red arm on the side of the box that shows the status of the mail. Incidentally, the purpose of the arm is to signal the mailman that there's mail to be picked up. Not only must you teach Jack to deposit the mail in your box, but also to tell the mailman it is there by pushing or bumping the mailbox arm up in the air with his nose.

Use your target stick to touch the end of the arm, and tell the dog to bump it until it is perpendicular. (See chapter 7, "Clicker Training.") Initially you will use the *"Bump!"* command, but you will change this to *"Arm Up!"* There are different commands for different demands. You are shaping Jack's behavior, but you are also shaping the commands. You will find that in a very short time Jack will know that he is to put the arm all the way up. He won't know that he's using it to signal the mailman, but the pattern will be set, and this is one less thing you'll have to worry about.

PRESENTATION: If using a step, make sure it is high enough for Jack to use his nose to bump the arm upward. Part of the reason for the separate command is to make the trick look even more impressive. When you show it off, your audience's jaws will drop as Jack, on command, puts the arm up. Explain that your brilliant dog knows it is a signal for the mailman (just a little white lie). Once the pattern has been set, Jack will automatically put the arm up (even if you don't tell him to). A laugh can be added *after* he is doing this trick like clockwork. Revise his training by immediately calling him back to you after he deposits the mail. In other words, *not* letting him put the arm up. Do that three times in succession for three days. The pattern will be set, and he'll stop putting the arm up. The fourth day, after he deposits the mail and starts returning to you, you will tell him to stay. As he looks at you, tell him *"Arm Up!"* You may have to repeat it a few times before he does it, but you have now started teaching him to return to finish the job. *Do not* send him back every time. One time out of every three to five times will suffice. When you are showing him off you will say, "Oh, Jack, you forgot to put the *Arm Up!*" This is guaranteed to bring the house down.

Putting the Arm Down

"PAW!" OR "HIGH FIVE!" "ARM DOWN!"

Yes, there is a "need" to have the dog put the arm down. The arm was left up to let the mailman know there was mail to be picked up. The mailman should have put the arm down after he picked up the outgoing mail and deposited incoming mail. Jack is more competent than the mailman. (You know what everyone says about the post office, but let me officially apologize to the postal service at this point. I don't want anyone going postal on me.)

The arm should not be up on an empty mailbox. There are two avenues for teaching this exercise: Use the target stick to move Jack's paw up to the back of the mailbox arm, and, through shaping, teach him to move the arm downward. The other approach is to use the High-Five trick and shape it into putting the arm down. As you see, the level of difficulty and complication is raised as we chain these tricks together.

Now we may also have to raise the level of the step that Jack uses to reach the mailbox. Equipment can be "chained" together in much the same fashion that trick sequences are chained. I cannot caution you enough: If you didn't build Jack a stairway to paradise alongside the mailbox, and steps must be added, then they *must* be solid as the Rock of Gibraltar. We will use the *"Paw!"* command to get the dog to paw the arm downward. Settle for a slight downward movement of the arm in the initial phases of the training. Show your pleasure and enthusiasm for a partial performance. Click and treat.

PRESENTATION: By changing the command to *"Arm Down!"* you make the trick more impressive. A funny routine would be sending the dog for the mail, and when he is halfway back to the house, you can say, "Hey, you forgot to put the *"Arm Down!"* Be aware that if you set the pattern by having Jack *always* put the arm down, you will not be able to throw in that extra little laugh.

Open the Mailbox

"PULL!" OR "TUG!" "OPEN MAILBOX!"

Remember when you duct taped the portable mailbox's floppy door to the bottom of the box? Now it is time to untape it so that the door can be closed.

1. Tie a piece of rope to the latch at the top of the mailbox and make sure the door works smoothly before putting Jack to work.
2. The initial command is *"Pull!"* or *"Tug!"* (see chapter 18), one of the foundation tricks for the well-trained dog. Later you can change the command to *"Open Mailbox!"*

There is a transition between pulling on a hand-held towel and pulling on a hanging rope. Before starting to work with Jack, figure out the direction in which the pull is most efficient and guide Jack into pulling in that direction. You can have the dog repeat without going through the whole routine. It is up to you to make sure that your dog is applying the correct force in the correct direction. He'll "feel" the difference, but he needs your guidance.

PRESENTATION: Getting the mail out of a closed box is really impressive. You can keep sending the dog for the mail before he starts opening the mailbox. The separation of the tricks enables you to show off before the complete routine is finished.

Pick Up the Room

"TAKE IT!" OR "FETCH!" "DROP IT!" OR "OUT!"
"PICK UP THE ROOM!" "WHITE!" "COLORS!"
"DRY CLEANING!"

Now this is *really* handy. Sure, it's a great trick, but it's an even bigger help. What is to be picked up is the question. Another factor is that it is not just picking it up but also putting it someplace. This trick is for female readers: Guys are the ones who drop the stuff there in the first place; men don't pick things up.

There are two approaches to picking up the room. Either teach your dog to pick up items by name, or just teach him and encourage him to pick up everything that is on the floor.

You may feel that there are too many different things for the dog to learn all the names. No problem! The more you teach your dog, the easier he is to train, and the more names of items you teach, the easier it is for him to learn additional names.

There will always be unnamed items on the floor, but a good retriever will eagerly pick up anything. The retrieve is the reward. Point and encourage him and he'll respond. It's party time for your dog, though you should still offer praise.

You need to have a depository for the stuff he picks up. For information on teaching your dog how to drop the items in a basket, see chapter 16, "Retrieving," which explains *"Drop It!"* A laundry basket will work. Now let's really get sophisticated. Have two laundry baskets: one for white clothes, the other for colors. Of course, you will have to teach your dog to differentiate between white and colors. At first you'll have to teach and use the commands, *"White!"* and *"Colors!"* but eventually Jack will learn to sort it out for himself, and you won't have to tell him. Despite what you have heard about dogs being color blind, they can tell the difference between white and colored clothes. They see things as if in a black-and-white film. Now add a third basket for dry cleaning. When you see Jack pick up dry cleaning, tell him to deposit it in the appropriate basket by giving the *"Dry Cleaning!"* command. You'll never teach him to recognize the difference between laundry and dry cleaning on his own. If anyone out there is able to teach his or her dog that, I have a fifty-dollar bill for you. (I have another fifty-dollar bill for anyone who can teach him the difference between light and heavy starch!)

PRESENTATION: Since all the males in the family are going to evacuate the area when it comes time to pick up, you can't show off for them. You don't want anyone to see your house looking messy, so you can't bring in friends and neighbors. Sorry, you can't "present" this! Well, you could get a job as a housekeeper. The training for the dog can be done as you are doing your normal housekeeping chores; I don't even recommend training the dog specifically for this. Start with a good foundation in retrieving, and a happy, motivated dog, and then just tell him what to do. You won't be giving too many commands. You will be busy whistling while you work.

Tour the Mall

"HIGH!" "STAND HIGH!" "MARCH!" "RIGHT TURN!" "LEFT TURN!"

If you live in the suburbs, the mall is not a location—it's a way of life. If you take your dog into the mall, he should walk upright to improve his visibility, both to see and be seen. This walking on his hindquarters can be a real turn-on for your dog and is an excellent exercise to build upon as you see how the tricks are put together and how they can be varied from the basic *"Stand High!"*

1. A lure-and-reward method is the simplest way to teach Jack to stand high. It takes a delicate touch to move Jack into the required position. Just hold that tidbit higher and higher as Jack attempts to move into the appropriate position to sniff it. Start with it one inch from the tip of the nose and slightly raised above the nose. The initial command is *"High!"* Use *very* short sessions, moving Jack by minute degrees to stand on his hindquarters.
2. This command is later changed to *"Stand High!"* as Jack starts elevating his body. You may start by having Jack in a sit-high position. (Which is the reason the command given here is just *"High!"* rather than *"Stand High!"*
3. If you get a *"Sit High!"* and he doesn't know that trick, seize the opportunity and work on that trick.
4. The body position is critical and the same in both the sit- and the stand-high exercises. The head must be over the thorax, the thorax over the hips and the hips (in the stand) over the hindquarters. In the sit high the hips and hindquarters are together. There must be a straight line down Jack's back to maintain the proper balance. Now, on

top of all that, his front legs should be tucked in close to his body. Jack doesn't know how he's supposed to line up these body parts, and it's up to you to teach him. The command now is *"Stand High!"* Once you have Jack in the stand-high position, closely observe how long he stays there. Just before he tires, give him a release so he can return to all four legs.

5. Explode into a rush of clicks, cookies, applause, praise, rubs, cheers, pats and love. Work on extending the time Jack stands on his hindquarters later. This is not a normal position for Jack, but many dogs revel in this position, particularly the smaller ones.

   I remember Go-Go Burroughs, a Miniature Poodle, walking on his hindquarters for blocks through the streets of Manhattan's fashionable Upper East Side. He would often do it without command and adored the appreciative glances and remarks that he received. You may have seen Go-Go as Sylvia Myles's dog in the Dustin Hoffman and Jon Voight classic *Midnight Cowboy*.

6. Simply getting Jack up on his hindquarters is not where it stops; now he has to move forward, and you can use tidbits or the target stick for this. Go for one or two steps, about two or three times in a row, then knock off.

7. The command is *"March!"* and Jack will walk alongside you for those couple of steps.

8. When you say *"Stay!"* he will stop in the stand-high position and wait for your next command. We are doing two things here. We are teaching the command and also getting Jack in condition to do it. He has never done this before, and, just as you wouldn't be in shape to suddenly get out of your couch-potato mode to run a marathon, neither would Jack be in shape to do this. He will learn this trick faster than you can get him into condition, so have patience.

9. You want to phase out the tidbit or target stick as rapidly as possible. As Jack's endurance builds up, you can get him walking for some distance, but do not overtax him. Even if

he really enjoys it, I wouldn't let him walk for more than a block.

10. Next, we are going to teach Jack his right from his left. Yes, he can certainly learn. I know some dogs who are better at this than people. Jack will follow you through the mall, but why not send him out ahead and tell him which way to turn. Let me caution you on this. *You* must know your left from your right. If you get mixed up, you will really screw up Jack's training.

11. Every time you turn to your right (and do it as a sharp, squared-off corner), say *"Right Turn!"*

12. The *"Left Turn!"* is the flip side of that trick. You will not have to use tidbits to lure Jack on these turns. With him alongside you, make the turn as you give the command.

13. Also use a hand signal and, if you want to, add the click and a tidbit. Enthusiastic praise and encouragement are easier to administer and can continue as the dog performs.

PRESENTATION: Make sure the mall will permit dogs. If your dog carries a little purse in his mouth, now there's a picture too cute for words.

Report

Here is a trick for future lovers. It is a great trick for those romantically inclined and can be used by more than just suburban residents. It is a graceful way of hitting on women (or men, depending on your interests). The advantage is that you don't need all the "mall training" mentioned above. Heck, you can do this with a young puppy. As a matter of fact, it is even better with a puppy. The trick consists of you pointing your puppy at your chosen target and saying, *"Report!"* The puppy wiggles over and—well, you have to take it from there, but this is a major icebreaker. Start talking about dogs and ask about his/her dog. If that person doesn't like dogs, then you're wasting your time: Why on earth would you want to know a non–dog lover?

1. The system is simple. You want to enlist the aid of a few different friends to help you train your dog. If you are having trouble locating able assistants, tell them that you will help them find a significant other. Have your assistant, treat in hand, squat down and call the dog, while you head him in the right direction and gently push him forward. (A maximum of five tries the first time out.) You may wait five minutes and try again, but don't have extended training sessions. And make sure those treats are small and delicious. The clicker also is a valuable adjunct in this training.

2. Have your assistant click right before the dog reaches her. Your initial training will take place in a quiet area, but you want to work toward a busier area. A great training area is a "horizontal" rather than "vertical" mall. A horizontal mall is one that is spread out over a large area. A vertical mall is a high-rise mall with multilevel parking in the basement. In the vertical mall, you can start practicing in the outer reaches of the parking lot and gradually move toward the center of the mall. The closer to the mall you get, the more foot traffic. People don't want to walk too far from their cars, and in close is where the bulk of the cars are parked. You can even enlist dog-admiring passersby to help you.

3. Your assistant should jump into the breach and say that you are training the dog and would they like to pet the puppy and give him a treat. Your assistant can oversee the proper rewarding of Jack by these extra helpers. Strive for distance training. In other words, get the puppy to travel a distance to your potential intended. Ten feet is a good distance. You do not want to be so far away that you cannot see if this is a really good-looking person. Let's be selective here.

Two warnings if you train at the mall: One, you have to watch the traffic and be prepared to quickly scoop your dog up. This is another advantage working with a young dog; you *can* pick him up. Don't try to pick up a two-year-old Komondor. And two, should you decide to do some shopping, don't leave your dog in a hot car. Be aware of the temperature.

PRESENTATION: You have to send me an invitation to your wedding if you succeed with this ploy. Even if I don't show up, you'll get a nice present. (The first boy should be named after me too.) The first presentation is probably not going to get you married, so why discuss it here? Remember, the follow-up chitchat doesn't appear in this book. You'll have to figure that out by yourself, but be prepared: You'll need to have thirty to fifty years of chitchat with your S.O.

12
TRICKS FOR THE RURAL DOG

The rural dog is used for a wide variety of jobs that are striking enough to be called tricks. Entire books have been written on this subject, and they've hardly scratched the surface. Here is an overview of some of the great tricks that can be taught to help around the farm/ranch/house, etc.

Herding

"WAY TO ME!" OR "RIGHT!" "COME BY!" OR "LEFT!"
"COME IN HERE!" "THAT'LL DO!" "TAKE TIME!" "STAY!"
Herding makes your dog more of a workhorse than a trick dog. But just because these actions are useful doesn't mean they aren't tricks. If you live in the country and want to use these tricks, it's reasonable to assume that you have animal sense because you have been working around animals. Understanding one or two types of animals opens you up to understanding a wider spectrum of God's creatures. Animal sense translates into dog sense, and that's a big plus. What we're primarily concerned with here are sheep and cattle. There are behavioral differences in livestock. Beef cattle and dairy cattle are different. There's even a difference between Jerseys and Holsteins. Let's hope your animal sense will help you learn a maxi-

mum amount in this section. Suffice it to say, there are some generalizing about livestock, and some terms will be used interchangeably.

Ideally, your ol' dog "Tray" is one of the herding breeds. (It's more difficult to teach what is not there genetically.) Tray's been a great dog so far and you're not going to "fire" him. His "hardness" and the difficulty of herding the stock you want herded are important variables. Livestock listed from the most easily managed to the most difficult, are:

Chickens
Ducks
Sheep
Calves
Dairy Cattle
Beef Cattle
Horses

In any species, female animals with young are the toughest to manage. A general approach to herding will be covered here because of the wide variation among species. Only you know what you want and expect from your dog.

The first and most important thing is that Tray must know his right from his left. He's smart and will learn more rapidly than you can imagine. The hard part is remembering that when Tray is facing you, his left and right are the reverse of yours; you *must* be continually aware of *his* left and *his* right. Another layer of complication is the shepherd's terminology. To have Tray go to his right, traditionally you say, *"Way to Me!"* and to the left, *"Come By!"* You have my permission to use *"Right!"* and *"Left!"* if you wish to minimize *your* confusion.

Visualize a clock. You, the shepherd, are at six o'clock. Tray, when in a balanced position, is at noon (unless you're a vampire, in which case Tray would be at midnight). Tray is not "wrong" when he is not precisely at twelve. Both of you are controlling the flock (or herd). When you are at opposite sides, this is referred to as being balanced. That balance is continually shifting and changing depending on the ever-moving flock. Tray should usually face the flock (and you) meaning that he is a mirror image of you and his left and right are the reverse of yours. It's your job to keep Tray's right and left straight in your mind.

Before starting on a training program, try to capture the left and right behavior every chance you get. *Your* location is all-important in teaching these exercises; even the terms used depend on *your* location. Your presence opposite Tray gives good, balanced control over the flock. If Tray, on the opposite side, starts to move the flock toward you, he is "gathering" or "fetching" the flock. If you were on the same side with Tray and moving the flock forward, Tray would be "driving" the flock. When herding cattle, Tray might be "heeling," biting the recalcitrant cattle low on their weight-bearing leg, or on the nose or head. Nipping is generally considered too rough to use on sheep or smaller animals.

1. Start out with Tray alongside you.
2. If he is to go to his left, you will tell him *"Come By!"* while sliding the back of your hand alongside his right cheek. Use hand signals, even if he seldom sees them. It keeps you in practice, and Tray *may* see them out of the corner of his eye.
3. When you send Tray out to work the herd or flock, he should run as wide as possible away from the herd so he doesn't frighten and scatter the stock by moving into their comfort zone. You want Tray to go out to the opposite side of the herd. Widen his approach with the judicious use of a cattle stick or shepherd's crook. (You thought those sticks were just for the shepherd to lean on!) The purpose of a cattle stick is not to whack the dog, but to guide him into moving wide around the herd. Start training in small pens so you don't have to run your buns off as you learn to guide Tray with the stick.

Teaching sides is superimportant. In a small area, ducks are good animals to start with. (And you *do* want to start in a small area.) Put the ducks in a pen and have Tray work them from the outside, thus preventing him from getting close enough to injure them. By setting the pattern with Tray working away from the ducks, he learns that he can control them without direct contact. Later, when you take the ducks out of the pen, the pattern of working them at a distance will have been established. Control Tray's movements with your voice, body language and cattle stick. Concentrate on sides because, like people, most dogs prefer one side (left vs. right) to the other. Work both sides, but put the emphasis on the side Tray prefers *not* to work.

I like the commands used in stock-dog work. Traditional trainers, especially in obedience training, have said that the commands must be short, crisp and precise. In stock-dog work, particularly in handling the "softer" dogs, trainers carry on a conversation with the dogs. (Softer dogs are the ones that are easier and not rough on the stock.) The longer commands, in a soft tone of voice, express a mood, and these dogs respond well to the delivery. The amount of force needed in managing stock and the breed that manages that stock, ideally, should be well matched. "Sensitivity" is a word that is thrown around, very often improperly. The sensitive dog or livestock are more likely to spook, shy or panic and react differently than the harder dog or livestock.

A good comparison is the Border Collie with the Louisiana Catahoula (Leopard) Hog Dog. The Border Collie is more sensitive and can be controlled by a softer, more flowing voice. Hogs are a lot tougher to manage than sheep, and in Texas they use Catahoulas to herd horses. The Catahoula herds tougher stock and must, in turn, be tougher.

Louisiana's range hogs are really hard to manage and have to be moved fast from under heavy undergrowth, have to be kept moving before they can regroup and balk. Sheep are worked more slowly. They're more likely to panic. Different breeds for different needs, and different commands for different demands. Now we're getting into the fine points, which deserve to be discussed.

Tractability, the ability to be controlled, handled and managed is a fine point, and should be considered more often in dog training. It is particularly appropriate in livestock management. Everyone thinks they want an intelligent dog, when in reality, what they want is a tractable dog, one that will do what you command rather than seeking to outsmart you.

Leaving your dog alone to collect and herd animals is not going to cut it, since he *has* to take direction from you. Do *not* leave Tray alone with the stock in the initial phases of training or he will develop bad habits in your absence.

To add to the complication, you must also learn (and teach) the whistle commands, but hold off on that until Tray is working pretty well in close. Life is complicated enough without introducing the whistle too early. It is *you* that will have your hands full rather than Tray. The purpose of the whistle is to control at a distance. The whistle will carry much farther than a voice, and a shrill whistle will carry farther than one less shrill. The voice is more controlled and permits you to carry on a conversation with Tray. Commands used by human shepherds indicate a conversation, commands such as *"That'll Do!"* to terminate a working session, *"Come In Here!"* to get Tray to come straight in to you, and *"Take Time!"* and *"Stay!"* to slow him down. Verbal rewards (and corrections) are better delivered by changing the inflection in your voice.

PRESENTATION: The work is the presentation.

Collect Eggs

"COLLECT THE EGGS!" "LAY THE EGG!"

If your dog is not retrieving properly, see chapter 16 "Retrieving." Start off with a couple of hard-boiled eggs. The advantage of this "training aid" is that it is inexpensive, has the right odor, will not break and is the right weight. The shell may get bruised or broken in the process, so it's good to have a spare or two. If you have a Pomeranian use robin's eggs.

Insist that your dog retrieve one egg at a time. Some dogs, if they get worked up, will attempt to work too fast and try to grab more than one. It is important to keep Tray calm and relaxed as he works. Have your dog gently deposit the eggs in a large, low, open straw-lined basket. You will control the deposit of these eggs with your tone of voice: gentle and not rushed. The command is *"Lay the Egg!"* (and it is delivered to the dog, not the chickens—the chickens' command will be covered in the sequel to this book). Your tone of voice can control Tray. *"Lay the Egg!"* is a different command from *"Drop It!"* or *"Out!"* It means the eggs are to be gently laid in the basket with the other eggs. Have Tray touch or bump the straw in the basket first before he deposits the egg to let him develop a feel for the distance to the straw. This can be done by gently caressing the underside of his jaw, keeping his mouth closed and slowing him as he lowers his head. An alternate approach would be to use your voice to control his movement, or use a combination of both.

PRESENTATION: Tray must, of course, get along fine with the chickens. Do not let him get among the sitting hens. Get the hens out of the henhouse before sending him to work. After a period of time you can actually have him retrieve eggs from under the hens, as long as he is slow and gentle in his approach. Otherwise, he'll end up with egg on his face.

Pick Up the Apples, Oranges, Lemons, Pears

"APPLE!" "ORANGE!" "LEMON!" "PEAR!" ETC., AND "DROP IT!"

This is an easier variation on collecting eggs. Call each piece of fruit by its name as a command, then tell the dog to *"Drop It!"* in the bushel basket. If you have a toy breed, have him retrieve beans—jelly beans.

PRESENTATION: Using the fruit's name adds a lot of class and style to the exercise. There is a practical reason for it, too, if you have more than one type of fruit. Different fruit falls off the trees at different times, and you want your dog to be selective. Even if you do not want him to be selective in picking up the fruits, you do want him to be selective as to which bushel basket he drops them in (unlike eggs, they *can* be dropped). Put a few of the desired fruit in each basket, and watch Tray deliver the named fruit to the proper basket.

These are the tricks that can save your dog's life. Many of them are easily taught—can even be taught in day-to-day living and thus require no extra time at all. These skills can and should be continually reinforced. If you really love your dog, *all* these tricks should be in "Nigel's" repertoire.

Doorway Safety Trick

Every time he reaches a door, it's Nigel's job to sit. It is your job to ensure that he sits. He should remain in this position until you tell him *"Heel!"* Simple! Think of the long-range effect: He won't be charging in or out of the door. Everybody's life is easier if *you* make sure he sits every time. No exceptions! There is no longer the rush to get through. Remember that a dog's Second Commandment is, "If a door opens, go through it." We'll change that. Incidentally the dog's First Commandment is, "If it drops on the floor, it's mine."

PRESENTATION: The presentation of this trick is more for you than anyone else. You can now carry a heavy grocery bag, walk up to your door and fish out your keys without Nigel jumping all over the place. He will sit like a gentleman and wait for you to open the door and say *"Heel!"* If you are leaving a room with Nigel, explain to the people staying behind what a gentleman Nigel is as he sits at the doorway and heels through life.

Traffic Safety Trick

The same procedure outlined in Doorway Safety applies here. Before stepping off each curb, Nigel must sit. The need for this training is obvious, but you can advance and enhance this by taking a little more time at each corner. Give the *"Heel!"* command without stepping off the curb, and it will teach Nigel that he's not only supposed to wait for the command but also for your forward motion. This is desirable from a safety point of view. If a car was making a right-hand turn, the driver might see you to his right, but the right front fender would obscure his view of Nigel, especially if the dog stepped off the curb. The dog is forbidden to step off the curb without your forward motion. If you are not smart enough to look both ways, it serves you right if a car hits you. I don't want you hit by a car, but my main concern is Nigel!

PRESENTATION: As simple as this exercise is, you will have passersby looking in amazement at the dog waiting at the curb. Where do you live? New Yorkers never wait for lights. Angelenos always do. Nigel waits for *you.* A dog that will sit on command and do as he's told amazes many people. Your explanation can include the remark that guide dogs for the blind "check" (stop) at every corner.

Auto Safety Trick

"HUP!"

The right rear seat is the safest place for your dog to ride. If you have a four-door car, that spot is safest because:

1. It puts Nigel well away from the driver so that the dog cannot annoy you or interfere with the operation of the vehicle.
2. The rear window is kept clear so the driver can use the rearview mirror.
3. The dog cannot paw the driver for attention.
4. The dog cannot pant and salivate down the back of the driver's neck.
5. The dog enters and leaves the car from the curb side.

The door is slammed on the leash, thus restricting the dog's movement. As an added safety measure, if possible, the leash is tied off on the door handle to stop the dog from pulling the leash through the door and to make sure there is no loose end that can snag. The door is locked, and the window is raised so the dog cannot jump out. Do *not* do this with an unattended dog. The dog is Hugo McGirr, a Labrador Retriever, trained at Olde Towne School for Dogs, Alexandria, VA.

The first part of the trick is getting Nigel to remain in that spot. A dog seat belt is the safest device to control him. If you do not have such a seat belt, a quickie solution is to keep the leash on Nigel and slam the car door on the leash and tie it off to the outside of the car. A simple loose knot stops Nigel from pulling the leash through the door. Doubling the leash and leaving the end inside the door, then knotting it outside the car is one solution. *Make sure the door is locked.* Make sure that you do not have the leash running through the lock area in the door jamb. Do not have the leash too long. Nigel does not need that much freedom. We now have a modified seat belt and are confining the dog to the area in which he is to remain. By your setting the pattern, Nigel will learn where he is to sit in the car. Do this every time for a month or two, and it will not be necessary to tether Nigel. Of course, if you encourage him to move into different areas in the car, you will upset the "invisible" training you have accomplished.

Next, Nigel should be taught to sit automatically when he comes up to the car door and to remain sitting after the door is opened. Nigel remains seated until he is told *"Hup!"* at which point he jumps into his seat. He should not jump into the car until he receives the command and should wait quietly, without a fuss. Even more important, when it's time to get out of the car, Nigel must sit until he is again given the *"Hup!"* command to jump down. This is a chapter on safety tricks, and remaining seated, waiting for a command, is safe. After you've parked, once again, Nigel sits, waiting for his next command. This enables you to assemble the kids, pick up your packages, get your keys in order, etc.

PRESENTATION: Every time Nigel rides in the car, put him through his paces. It will take less time than wrestling and struggling to get him in and out of the car. If a passerby stops to watch you, make Nigel wait a bit longer before giving him the command. Show off and work on the exercise at the same time. Out of the corner of your eye you will see the approving nod, the amazed face. Another big advantage of this trick is that Nigel is conveniently getting in and out on the curb side of the car.

Elevator Safety Trick

Now you're getting the idea. The elevator trick is another one of those invisible training jobs that you can do as you go through life. Avoid busy elevators at the beginning of this training. If you find many are full, be prepared to miss one or two.

Nigel should remain seated, in the heel position, until you give him a command. He shouldn't move when the elevator door opens. Believe me, this is not the last elevator out of town. When you enter the elevator, go to the far right corner, turn and have Nigel sit in the heel position with both of you facing out. This gives Nigel protection on three sides, leaving only one on which you have to protect him from an unseeing passenger accidentally stepping on him. There will be a lot of opening doors to tempt Nigel, but he should remain in position until you tell him otherwise.

PRESENTATION: A well-behaved dog that doesn't frighten other passengers is the ideal presentation. Do realize that some people are frightened of dogs. Pay attention, and if you see a fear reaction on the face of someone already in the elevator, wait for the next one. This is Nigel's and your presentation. If you are already on the elevator and somebody entering appears frightened, it is up to him or her to decide whether or not to wait for the next car.

Stairway Safety Trick

"EASY!" OR "SLOW!"

A major problem with dogs is that they want to go running up and down flights of stairs like little kids. It's hard to prevent this, and if you're holding on to the leash, a charging dog can be disastrous. The trick is to slow Nigel down. The command to use is *"Easy!"* or *"Slow!"* This command is delivered in a slow, soft drawn-out tone of voice and should be used anytime you want to slow Nigel down. You can do some preliminary training by using this command when out walking and he pulls on the leash. A slight leash correction should be used with the command as Nigel pulls. This is the fast way to teach the *"Easy!"* or *"Slow!"* command, but it requires more skill to accomplish on a stairway than when walking on the flat, so we'll do it the easy way first.

1. After preliminary training on the flat, go to the first step of the stairs and have Nigel sit.
2. Go to the second step and have him sit again. Once he's got this down, move up to two steps at a time, then three. This step-by-step approach will do the job. Just don't be impatient. What's your rush? If it takes a minute or two longer, that's better than tumbling down the stairs. Anytime Nigel forges ahead, plant your feet and tell him *"Easy!"* or *"Slow!"* and if possible, give a leash correction. Watch your step on the steps. It's a question of *your* balance. Nigel has four on the floor, and you have two in the shoe. Not only does he have twice the feet on the ground, but he also has a lower center of gravity. Limited space and balance are added to problems. Step by step, you will slow him down. Use the same procedure descending the stairs. It will take you an extra two minutes per flight of stairs. If you do it *every* time for a week, Nigel will be trained.

PRESENTATION: When the neighbors see that Nigel is no longer dragging you up or down the steps they will want to know why the improvement? Tell them you sat down and had a heart-to-heart talk with him.

Hasty Muzzle

The purpose of the hasty muzzle is for short-term use in an emergency situation. Do not leave Nigel unattended with the muzzle on.

With you on the dog's right side (the heel position), wrap the hasty muzzle under the jaw once and . . .

With the dog sitting at the heel position, with your left hand grasp the six-foot leash at its snap and say *"Muzzle!"* With your right hand, grasp the free end of the leash and run the leash under Nigel's chin, over the top of his snout, under his chin again and over the top (that's two times around his muzzle). The right hand holding the leash then continues its journey around to the left of Nigel's neck, behind the back of the neck, and joins the left hand. (Ultimately, we will tie the ends together.)

Slide the whole leash off Nigel's head and release him with praise. Repeat this three times a day. After a week you can start tying a square knot where the ends of the leash meet. The reason the knot is not tied for the first week is that you are working on your ability to wrap the leash around the dog's head. After you feel comfortable with putting on the hasty muzzle, you can then work on the square knot in a more relaxed fashion. Furthermore, we do not want Nigel to be too uncomfortable while you are learning. This training is more for *you* than him. Nigel is much smarter than you and will pick it up quickly.

After Nigel is acclimated to the muzzle, have him wear it a little longer. Five minutes is not too much time.

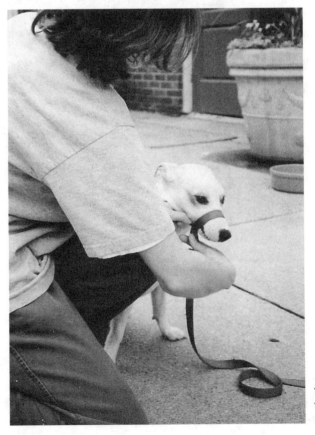

. . . wrap it twice around the dog's muzzle . . .

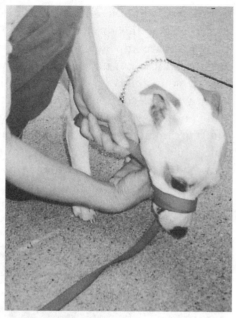

. . . run the leash under
the dog's jaw for the
third time and . . .

. . . around the back of
the dog's neck and . . .

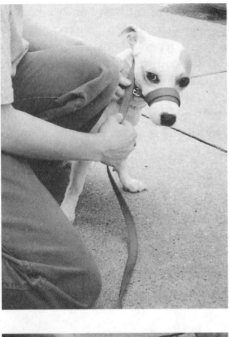

. . . bring the leash around to the right-hand side of the dog's neck and . . .

. . . tie a square knot on the right side between the neck and jaw. The dog here is Buster Dicken, a Jack Russell Terrier, with his trainer Jane Winchester of Olde Towne School for Dogs.

Bull breeds need a different tying of the hasty muzzle because of the head shape. Face the dog with the leash in a loop in front of the dog's muzzle, with equal lengths between your hands. The loop is crossed over at the top of the loop and is tossed over the muzzle. With the loose ends, one in each hand, gently tighten the leash above the snout, then drop your hands down while crossing the leash under the snout, passing both ends back behind the neck, where the leash is secured with a square knot.

PRESENTATION: Use the hasty muzzle when you take Nigel in for his shots. *You* will be showing off to your vet, rather than Nigel: Though Nigel does need training to accept the hasty muzzle, your veterinarian will be more impressed with your skill in handling the dog. Should you have a veterinarian who doesn't permit you to handle your own dog, you can still use this hasty muzzle in a dire emergency.

Pool Safety Trick

"OUTTA THE POOL!"

A pool can be deadly for the untrained dog. I know, I know, you've heard that all dogs can swim, and that's true. But it doesn't mean that a dog can swim forever. What's the problem with pools? Your dog must learn how to get out of the pool. (If you don't want the dog to go into the pool, you'll have to get another book to cover that problem.)

Guide Nigel into the pool. Leave the leash on him, or—better yet—put a thirty-foot leash on him. (If you tie a stick in the leash handle, it will float.) Then tell him *"OK, Outta the Pool!"* He'll look at you, and you'll gently guide him over to the spot where he's able to climb out. If there's no obvious climbing-out spot, you'll have to make one. Three or four times are the minimum that you'll need to practice this with Nigel. Then check him out every four to six months. The main purpose of this trick is to show him where he can get out of the pool.

PRESENTATION: When your friends and neighbors are hanging out at your pool, change the command slightly and try to sound as if you're a lifeguard. Say *"OK, You Kids Get Outta the Pool!"* and watch Nigel come charging out.

Raus!

You want Nigel to leave the room, and you say one word to him and he is gone! You can't even get the kids to do that. It is soooo easy! And so useful and grand and impressive and handy and safe. It also takes about ten minutes to teach. You'll use an aversive here. A benign aversive, but an aversive nonetheless. As this is a safety trick, you'll start teaching it in the kitchen. We would prefer a room with only one doorway, but that is not an absolute. The command is taken from the German *"Hier aus!"* (Get out of here) which is generally shortened to *"Raus!"* I like it because it sounds like its meaning. A genuine onomatopoeia.

Why the kitchen? Because there are a couple of dangerous scenarios that can take place there. One is a grease fire on the stove, with Nigel excitedly barking. You are busy firefighting and do not have time to contend with Nigel. Tell him, *"Raus!"* and he leaves the room. Another scenario might be when a glass breaks on the floor and you want Nigel out of there before he steps on the broken glass. Same solution! (Make sure you do not send Nigel through the glass field.)

Make a "beanbag" and put it on a counter, as far from the edge as possible. A beanbag is a brown paper bag with a scant handful of uncooked rice in it. Blow the beanbag up like a balloon and twist the top to seal it. You now have a giant rattle. Next, position Nigel between yourself and the door. You want to "herd" him out of the kitchen. Tell Nigel *"Raus!"* and attempt to hit him with the beanbag as he scurries out the door. It isn't necessary actually to hit Nigel, but *try* to smack him. (It won't hurt if you do connect, honest. Hit yourself over the head with the beanbag for proof.) Make sure you chase (herd) him all the way out the door. Do *not* do this more than three times in a single session. Wait after each *"Raus!"* After Nigel has settled down, you can call him over to you. Give him a lot of encouragement and pats or a cookie. *Do not* overdo it. A maximum of three times the first day, then once every other day for a week is fine. Follow up with an occasional reminder once every four to six months. Try this exercise in other rooms as well. You don't have to start from scratch. Nigel knows the command, so just do the exercise once. Phase out the beanbag, but keep it handy.

PRESENTATION: You have houseguests and you have hors d'oeuvres on the coffee table. Nigel has just said hello to your newest guest and is eyeing the hors d'oeuvres. You boom out *"Raus!"* and to everyone's amazement he gallops out of the room.

Move or Yield or Excuse Me

We ask very little of our dogs. But one of the jobs your dog has is to stay out of your way. It's his job because he's closer to the ground than we are and can see what's going on down there. On the other hand, you don't want to step on Nigel either. When possible, you have an obligation to warn him. The younger he is when you start this, the better and more useful the results.

Nigel is lying down, relaxing. He is finally quiet, and you really don't want to disturb him. Choose your command well. What do you want your tone to be? Commanding? Requesting? Or indignant? *"Move!"* is delivered in a commanding tone of voice. *"Yield!"* is delivered in a requesting voice. If you indignantly say, *"Excuse Me!"* in a rising tone of voice, it becomes quite funny. The tone of voice is not for the dog per se. It is for comedic effect. Once you decide on your command and the appropriate tone of voice you have to stick with it.

Before we decide what tone/command to use, let's see what we'll do.

1. Make a three-quarter turn toward Nigel and, using very short steps, make a shuffling sound, raising each foot after each shuffle.
2. If Nigel doesn't move, nudge him with your feet. You've just moved Nigel. Walk away.
3. Should Nigel come over, you can pet him.
4. When Nigel relaxes again, repeat the exercise. If he doesn't lie down again, don't worry. You'll catch him the next time around. Your purpose is not to deprive Nigel of rest. You want to get him at a time when he is not expecting to be given the command.

Train for this command periodically, not consistently. Though you could give Nigel a *"Down-Stay!"* command and then move in on him, that wouldn't be fair. Always try to be fair to your dog. Don't give him conflicting commands. Now, an argument could be made that they are replacement, not conflicting, commands, but why do it if it isn't necessary?

PRESENTATION: The best presentation is made with the command *"Excuse Me!"* delivered in a haughty, superior tone. That is really funny and doesn't require a lot of introductory explanation of what you're demonstrating.

Step Over Your Dog

"STAY!" OR "DON'T MOVE!"

The deal we made was that your dog would be obedience trained before you use this book to train him further. My contention is that a good obedience course will have already taught this trick. But in case your dog isn't trained to do this, here's how it's done.

Your dog must remain stationary on command when you step over him. Here we have an Australian Cattle Dog, Joey Mejias, remaining stationary when his owner and trainer Sandy Mejias steps over him.

1. Start with your dog in any position: down, sit or stand. Down is recommended because it's the steadiest position, and no matter how big a dog or how small you are, the downed dog can be stepped over—just about.
2. Try this with the dog in the heel position. You're on his right side and you say, *"Don't Move!"* Then slowly and cau-

tiously, step over Nigel. If he seems a bit nervous, calm him down with soft talk. As he calms down, repeat *"Don't Move!"* a couple of times.

3. Now it's time to straddle Nigel. Stand over him with one foot on either side of his body. Next, move forward in the straddling position to Nigel's head.

4. Then circle around Nigel until he is again in the heel position.

5. After repeating this a couple of times you must stand directly in back of Nigel and, straddling his tail, move forward from rear to front. Take it easy. We're in no rush, and with the average dog we can cover this in a few minutes. If the dog seems too nervous, terminate the training and start over tomorrow.

6. The hardest part of the training is the last step. It sounds simple, but it will bother Nigel. Straddle Nigel and walk from his *head* to his *tail*. Once the dog accepts this, you're home free. Say you're in the kitchen on Thanksgiving Day. Nigel is waiting for the opportunity to obey the First Commandment: If it drops on the floor, it is mine. You have taken a huge hot turkey out of the oven. You want to put it on the sideboard. Tell Nigel *"Stay!"* and you can step over him.

PRESENTATION: Using the command *"Don't Move!"* makes the trick more interesting, and this is the way to present it. After you've stepped over Nigel and straddled him, run around and jump over him. That is the frosting on the cake. As you can see, this is the flip side of the previous trick. There is absolutely no reason for not teaching Nigel both these tricks.

Focus or Pay Attention

If your dog is paying attention to you, he won't be distracted and get into trouble. But there are sooo many interesting things out there! (You should be the most interesting thing to your dog.) Teach him to focus on you all the time. If his mind wanders, simply tell him to *"Focus!"* and his attention immediately comes back to you. This safety trick takes more work than any other trick in this chapter. Not only does it take more initial work, but you also have to continually reinforce the focus exercise. Every time Nigel is distracted, it's your job to step off swiftly in the opposite direction and give the command, *"Pay Attention!"* followed by a snappy jerk on the leash. I know you don't want to correct your best buddy, but Nigel has to learn when he's doing something wrong, as well as when he's doing something right. You'll notice almost immediate improvement. He'll pay more attention to you. (However, improvement will be immediately lost if you don't keep working on it.)

1. The ideal setup is to have the dog in the heel position, with the distraction coming from his left flank.
2. Move off rapidly to Nigel's right flank and tell him to *"Focus!"* or *"Pay Attention!"* The reason for stepping off in the opposite direction to the distraction is because Nigel won't be able to see your body movement; this will make him pay more attention to you, which is the name of the game.

Now I don't expect my dogs to pay attention to me 100 percent of the time—just most of the time. I want a dog that I'm working with to have a chance to get out there and smell the roses as we work together. We're working together, but I'm the boss because I *think* I'm the smarter one.

ALTERNATE METHOD: Rather than giving a leash correction you can give the command, step off to your right and then treat Nigel. You will always be ready to practice the previous method. In this method you must have food handy to dispense.

PRESENTATION: When showing off this trick, the best command is *"Pay Attention!"* rather than *"Focus!"* You give the word, and Nigel immediately looks into your eyes. Every time his mind wanders, repeat the command. His head racks around, and he looks at you. This is the result of all this work. The real and important result is Nigel paying more attention to you even when you don't tell him to do so.

The Ultimate Emergency

"HURRICANE!" "EARTHQUAKE!" "TWISTER!" OR "TORNADO!" "FLOOD!" "CYCLONE!" "SHSS-SHSS!"
The above disasters strike terror in our hearts. The disaster word you choose to teach varies depending on where you live—and your level of paranoia. Being prepared is always the best idea. If you worry that much, I would suggest some preparation on your part:

1. First, check with your local emergency-preparedness organizations for instructions regarding natural disasters.
2. Check with your local shelter or humane society for their emergency recommendations. Most shelters have emergency-preparedness plans. You should be aware of their policy on taking in dogs during and after an emergency.
3. Keep a spare leash by your bed.
4. Have a crate large enough for your dog available for such emergencies.
5. Have a collar made for Nigel with a metal ID tag bolted at each end to the collar. Your name, address, telephone number and the word "Reward" should be etched into this tag. The collar should be emergency orange in color and have reflector tape on it.
6. Get in touch with me for my free "Earthquake Emergency" flyer.

The procedure for each one of these commands is the same; the location varies depending on the emergency, and the emergency varies depending on the section of the country in which you live. Who made the rule that there is a different, major life-threatening emergency for each section of the country?
Before the emergency arises, select the spot where you want

Nigel to go. This is the spot he will go to on command. Can you teach more than one location? Sure! Should you give each one a separate command? Yes! The truth is that one spot is really all you need for most emergencies, floods excepted. In this case, it would be wise to select the highest inside and the highest reachable outside parts of the house. The safest spots in the house are:

Hurricane—Under a doorframe in the center of the house, or in the cellar.

Earthquake—Under a doorframe in the center of the house. A safer spot is outdoors, away from buildings and other structures.

Twister or tornado—In the cellar, particularly a storm cellar.

Flood—The highest reachable part of the house, preferably on the outside.

Cyclone—In the cellar, particularly a storm cellar.

1. Start off by putting your dog in the chosen spot. Say *"Cyclone!"* or the appropriate disaster name.
2. Tell Nigel to stay, then walk away about five feet and call him.
3. Repeat the command and lead him back to the spot while giving the command.
4. Click and treat the dog, give a *"Stay!"* command and move away.
5. Call him again and repeat as above. Do that three or four times, then, rather than leading your dog to the spot, *send* him to the correct location.
6. Start to lead him to the position, then, two feet away, you should "push" him forward into the right spot, all the while repeating the command. Now, this pushing is not a physical push, but a psychological push. You physically lead him away from you with your hand and then continue the hand and *mental* movement. Praise, click and treat.
7. Move farther and farther away from the assigned spot, thus sending Nigel farther each time. It doesn't matter what posi-

tion he winds up in, but sit works well. Once he finds the spot, call him back to you and praise and repeat.

8. The next level of this trick is to start using a herding technique. The way you drive a dog into the correct location is to gently shoo him. Move forward and gently say, *"Shss-Shss!"* Your hands hang down from your wrists at elbow height, palms facing you. You make the motion of brushing Nigel away as you herd him into the right spot. In herding, you want to line Nigel up between you and the spot and "chase" him into the right location. Repeat the command and reward him. Here is a good place to use the clicker. You are not on top of Nigel, and the clicker rewards him at a distance.

We're working on distance, and you want to be able to do this from any part of the house. Start close to the assigned spot and work back to the farthest reaches of your house or apartment. Can you work Nigel on all of the above commands? Of course you can, but it's not practical. No section of the country has all these problems. You can even teach your dog to go to a spot outside the house, but remember that Nigel is going to be as nervous as you are and may bolt when the big one comes along. Practice once a week after Nigel has it down pat, and always show off for visitors. Vary the spot from which you give the command, and have him stay for longer periods of time before recalling him.

PRESENTATION: Any time you have company, steer the conversation to natural disasters. This is easy to do if your friends and neighbors are as paranoid as you. Then spring your trap. Explain that it's important that Nigel know where to go in case of a _____ (you fill in the blank). Tell your guests why he is going where he is going. Nigel knows exactly where to go, and he moves to his assigned spot and gleefully sits there and wags his tail. When Nigel does this trick, you want to work on really long stays in the spot. If you work for a company that continually moves you around the country, you can teach the appropriate command for the area in which you live. We haven't mentioned fire because we use no command for that. Instead, it is your responsibility to *lead* Nigel out of the house as you'd probably do in an earthquake. It is important that you keep him as calm as possible under a stressful situation.

14

TRICKS TO EXERCISE YOUR DOG
WITH MINIMUM EFFORT

This is great! Everyone is concerned with giving his or her dog enough exercise, and this is how to do it with minimum effort. We all should run five miles every morning before breakfast and take our dogs with us. We all know this is not going to happen.

Does your dog need more exercise than you do? That depends on how active you are. Activity should be regular rather than intermittent. Your dog will become more of a couch potato, as you will, with less exercise. Figure out what you want him to do and then keep it as regular as possible. The retrieving tricks are ideal. You must participate in your dog's workout, but you can do that sitting on your fat behind. Some of these exercises really get the dog worked up and get his endorphins flowing. This will make both of you feel good, and he'll be on a natural, drug-free high.

Chase a Light Beam

This is a great trick for exercising your dog. Some dogs just take to it naturally, and others have to be trained. If your dog has an aptitude for light-beam chasing, wonderful! If not, and your dog likes Frisbees, start with that.

1. Make a small hole on the side of a dark-colored Frisbee through which to attach a string. (If you have a soldering iron or wood-burning tool, just heat it up and burn a hole through the edge.) This hole will ruin the aerodynamic quality of the Frisbee, but so what! This is fun for your dog.

2. Start teaching this trick at night. Turn the lights down low. You do not have to shut them off. If you have a night-light on, or a light on in the next room, you will be able to see well enough not to fall over your own feet.

3. Bring in "Brock" and start slowly shining a flashlight or a laser beam around on the ground. If Brock shows no interest, then toss down the Frisbee with the string attached.

4. As soon as he is focused on the Frisbee, shine the light beam in the center of it. (It's best if you have a flashlight with a handy ON-OFF switch.) The purpose here is to switch Brock's interest from the Frisbee to the light beam. The ON-OFF switch helps you tease his attention. Verbal praise is the reward to use here. (Both your hands are too busy for anything else.)

5. A great deal of verbal encouragement in an ongoing conversation will get Brock going. Keep his interest in the Frisbee up. When his attention starts to lag, it's time to knock off the training session. You can work longer sessions of fifteen to twenty minutes as long as Brock is interested. The purpose here is to shift his interest from the Frisbee to "playing" with the light beam. As his interest shifts, *do not* overwork the light beam. You want to gradually divert Brock's attention away from the Frisbee on to the light beam. This can take up to six sessions of twenty minutes each in the worst-case scenario.

PRESENTATION: As Brock becomes more and more interested in chasing the light beam, you no longer need to dim the lights for this self-rewarding trick. For theatrical effect, work him up to following a colored light. The new laser pointers come with different silhouettes and can be used in daylight just about anywhere. The more worked-up the dog, the funnier the trick. Now you not only have a good trick, but a great additional training tool. The light beam can readily be converted to a lure useful in training Brock. It can be used in a similar manner to the target stick.

Half Turn

"TURN!" "RIGHT!" "LEFT!"

We are starting to build on a series of tricks. Chasing the light beam helps prepare for these tricks.

1. With Brock standing and facing you, hold a piece of food in your left hand. While moving that hand to the left, tell Brock *"Turn!"* Keep your left and right straight. You are a mirror image of your dog (and this can add to your confusion). Your leftward movement lures Brock to his right with that piece of food, and you deliver it to him as he turns his head to his right. When he takes the lure, click.

2. Do this three times to Brock's right in six-minute sessions, using the command *"Right!"* Get ready for a little juggling now.

3. Switch the food to your right hand this time (the clicker is in your left). Repeat as above, this time saying, *"Left!"* (Later, you'll change these commands to *"Turn Right!"* *"Turn Left!"*)

4. Go back and forth between left and right with this, and remember that we want Brock to begin moving not just his head but his head and shoulders. Work it up to moving his head, shoulders, whole body. You should alternate between left and right.

5. Your first session can be a bit longer, but as soon as Brock shows the slightest loss of interest, stop. Do not go on for more than seven minutes, no matter how much he enjoys it. If you are all worked up and do not want to stop, switch to another trick (preferably with a different reward).

PRESENTATION: If you want to start showing off early, give this a try or two. Before Brock has the trick down pat, you'll find that he'll respond to your body language. Moving your body to the left or right will have him turning to the right and left. Subliminal sensory cues will start to develop here (see chapter 8). Without realizing it, you will be twisting your body in a characteristic fashion that Brock will pick up on. You're giving him extra information, and that is not bad.

Chase Your Tail

"RIGHT!" "LEFT!" "REVERSE!" "SPIN!"

Even if you have one of the docked breeds, you can still get your dog to chase his tail. Some dogs are prone to tail chasing, and if you can catch the behavior and click on it, or put it on command, you're halfway there.

The previous tricks have set Brock up for this trick. Enticing Brock to chase his tail can be done with two great dog-trick training tools: masking tape and peanut butter. Both these items are easy to handle, inexpensive and will stick to things. Not only will they stick to things, but when you pull them off your skin (or your dog's) there will be no painful ripping. Peanut butter appeals to the dog's taste buds, and masking tape annoys him. (You might even say that masking tape is a pain in the tail.) Both these tools become self-rewarding: removing the tape and eating the peanut butter are self-rewards. The chasing also develops into something self-rewarding. It can be addictive to Brock because it gets the endorphins flowing.

We are going to use the *"Right!"* and *"Left!"* commands introduced previously, getting Brock worked up.

1. Stop Brock mid-turn and immediately give him the *"Reverse!"* command along with the hand signal (the hand moving in the opposite direction), and he will switch.
2. The *"Spin!"* command is a variation on the above. We do not have Brock focusing on his tail at this point. Right now he is focusing on spinning. You want him to focus on his tail.

3. If you want to use peanut butter, you need a dog that has hair on the end of his tail, and don't say all dogs have hair on their tails. I mean you want a dog with a tuft of hair on his tail. The hairless Chinese Crested Dog has a tuft of hair on his tail, but the Manchester Terrier, while it has hair on its tail, does not have a tuft of hair there. You need that tuft of hair to work in the peanut butter. Yes, you can put peanut butter on the shorthaired Manchester Terrier's tail, but you are better off using masking tape because it will last longer on the tail.

4. Alternatively, put a tail on the tail with a two-inch extension of tape. Now hold the tip of the tail right under your dog's nose and let him taste the peanut butter, or tease him with the tape. He will not be able to reach it on his own at this point. You want him to try to catch it once he gets started, and he might be able to do that if he picks up enough speed and extends (stretches) his body enough. These exercises will increase your dog's suppleness.

ALTERNATE APPROACH: A "marking" approach will work out really well here. A target stick can be used, but I would recommend using the laser pointer, since you have already trained Brock to respond to it. The target stick or laser pointer eliminates set-up time. The appearance of the target stick or the laser light prepares Brock to follow one or the other.

ANOTHER ALTERNATE APPROACH: *"Spin!"* can be taught through modeling or molding, i.e., manually teaching Brock the movements. This is sometimes called a "compulsion" method. An important point to remember is that you're better off choosing one method from the start and following it through. If you switch back and forth, Brock will learn nothing. But you can use other techniques to *augment* what you're working on.

With the dog standing in front of you, spin his head and shoulders to his left while you push his right hindquarter to his right and say *"Spin!"* You will push on the right shoulder to his left (your right) with your left hand, while your right hand pushes on his left hindquarter to his right (your left). Once you have him spinning, add the *"Reverse!"* *"Left!"* and *"Right!"* commands.

Note: Back chaining, (see chapter 7), starting with the last part of the trick first and moving backward, is an effective technique, but trick building is better than back chaining. It is a point of view. Do you want to do a certain trick and build it from the back to the front? Is that an effective way to teach an extended (multipart) trick? Well, it is effective, but this book's approach is different. Rather than have the tail wagging the dog, why not build rather than back chain? Teach a series of independent tricks that will each stand alone. If they *grow* from other tricks, that is all well and good. Either approach will accomplish your mission, but building will teach more tricks, so why not take the scenic route and make an interesting side trip or two? If you add a dash of imagination, you will end up with a dog that does more interesting and different tricks. Don't back chain! Build! Here we have built on a number of tricks. Not merely spinning, but spin right and left and do reverses, chase your tail and chase a light beam. One trick is built into five or six.

PRESENTATION: This is a great trick that can be performed anywhere. When you start saying *"Right!"* or *"Left!"* the audience will be impressed, but the *"Reverse!"* makes it the ultimate performance. When showing off a series of different tricks, return to the tail chasing as the last trick, but call it "spin," and your audience will think it's a different trick. Point out and point up the command by explaining that the dog is now spinning and not chasing his tail. It is all in the presentation.

15
BALANCING TRICKS

Here is a dynamic collection of tricks that can be built upon and, as a matter of fact, *should* be built upon. As you begin to build a repertoire, your dog will enjoy working even more and work even harder for you. The pleasure of work is often reward enough for dogs. The downside is that the training takes time, patience and a very soft, steady hand. To teach many of the tricks in this book, you can just jump in and start, but not these. These tricks require a close relationship with your dog that develops through extensive previous training. You want to develop your dog's love, understanding, respect and willingness to please and work along with you. Each one of these tricks can be done in a variety of positions: sitting, sitting high, down, walking, walking on hindquarters and even in the kiss-my-ass position. Not only do you need a steady hand, but also steadiness on the part of the dog. Balance is important, so start with the sit-stay position. This position is steady, easy, controllable and requires less bending for you. If either one of you becomes bored with a trick, move on to another. A high-energy, active trick can be alternated with a relaxing, low-energy trick that requires more patience than action.

Balance and Catch

"BALANCE!" "TOSS!" "CATCH!"

Here is one of the tricks that I "invented." It's actually two tricks in one, and the dog teaches herself the finer points of the last part. (Every dog develops their own method of flipping a tidbit up and catching it.) You work together on the middle part. The first part is the sit-stay, which "Suzette" should have no trouble performing. It is the simplest position from which to start for all these tricks. With the dog in the sitting position, take a tidbit and place it on her muzzle. There is a slight depression right behind the nose that the good Lord made *just* so you can teach your dog this trick. Try to use tidbits that are flat on at least one side so that they do not roll off. *"Staaaaay!"* is delivered in a calm, drawled-out tone of voice and immediately followed by *"Toss!,"* the command you give to release your dog from the stay position, allowing her to scarf the tidbit. This is the middle third of the exercise, where you and Suzette have to work together. You are taking your time and calming her down; she is learning the self-control needed to remain steady. Now, you still may have your fingers on the tidbit when you say *"Toss!"* but you do not say *"Toss!"* when she is in a wiggley-waggley mood. Get as much calmness, steadiness and self-control from her as you can, even if only for half a second. You and Suzette will increase the period of steadiness. Remember that you are helping Suzette build up her self-control, an important starting point in balancing exercises. The period of self-control will increase at the same time the relationship between you and Suzette broadens and deepens. This will be so subtle that you do not even notice it, but it will form the basis for future training success. The bonus offered by this exercise is steadiness and self-control, as well as increasing the period of self-control and eagerness to perform.

PRESENTATION: Hopefully, you will graduate to more complex variations of this trick, but if you do not, this trick stands by itself. Adding and changing commands can touch up the presentation. *"Balance!" "Toss!"* and *"Catch!"* add three commands to the repertoire with virtually no extra work. On the command *"Toss!"* Suzette moves her head, flipping the tidbit in the air, then catching it. The pattern has been set and the dog knows what to do. It is your job to deliver the commands with split-second timing so that it looks like the dog is working to your command rather than merely doing the routine. As far as "training" her to catch the food, she'll train herself. You'll take the credit but she did the job.

Balance an Egg 1

"EGG!"

Start off with a hard-boiled egg, and position the egg far up on the muzzle, by the dog's stop—the space between the eyes. The narrow portion of the egg should be pointed down toward the nose. Before starting, tap the side of the egg slightly, making a flat indentation in the egg to keep it from rolling off the muzzle. Start with the command *"Egg!"* which will be a secondary cue. (The primary cue will be the dog seeing the egg.) You are now teaching a different procedure from the Balance and Catch trick. Different item, different location, different command, but the work on the previous trick is essential to gradually move the dog into this variation. We start with the easy stuff first. When the dog has held the egg steady for several seconds, gently remove it, and click and treat the dog. Extend the period of time that the egg is held. There is no *"Toss!"* and *"Catch!"* at this point in the trick. If you are eager to go on to the really advanced, impressive stuff, go forward and read "Balance an Egg 2."

ALTERNATE APPROACH FOR ALTERNATE BREEDS: The length of muzzle on some breeds makes this trick impossible. The Pug, Affenpinscher, Brussels Griffon and Shih Tzu are a few examples of breeds that have muzzles that are too short. If you *really* want to teach this trick, get some pigeon eggs or use a jelly bean. For breeds such as the Bulldog and the French Bulldog, dent the bottom (wide end) of the egg and stand it upright on the nose.

PRESENTATION: While you have started with a hard-boiled egg, in the actual presentation you want an uncooked egg. Remember that an uncooked egg also can be lightly tapped to flatten one side, yet not break apart. Have the dog hold the egg for about thirty seconds. Anything longer than that will be boring to the audience. An egg is an egg, but the audience has to be guided into being impressed. After removing the egg, break it with a flourish to show the audience that it is an uncooked egg. If you are doing a comedy or clown act, the breaking of the egg can be done on your forehead.

Balance an Egg 2

"EGG!" "TOSS!" "CATCH!" "ROLL!" OR "SLOW!"

We are now back to the hard-boiled egg. This is truly building on a trick. Combine the *"Toss!"* and *"Catch!"* with the balancing of the egg. Yes, we are going to teach Suzette to catch that hard-boiled egg. Remember that this trick is lacking the built-in immediate food reward. You have to deliver the reward rapidly, and a clicker or verbal reward would be highly recommended here. Suzette will probably, at least in the initial phases of the training, rotate her head and roll the egg into her mouth, which is fine. The contrast of tossing the food in the air and catching it makes the trick even more impressive. If she does toss and catch it, go with that performance. You can keep the slow roll, if you wish, by making sure that Suzette remains calm and is not worked up prior to the command *"Roll!"* or *"Slow!"* The *"Slow!"* command can be used for slowing Suzette down in a multitude of exercises. Deliver the *"Slow!"* in a *"SLOoooooow!"* calm tone of voice. After the exercise is completed, remove the egg from Suzette's mouth and then get her worked up with exuberant praise. If she jumps and bops around, it is good for the misdirection, as you shall see in the Presentation. (Misdirection is a magician's term for diverting the audience's attention away from what you do not want them to see.) You have the ideal distraction in Suzette.

PRESENTATION: The final flourish on this trick is dictated by the individual dog and further influenced by her breed. Most retrievers, such as Golden, Labrador, Flat-coated, Chesapeake Bay and Curly-coated Retrievers, have "soft mouths." They are predisposed (genetically) to hold things gently. Other breeds, such as Border Terriers and Kerry Blue Terriers, grab with a firmer grip. This will determine whether or not you are going on to use uncooked eggs. It will also determine the commands that you are going to use. The command and the tone should match the dog's performance. *"Toss!" "Roll!"* and *"Slow!"* are some of your choices. If using a hard-boiled egg, as you remove the egg from her mouth, you exclaim, "Look how happy Suzette is!" With your left hand extended in the direction of Suzette, slip your right hand, holding the hard-boiled egg, into your jacket pocket and exchange for an uncooked egg. Put the egg back in Suzette's mouth and have her give it to an audience member. Kids are always good. Then have the child break the egg. The perfect misdirection. Dishonest? No, this is show business. Remember to always bring spare eggs. Also make sure that all the eggs are the same color.

Balance a Book

"SCHOOL DAYS!"

This is easier than you may think. It is an extension of the preceding balancing tricks. We will get into the fancier stuff later on. *"School Days!"* is the command as you gently elevate Suzette's head so its top is as level as possible in order to balance a book. The book should extend beyond her head somewhat, but not too much as this increases the balancing problem. With dome-headed dogs, such as the Papillon and Newfoundland, use a soft-covered book. If it flops over, make sure that it doesn't obscure the dog's vision. Most dogs have flat heads, and you can use a hard-cover book. (Don't use the Manhattan telephone directory; pick something that is not too heavy in relationship to your dog.) Steady the dog and have her hold the book for longer and longer periods of time. This is practice, so Suzette will be required to hold it longer than she will when she is performing. We are also setting her up for the more intriguing variations on this trick. As she does this, we relax her by gently petting, caressing and calming her. This is not the time to use a food or clicker reward. The clicker will cause a quick head movement that will topple the book. Ditto a food reward. You won't be able to get it into her mouth before the book falls. On top of all this, the swallowing of the food will cause undesirable head movement, and you'll also have ruined her calm, relaxed mood.

PRESENTATION: Stacking one book on top of another impresses every one. Choose your books carefully. Don't use books with slippery covers. A rough surface prevents sliding. If your books have a slippery surface, there are a number of solutions available to minimize this problem: a product called "Tacky Finger," available from stationery stores; rubbing the cover with rough sandpaper; coating with Coca-Cola or some other sticky substance. You can even use Velcro between the books, although that is a bit more obvious.

Sit High or Beg

Now, if your dog didn't teach herself this trick, it's up to you. If she did teach herself, I want you to humbly take the credit. Suzette won't mind! You are a team. Suzette usually gets credit for her brilliance rather than you for your hard work. Position in life is everything, and nowhere is that more true than in this trick. Suzette must learn to sit squarely on both hindquarters. Just as you build a house from the foundation up, this trick is built from the hindquarters up. Some dogs try to do this with a twisted spine—and some even succeed—but it's an unstable position, so attempt to get the dog's body properly aligned.

A dog begging. Mug-Z, the great trick dog, doing an old standard. Mug-Z was the first dog on David Letterman's "Stupid Pet Tricks."

Timing and touch will be all important. There are a couple of different approaches in teaching this important trick. You've been reading about the balancing tricks, which are quite impressive. Do them with Suzette sitting high, and you'll bring down the house. These tricks are synergistic, more powerful than the sum of both parts.

First, Suzette has to be taught to use her body properly. The position from bottom to top has the dog sitting squarely on hindquarters, thorax squarely over the hindquarters, paws tucked in close to the body, neck rolled back over the spine and head positioned over the neck. Positioning of the head in relation to the neck is tricky. A good description is that the neck should be *arched* like a swan's. You won't see that exaggerated arc in the neck, but that's the idea. It could be further described as like a cadet in military school "bracing," racking the chin in with the head back and over the spine. Dogs have a long lower jaw and cannot rack their chins in, but it is this feeling (or mood) that is important for the proper body position—a ramrod-straight back with the *entire* body aligned. Dogs sometimes will attempt to balance themselves by reaching out with their paws. Discourage this. While Suzette may feel that it is necessary for her balance, she is wrong. It will throw the balance of her body off.

The easiest way to teach this trick is with lure and reward. With the dog in the sit-stay position, hold a piece of food over her head and encourage her to elevate her body to keep the food in view. You can start off by doing this every time you feed your dog. It's simple and only takes a few seconds before each meal to establish the trick. Always take the easy way out and push that invisible training.

Here are two ways to teach the Sit-High trick: the corner method and the Charlie Chaplin method. In the corner method, place your dog against a corner of the room and gradually lift her up with the leash attached to her collar. Suzette has a sense of security with her back to the wall and support on either side. I prefer the Charlie Chaplin method because you are able to be in closer physical contact with your dog. Stand with your heels together and your feet splayed out. Suzette does a sit-stay between your feet and facing in the same direction as you. Gradually pull her up by her collar. As you raise Suzette into a sit-high position, start scratching her chest and exert an upward thrust, taking the pressure off the collar. You are modeling Suzette into position; massaging, scratching and modeling. Slide your hand up her chest to the point of the breastbone and scratch her there.

She may be extending her head or paws forward to "assist" in gaining her balance. If the paws reach out, flick them with your thumb and forefinger. If her head goes forward, gently guide it back into position by applying mild pressure to the top front portion of her head or scratching her stop as you position her head properly. You do not have any walls in your way, and you are as close to Suzette as you can get.

PRESENTATION: The élan that you generate when you add the sit high to any of these balancing acts is amazing. The sit high, or beg, is not really "added," however. The dog is in position, and the object to be balanced is then added. This sequence is much easier to teach. The elements can be taught simultaneously, should you so desire. Ultimately, your dog will go right into the sit-high position, but you do not have to wait until that point is reached before showing off.

Balance a Teacup and Saucer

The saucer is balanced on the muzzle. It should be set well up on the muzzle, with the edge on the dog's stop. Try a couple of different-size saucers to see which fits best. Once the size is determined, buy a plastic cup and saucer to keep costs down. There will be mistakes. If you don't have plastic, work Suzette on plush wall-to-wall carpeting. Take your time, and work in short, frequent sessions.

PRESENTATION: Fragile-looking china will add to the act. Worse-case scenario is that Suzette will drop it, and the audience will see that it's the real thing. Make sure you have spare cups and saucers. Broken china and glassware must be immediately swept up to protect your dog's feet. See *"Hold the Dustpan!"* in chapter 19 and *"Raus!"* in chapter 13 for dealing with just such an emergency.

Balance a Bird

This requires as much training of the bird (or birds) as it does of the dog. A wooden dowel in the dog's mouth with a live parrot on either side is an impressive trick. Adding another bird on top of the dog's head is the *pièce de résistance.*

Sit High on a Pole

"HUP!" AND "SIT HIGH!"

Place an eight-inch-wide, four-foot-long plank on two steady sawhorses. Thickness of the plank depends on the weight of the dog. We don't want the plank to bend. Try one half an inch thick. Read ahead to learn about "walking the plank," and you might very well decide to make those sawhorses flights of stairs. Tell Suzette *"Hup!"* to command her to jump up on the plank. Then tell her *"Sit High!"* a trick she's already learned. No problem! She's just doing it in a different location. Narrow the plank gradually so that Suzette is ultimately balancing herself on a two-inch plank. Watch how she daintily jumps up on that narrow plank, putting her entire heart into what you are asking of her. Now it is time to substitute a pole. You must make sure that the pole is firmly anchored to the sawhorses. For strength and diameter I'd suggest a clothes-closet pole. This will hold even a Mastiff. Later on you can substitute a broom handle. But watch the diameter if the dog is over sixty pounds. A metal mop handle is a good, strong alternative.

PRESENTATION: Drumrolls always add a lot to any demonstration. Picking up the pole after Suzette performs helps milk the audience for applause. The thinner pole is more for your (and Suzette's) self-satisfaction. The audience will not appreciate the harder work required to balance on a thinner pole unless you show Suzette first getting up on the clothes-closet pole and *then* go to the broom handle. Make sure you highlight that accomplishment. Here is a worthy rule of thumb in teaching tricks: The more difficult the trick is to teach, the less it's appreciated; the easier the trick is to teach, the greater the applause.

Sit High on My Back

"HUP!" "HIGH!" "GET DOWN!"

This trick requires a bit of work but is very impressive. A flat back is an asset. If, like me, you are rotund, it becomes more challenging, but not impossible. Doing this by yourself makes it that much more difficult. An assistant with a real feel for dogs will speed up the training. Practicality dictates that you do it by yourself so that you can practice anytime and anywhere.

With the leash on your dog, lie facedown. Talk and guide Suzette into position sitting on your back. Leading and guiding Suzette onto your back when you are facing down is a real problem, but it will be worth the trouble for this most impressive trick.

Once Suzette gets the idea, you can move to the next step, which is with you on all fours. Throughout this training, use a clicker or verbal praise as reward. Food reward is ineffective here because of the delivery problem. If the dog is properly clicker trained, food delivery is not necessary. The click is the reward and a reminder that food will be delivered later.

You will have Suzette do a sit-stay, and you will get on all fours in front of her. Both of you will be facing the same direction. The leash will be slung over your right shoulder (if you are right-handed). Tell her *"Hup!"* as you guide her onto your back. At this point you can interject some table work with Suzette. Have her jump up on the table while you partially hide under it. You then can come out from under the table and have her sit high every third time. Just the *"Sit!"* is sufficient most of the time, but throw in an occasional *"High!"* so she understands the goal. Now let's leave the table and get you back on all fours and her on your back. When finished, tell her *"Get Down!"* at which point you'll shower her with praise.

The author, Captain Haggerty, when he was in the U.S. Army K-9 Corps, with a German Shepherd sitting high on his back.

This trick is ready (but not polished) when you are on all fours with Suzette sitting high on your back. Be prepared to put in *a lot* of work on the all-fours position.

The next step (and don't rush it) is for you to stand up in front of her, knees bent and bending over. Keep your back as level as possible. Make sure, when she jumps up, that she sits squarely on your back, facing forward. Now we have a trick! We are not stopping here. We want to have her sit even higher up on your back. Ultimately, we can get Suzette to sit on your shoulders. She doesn't have to leap to your shoulders. Just to the flat of your back. Then you slowly stand straighter and taller as Suzette moves up your back.

PRESENTATION: Your dog should be facing in the same direction as you. It's a small point, but if Suzette faces in the opposite direction, it presents a defused picture (and believe me, people will want to take pictures of this). Having the dog balance something after she is sitting high on your shoulders presents a problem unless you get a petite person to climb up on an A-frame ladder or step stool to put something on Suzette's nose. That makes Suzette appear even higher.

Walk Tall

Walking while balancing a book on her head is easier for Suzette if she is walking on her hindquarters. She has already learned to carry her head properly, with the top of the skull parallel to the ground. When she is on all fours, the tendency is to hold her head at more of a slope. She can be taught to walk on all fours with her head at the proper angle, but it is going to take a good deal of work. See chapter 11 for the Tour the Mall trick. We are building on that Tour the Mall trick. Suzette has been trained to balance the book on her head in the sit-high position, and this is an extension of that exercise. Once that foundation is built all that's required is a steady hand and a bit of patience. You have already done the hard work! Put in a little effort to make a dynamite trick.

Walk the Plank

This is more of an agility exercise than a trick. It's listed here to get you interested in agility training and competition, but more importantly to prepare Suzette for other tricks. A few considerations: Make sure that the catwalk or plank that you use is rigid, with as little flexing as possible. An unsteady surface is too upsetting to your dog. A good height for the plank is about level with your waist. There should be a strong flight of stairs leading up to and down from the plank. You might see if there is an agility club in your area and use their equipment rather than building your own, but you'll need different equipment from the standard agility stuff. Ideally you would have these two flights of stairs fitted so that you can vary the width of the plank to be used. This is not a book on obstacle construction, but heavy-duty metal clamps that can be bolted down at different locations (widths) on the top steps are ideal. Another quick tip is that, in teaching a dog to climb stairs, it becomes more difficult if she can see the ground between the steps. Close the steps off with wood or cloth so that they appear solid to your dog. You want to work the width of the plank down to three inches (or less). If using a longer plank, you'll need a monopod (pedestal) to support the middle of the plank to ensure steadiness. A shaky surface really discombobulates dogs because their balance and location sensors are different from ours. Shaky surfaces may be introduced later in the training, but not in the early phases. Your job is to walk alongside your collared and leashed dog. Encourage and guide Suzette up the steps and out on to the plank. Your job is also to be there for emergencies—ever ready to catch and assist her if she makes a false step. Do not introduce shakier surfaces unless it serves a useful purpose. Walking that three-inch-wide plank is a great trick. Increasing the height of the plank increases the trick's impressiveness, but it can increase the weight and cumbersomeness of the "prop" as well.

PRESENTATION: Clamp the narrow plank onto the two flights of stairs and rest it on the pedestal in the middle. At the end of the trick unclamp the plank and show the audience how narrow it is, accompanied by a drumroll. We are getting into tricks for audiences here. You are starting to manufacture equipment (props) for your "dog act." Make your props/obstacles as versatile as possible. Read ahead before you make anything. We want versatility, steadiness, durability and lightness.

Walking on a Double-Rope Bridge

Now we are getting into really tough stuff—but not impossible. As I mentioned at the beginning of this chapter, the training you give to your dog develops her love of work and willingness to expand her bag of tricks. If you reach this level or have her balancing herself on a single pole, you have done your homework. Now for some fast information about ropes. You want manila rope, but not the *real* manila rope. There is a composite rope that is much less expensive but has all the characteristics of manila (e.g., is less likely to stretch than other ropes). Anything less than one-eighth inch is cord and anything over that is rope. You want one-inch rope with as high a SWL (safe working load) and ST (breaking strength) as manila. Cut two lengths of rope, using pruning shears, and wrap electrician's tape around the ends to prevent unraveling. Attach the ropes to the two flights of stairs, to either side of a four-inch-wide plank. Use duct tape to tape the ropes to the edges of the plank at intervals of four inches. It's important that the ropes be taut. In time, you'll use a narrower plank so that you can gradually move the ropes closer together until Suzette actually is forced to walk on them. When she is working well on the two ropes, remove the plank. Without the plank, there will be a bit of spring to the ropes. The reason you use "manila" rope is because it isn't supposed to stretch. Believe me, all rope stretches, and so will yours when you string the ropes without the plank. Put the monopod (pedestal) in the middle, and tape the two ropes to it. This will steady the ropes and reduce the stretching. Later you can remove the pedestal. As far as the time frame on teaching this trick goes, be prepared to spend as much as six months of daily work.

PRESENTATION: The important thing from the point of view of the audience is that Suzette is walking on *rope*. Don't worry about its thickness. Too thick will not register with the audience, which usually only recognizes something when it is pointed out to them. Dwell on the rope, not the thickness, unless you have worked Suzette down to thin rope. Play with the distance between the ropes for the most dramatic effect. Six inches between the ropes is quite dramatic. Increasing height will increase the impressiveness of the trick too. But always keep your dog's safety in mind.

16
RETRIEVING

To Retrieve or Not Retrieve—
That Is the Question

With retrieving, the whole world of dog tricks really opens up to you. A good *reliable* retriever is the pride of all dog trainers. The key word is "reliable." How reliable is reliable? First time, every time is reliable. Why first time, every time? If "Garcia" is on a movie set and has to carry a message from point A to point B, you don't have time to play games and entice Garcia to carry that message with the meter clicking at over $20,000 per hour. If Garcia is in one of his moods, you may need something to "make" him carry the missive from point A to point B. The director doesn't have the time to sit down with Garcia and discuss his motivation. The producer will be wasting his time if he discusses production costs with Garcia.

If your ambitions don't extend to becoming a "showbiz mom"—if it's just party tricks you're after—you don't need a reliable retriever, and you may not want to be so "tough" on your dog. Good! Don't be. This is a conscious choice that you must make.

Others of you will be overachievers and will want your dog to be 100 percent "reliable." You refuse to be embarrassed on a film set, or anywhere else for that matter. There is something in here for you too.

Choose your method of training wisely. Trying something once is not a fair trial. Study the different methods and follow through on one of them. Any single method will produce results if you follow through on it. If you are confused as to what you want, then I'd suggest having a consultation with a trainer who prides herself on developing the type of retriever that you want your dog to be. She'll set you on the right path. That expert opinion can help you decide on which path to take.

A Retrieving Warm-up

TAKE YOUR DOG FOR A WALK IN THE WOODS

A romp in the woods is a good warm-up for your dog. If you are a city-dweller, you're going to need a car to get to the woods. Let us see what Garcia's natural inclinations are when it comes to retrieving. Let's also give him a chance to use his nose. The next chapter, "The Knowing Nose," goes into scent in more detail, but this doesn't mean that Garcia can't use his nose until you have read chapter 17. During this walk in the woods, Garcia may proudly pick up a stick. If you ask him properly, his previous training will have him bringing it to you. Toss it out again, and the games will begin! This playful interaction will give Garcia maximum exercise, with a minimum amount of effort on your part. It will also get him to use his nose. Next time he brings the stick back, trim it down, break it in half, disguise its appearance. Now toss it in a pile of other sticks, and Garcia still will bring back "his" stick. Wow! We're on to the next chapter already!

The Play Retrieve

The play retrieve is fairly straightforward. Toss out the stick and the dog brings it back. Party time! A big game! Any dog can do it, not just the retrieving types And this requires no discussion. It is the most natural thing for a dog to do—and besides, it's covered in chapter 11.

The Clicker Retrieve

"TAKE IT!" "OUT!"

This is a nice easy way to start off on retrieving *and* a good way to start clicker training your puppy.

1. Sit on the floor with your puppy Garcia and relax. If he comes over to you, ignore him.
2. Toss out some toys. Should he go bounding over to one toy and pick it up, you should click and treat.
3. Click on the picking up, and if he brings the toy back to you, click and jackpot! But you are not going to be that lucky. What will probably happen is that Garcia will move toward one toy, you'll click, and he'll come over to investigate the sound. When he comes over, treat him.
4. Ignore him as he wanders around, but when he heads in the direction of one of the toys, click and treat.
5. The next time, you want him to move even closer to one of the toys before you click. You will raise your standard of performance each time. You're shaping his behavior.
6. If Garcia doesn't improve, you don't click. Four minutes is fine for the first session.
7. Walk away. Pick up the toys when he's not looking and set them aside for your next session.
8. Our purpose here is to get Garcia closer and closer to the desired object "to be retrieved." One, two or three items can be tossed out initially. Observe Garcia and see which one or ones really intrigue him.
9. Click in an escalating manner with the attitude of, "You do me a favor, and I'll give you a click followed by a small bit of delicious food." Feel satisfied by small improvements as long as they are improvements. Keep going step by step no matter how slowly.

If Garcia *does* go bounding out there to grab a toy and proudly bring it to you, click and treat. These sessions will probably last about three or four minutes—easy and relaxed. The hardest part is getting up and down from your spot on the floor. No rush. Relax! You're using the tortoise-and-the-hare approach. Slow and steady wins this race. Remember, if Garcia loses interest, get up and walk away. You lose interest when he loses interest. Even if he is attempting to manipulate you, don't worry. Manipulation attempts by dogs are extremely difficult to spot. As a matter of fact some trainers are not even aware that dogs do attempt to manipulate them. Time and experience will dictate when to do a "test run" to see if you are being manipulated, but that is beyond the scope of this book, so no recriminations, simply walk away. We like to finish on a high note, but this is the exception that proves the rule. Your attitude becomes, "Even though you have lost interest, Garcia, I haven't lost interest—I'm simply going elsewhere." Now, if Garcia is really clever, he may start going through all sorts of gyrations as you walk away. He may offer you all sorts of behaviors. Here we separate the men from the boys. What do you do? Do you go back, or do you continue to walk off? Either answer could be correct—this time. He has enticed you back by offering a number of keen and new behaviors. If you are not mentally set to click those new behaviors, it still isn't a total loss. He will try you out again. *Do not* let him always control the situation. Go back only if you are mentally geared to take advantage of the situation and click his behaviors. If not, just walk off into the sunset as if nothing happened. There is always another day. The "other day" can occur a half-hour later.

When Garcia sniffs a toy, be sure to click. These clicks are followed by a food reward. You are into the home stretch once he puts his mouth on the toy. This is where you are breaking through on your clicker training. There will be a shorter wait between individual improvements. The completed exercise is the return of the toy to your hand. Now when you click and he brings the toy to you for a treat, start introducing the command *"Out!"* for dropping the toy into your hand. Common sense tells us that Garcia can't keep the food and the toy in his mouth at the same time. As Garcia's retrieving improves, you can reduce the frequency of the rewards and start putting in a variable reinforcement schedule.

The Forced Retrieve

"Forced Retrieve" even sounds terrible, but it isn't as bad as it sounds and is quite effective. Simply put, you will "make" Garcia retrieve. If he decides he doesn't want to retrieve (and even the greatest of retrievers go through this stage), you have a fall-back position. You have the "tools" standing by to make him retrieve.

First, you are going to teach Garcia to retrieve a four-inch-long wooden dowel, small enough to stick in your back pocket—something you can't do with a bulky dumbbell. You can get this rounded piece of wood in any lumberyard. A dowel can be bought in just about any diameter and length, so pick one that is the appropriate size for your dog. If you are frugal, you can saw off a piece of old wooden broom handle and get the dowel cost free.

1. Hold the dowel in front of Garcia's mouth.
2. If he moves his head away, keep the dowel right there in front of him. Should he open his mouth (which he probably won't) plop the dowel in and praise the dickens out of him. Don't worry if he drops it. We just want him to learn to take the dowel first.

The principle here is that the "annoyance" of the dowel in front of and following Garcia's moving mouth will require an action on his part. Try it yourself. Have someone hold a dowel right in front of your mouth and, as you turn your head, that dowel stays right in front of it—annoying isn't it? The minute Garcia opens his mouth and the dowel is plopped in, not only is the annoyance removed, but there is the immediate reward of an affectionate rub. Getting Garcia to take the dowel may take five minutes to achieve. Now, here is another place where a food reward is inappropriate. You can't have the dog hold the dowel and take food at the same time. (You are using a force method here, so you need not worry about the food reward. This is just an aside to help you better understand some dog-training theory.) The initial phases of this training probably will be slow and boring for you. It takes patience. Keep that dowel in front of Garcia's mouth, and expedite the process by using his collar to force his mouth open.

1. With Garcia in the heel position on your left-hand side, slide the collar high on his head and slide your left hand inside the collar so that it is between the right side of the dog's head, at juncture between the neck and head, with your palm facing you.

2. Twist your hand clockwise, forcing Garcia's jaw open and his head forward, say *"Take It!"* and plop the dowel in his mouth and praise the dickens out of him.

3. Again we are not worrying about him dropping the dowel. We just want him to take it. While it appears that we have just put the dowel in Garcia's mouth, there is a subtle difference between putting it in his mouth and getting him to "hold" the dowel and what we just did. Many people use the *"Hold!"* command while forcing the dog's mouth open, putting the dowel in, then holding the mouth shut. We have made him open his mouth himself, put his mouth on the dowel, and have given him a wonderful reward. Note that Garcia hasn't grabbed the dowel in his mouth. He has merely opened his mouth and accepted the dowel. We are building (shaping) on this behavior. Slow and steady wins the race, remember.

4. Once Garcia is reaching for and taking the dowel himself, it isn't even necessary to use the *"Hold!"* command, because you simply tell him to *"Take It!"* again.

5. Your next step with retrieving is to get Garcia to *reach out* for the dowel. Get him to reach farther and farther forward, an inch at a time. As he is reaching forward, you are lowering his head by lowering the dowel.

6. The goal is for him eventually to pick up the dowel off the ground.

7. This is hard work for both you and your dog. Keep moving that dowel forward and downward, and *make* Garcia reach for it.

8. Once the dowel is picked up from the ground, you're almost home free.

9. You will reach a point (or maybe two or three points) where Garcia will refuse to pick up the dowel. Just reaching for his collar will make it unnecessary to apply the pressure. Once Garcia sees you coming he will pounce on that dowel. Don't let him! Hold him back. Frustrate him. That frustration will increase his desire to pick up the dowel (in order to avoid your correction). Now, I just got off the Internet with someone I was explaining this to. Both he and his dog Niner look forward joyfully to these training sessions, where the dog is compelled to pick up the dowel. So "forced retrieve" *isn't* as terrible as it sounds.

At this point, you will start varying the location of and difficulty in retrieving the object. You will also be changing the items retrieved. You now have a reliable retriever. The one thing that makes him reliable is your ability to correct him should he decide he doesn't want to do it.

The Retrieve Wrap-up

It is now time to have Garcia forget about the dowel and pick up whatever you want him to. Do not immediately jump into something supertough. Gradually build up to that supertough object that you want him to retrieve. If you have no ultimate object in mind, keep changing size, shape and texture for variety. Wallet, car keys, handkerchief, pen, pencil, beeper, TV remote, scraps of paper—almost anything you have handy is a good choice. Let's make a new rule for you. From now on, anytime you drop something, you'll have Garcia pick it up. It's too easy to fall into the habit of using the same item over and over again. Ultimately, you'll be able to get Garcia to retrieve a dime off the sidewalk. (A nickel is not acceptable and only worth half as much.)

Retrieve Toys by Name

1. Start off with a ball.
2. Place the ball in front of Garcia and tell him *"Get Your Ball!"* Do that three or four times, then put Garcia's favorite toy alongside the ball. (If the ball *is* his favorite, you'll have to adjust accordingly.)
3. If he seems to be going toward his favorite toy, give him a cautionary "No," a soft delivery of the word spoken in more of an advisory tone than as a correction.
4. Have Garcia get the ball two or three times, then remove it.
5. Tell him to get his Kong, if that is the favorite toy, and have him get that three or four times.
6. Then put the ball back and tell him to get the ball. Be ready with that cautionary no in case you need it. Work on two toys for the first week, and then start adding a new toy a week. You will be pleasantly surprised at how rapidly Garcia picks up the different names. You must get at least one toy for Garcia that will not float and work this into his drill. Keep reading to find out why.

PRESENTATION: The names you give to the toys can enliven the presentation. If there is only one ball out there and it is red, tell him to get his red ball. "Bear" is a good name for a toy, but it becomes cuter if you call it "Teddy Bear."

Retrieve from Underwater

This is a piece of cake.

1. Go out for another walk in the woods and look for a small pond.
2. Let Garcia watch you toss his heavier-than-water toy into the water near the edge of the pond. Not too deep! The water should be just covering the toy.
3. Send Garcia out for the toy. In succeeding sessions you will toss the toy farther and farther, into deeper and deeper

water. Now we are setting the pattern. You can switch this retrieve exercise to other bodies of water.

4. Now, if you are one of those city-bound cliff dwellers, you could start gradually filling your bathtub. But try to take that walk in the woods. You'll both be better off for it.

PRESENTATION: An impressive trick, but you can't carry a country pond with you on your trips downtown. Take the water as it comes. A word of caution! Hose your dog off every time he has been in water. Swimming pools contain chlorine; ocean water contains salt; and fresh, sweet or branch water can contain bacteria. Please be caring and careful about your dog's health and safety.

Retrieve a Fish out of the Water

More retrievers teach themselves this trick by accident than people teach them on purpose. As a matter of fact, most duck hunters want to stop their dogs from retrieving fish. If your dog wants to bring home a fish instead of a mallard, why not?

Regal Barth, a Golden Retriever, in the water with a fish that he caught . . .

. . . coming out of the water, Regal, owned by Mike and Kathryn Barth, gently holds his prize . . .

1. Start off with a weighted, dummy fish.
2. Expand that dummy fish to at least three dummy fish of different sizes. If Garcia is retrieving dummy fish with a degree of regularity, realize that he is retrieving a recognizable object under water.
3. The next step is to find a small, shallow, clear pond.
4. Toss in a live fish along with a like-sized dummy fish. If the pond is too big, find a smaller one, or use wooden planks to contain the live fish in a small, shallow area of the pond. Garcia may be alert to the movement of the live fish.
5. Send him for the fish. If he retrieves the live fish, lavish him with praise. Should he retrieve the dummy fish, praise him and remove it from his vision. Do not put it back in the pond.
6. Now it is time to send him for the real thing. If the fish is okay after the first trial, toss it back in to be retrieved again. Do this a total of three times. In no time at all, Garcia will develop a passion for snagging live fish. Control is important

in all types of training, particularly here. You don't want Garcia going over his limit. In fact, I want you to go out and get a fishing license. I don't want State Fish and Game to lock you up before you've finished reading this book. Do you really think the game warden is going to believe it when you tell him that your dog caught the fish?

PRESENTATION: Don't worry about the presentation. Your dog is going to do it all. He'll enjoy the cheers, applause and energetic comments (mixed with some snickers).

. . . Regal delivers his fish to the hand of John Swinford.

"Retrieving" an Irretrievable Object

"SPEAK!"

The London Metropolitan Dog Section (Scotland Yard) has an exercise called "Retrieving an Irretrievable Object," which seems to be a contradiction in terms. It is not. It is used for search work in which the dog is assigned the task of finding contraband or some form of unspecified equipment by scent. If the dog found a safe, say, he wouldn't be able to retrieve it, so he would bark. (More on the behavior of scent in the next chapter.)

Now, what would you expect Garcia to do? Well, he should bark, and often a dog that has reached this level of training will start doing that out of frustration. If not, simply command him to *"Speak!"* when he finds an irretrievable object. The idea is that he calls for help with the found object. This is one of the few tricks in the book that I feel is more than your dog needs. If he were a full-time police dog, I feel that it would be an excellent trick, but it would be his job rather than a trick.

The Ultimate Retrieve: Retrieving a Steak

How can we top retrieving a fish out of water, a dime off the sidewalk and, of course, an irretrievable object? How about a T-bone steak? Now that is impressive! You want a dog that is on a controlled diet. Straight dog food, no table scraps, no people food. If you want to use a food reward, try to use the blandest possible. The idea is not to let Garcia taste what he is missing.

1. Coat the largest Milk-Bone you can find with clear shellac. That will keep it from breaking when tossed and from being tasted when carried.
2. Work Garcia on that bone over and over, then substitute an unshellacked Milk-Bone. Now, if you are using food reward *do not* reward with the same stuff he is retrieving.
3. Next, get a big piece of inexpensive meat. Shellac that too!

The shellacking will preserve the meat and prevent the taste from entering the dog's mouth. The purpose of the shellac is not to make it taste foul. It is to keep the taste away from the dog. Also it will contain and restrict the odor, which is more of a temptation than you realize. A housekeeping tip: Refrigerate this meat between training sessions.

4. Have Garcia retrieve, retrieve, retrieve that coated meat.

5. Store the shellacked meat in the freezer section of the refrigerator when you are not using it. Freezing the meat will minimize the decay, further reduce the odor and help contain the taste. Meat will continue to decay under the shellac. You will be able to smell it, and Garcia will too. That stinky, rotten, smelly odor will be like caviar to Garcia, but he is learning to retrieve. When you begin working him on unshellacked meat, watch Garcia like a hawk. You are there to make sure he doesn't try to eat it. There are a couple of reasons why you use cheap meat. One reason is because it is cheap. Another is that tough meat is tougher to gulp down than better cuts of meat. You are standing by to stop an imprudent move on Garcia's part. You will pounce on him and drag the meat out of his mouth if he attempts to consume his prop. Make sure that it is a *big* piece of meat. Of course, Garcia may never even try to eat the meat. Use the cautionary no here if you feel he is thinking about taking a bite. He won't be able to swallow a large piece of meat.

PRESENTATION: Here is a real moneymaker. Show off your dog at a local bar that serves food. When people show their amazement at his retrieving ability, deliver the throwaway remark. "I bet he'd retrieve a steak without eating it if I told him." A "dive" is the best bar to go to for this hustle. This type of bar has the clientele you need, the tough meat and, most important, you'll be allowed to bring Garcia into the place.

Get a Cold One

We have Susan Muick to thank for this one. It is a combination of a number of tricks. The idea is to send Garcia to the refrigerator to bring you a cold beer. Sure, a cold soda can be used, but it lacks the humor of a beer.

The sequence of performance will be:

1. Go to the refrigerator.
2. Open the door (using a knotted towel as a handle).
3. Remove a beer.
4. Put the beer down.
5. Bump the door shut.
6. Pick up the beer.
7. Deliver it to hand.

At this point, Garcia hopefully knows most of these commands. If not, teach them to him before progressing with this training. Going to the refrigerator will have to be taught.

1. On the command, *"Get Me a Cold One!"* lead Garcia to the refrigerator.
2. You will have tied a towel to the refrigerator door handle and will tell Garcia *"Tug!"* (see chapter 18).
3. Show Garcia the beer bottle on the bottom shelf and tell him, *"Take It!"* Make sure Garcia has easy access to the beer bottle and that moving it won't cause anything in the refrigerator to shift.
4. Have Garcia gently set the beer down.
5. Point to the front of the refrigerator door and say *"Bump!"* (chapter 9), getting Garcia to shut the door.
6. Tell Garcia to pick up the beer and deliver it. Do this six times, then wait one to four hours before repeating the sequence. Five sessions should have Garcia rocking steady on this trick. One thing that you want to do is get farther and farther away from the refrigerator as you give the command.

You should be able to send Garcia from one side of the house to the other.

PRESENTATION: A beer bottle may not be the easiest to retrieve, but it is the most effective for this trick's presentation. Don't use a glass bottle. Plastic is lighter and safer. If you have a party at your house, this will be a very popular trick, particularly at Super Bowl parties. Please note that your beer consumption will go up, and this is not my fault.

It Makes Scents

Scent is most fascinating. Once you show your dog how to use his nose, he'll use it all the time and will enjoy life much more. It will be as much a pleasure for him as it is a trick. His sense of smell is vastly superior to yours. For example, what does ordinary table salt smell like? You feel it has no odor. A trained dog can detect this "odorless" product diluted 100,000 times. Now, that is a knowing nose. Trained dogs can smell someone 150 to 200 yards away. (Did you take a bath lately?) Actually, a dog can smell someone farther away than that. The terrain and vegetation block the scent from the dog. I had dogs regularly picking up men at half-mile distances when I was training dogs and men at Fort Ord, California. Dogs can more easily distinguish a person's odor than the FBI can distinguish fingerprints. Even with twins, who have similar scents, dogs can recognize the similarity and the difference.

Some General Information on Scent

You need to understand how the dog's nose works in relationship to the available scent. Scents are either ground or wind borne. The scent is the same. It is the behavior of the dog in relationship to the scent that is different.

For example, a Bloodhound's work as a man-trailer is to pick up scent that the person has left behind. The breed is used for finding lost children, escaped criminals, mentally disturbed people and those leaving the scene of a crime. The man-trailer, or tracker, smells where the person *was*. The dog working on wind-borne scent smells where the person *is*. The man-trailer needs an approximate starting point; and the wind-scenting dog searches an area where the person is believed to be. Interestingly enough, the conditions that are ideal for each searching technique are almost reversed. Foggy weather is good for tracking and poor for wind scenting. Windy weather is good for wind scenting but poor for tracking. This subject can get complex.

Should you decide to go into this type of searching, you need a lot more information than is contained in this short chapter, but that doesn't mean you can't teach "Holmes" a wide variety of tricks using his nose.

Let me reiterate that the difference between scouting and tracking is that the wind-scenting, or scouting, dog is locating where the person *is* and the man-trailing dog is going where the person *was*. It's all odor, and the odors don't behave any differently. What is different is *how* the dog uses the odor.

The way a dog uses his nose is genetic. Bloodhounds, Beagles, Bassets and similar breeds hunt with the head low: wind-scenting or scouting breeds, such as German Shepherds and Dobermans, hunt with the head high. Can they be crossed trained? Of course; but I don't recommend it. I am a purist and feel that each dog should be trained to specialize in hunting one way or the other.

Let me give you an actual example, of specialist dogs used in combat by the ever-creative British Army in Malaya. They had a problem with guerrillas who would run rather than stay and fight. The Brits would be on patrol with a scout dog and locate these guerrillas at a distance. The guerrillas, of course, would break and run in different directions. As soon as they were initially located, the English would call for a chopper to carry in the man-trailers. As soon the man-trailers were off-loaded from the helicopter, they ran the hottest trails leading from the enemy camp. Many of the guerrillas were captured. Different breeds for different needs.

Holmes can be trained to pick up the scent of a specific object or the scent of a person on an object. Golf balls have a characteristic odor. Why not make money finding lost golf balls on your local course? People have a characteristic odor too. Why not have your dog retrieve your hat out of a pile of hats?

Live scent is the odor of a person or thing. A dead person's odor is "live" odor too. The decomposing body (hey, this is supposed to be a fun book!) is producing an odor. The just-handled stick is tossed and it contains dead odor (of the tosser). Now, the stick itself has a characteristic odor that the dog could be taught to distinguish, but he will do this on his own. We want him to gravitate to the stick that you have touched and handled.

Dogs gravitate to the most recent, "hottest" scent. If the dog is working on where the person *was* he will prefer the hotter odor. The odor to start working Holmes with should be yours. Not only is he already familiar with your odor, but you will always be around.

Cold scent and cold trails are older odors. For a trailing dog, the hotter or more recent the trail, the easier it is to follow. How cold a trail can a dog follow? Once three or four hours pass, the trail is starting to get too cold. There is one fairly well-documented actual case where a dog ran a three-day-old trail, and there are even some that claim that they have run colder trails in actual cases. I find the three-day-old trail hard to believe. That's three days of changing weather and wind dissipating the odor. The only one who can give us the definitive answer is the dog, and he ain't talkin'.

Scent Tricks for Fun and Profit

See chapter 16 and read "A Retrieving Warm-up" for a great way to teach Holmes (or Garcia in that chapter) to start using his nose. Retrieving and scent work go hand in hand. That walk in the woods is a great starting point and will prove to you that your dog can do these amazing tricks.

Passive vs. Active Alerts

A passive alert has the dog sitting alongside the object that he has found. An active alert has the dog grabbing hold of the found object. Retrieving is the motivating factor for active alerts. *Please, please, please do not train for an active alert for explosives detection.* From the presentation point of view, the active alert is the more impressive. Holmes has found "it" and is charging forward with it to get his reward with all the enthusiasm of a kid under the Christmas tree or an adult with the winning ticket at the lottery office.

Handling the Odors

A major consideration is the actual handling of various odors. This is particularly important in the training of drug- and bomb-detection dogs. The dog's sense of smell is so keen that he will often select other odors to pick up on. For tricks, this is not as critical as it is in military and paramilitary work. There are a lot of "ambient" odors that can attach themselves to an item. These odors can "foul" a training session. Let us look at a couple of actual cases.

A training officer keeps the training aid—a one-pound block of explosive—in a bag in his car. The dog, handled by someone else, is trained to detect the explosive. But the dog starts picking up the odor of the particular training officer who is hiding the explosive for the training session. The dog is also picking up on the other odors in the bag and in the car.

Another example is when I train a marijuana-detection dog, I feel that he's ready to graduate when he can pick up on the scent of only three marijuana seeds. I place the marijuana seeds inside an airtight plastic 35-mm film canister. Now, that's a pretty good test! There are a number of potential flaws with that test, however. If this canister is used consistently, the dog may very well pick up on the plastic canister. Furthermore, if the same three seeds in the same canister are used over and over again, the dog will start to pick up on the odors of dogs that have gone before. Does this sound bizarre? No, not really. There are actual cases of these and similar confusions occurring. The pros concern themselves with these problems because they will affect the testimony given in a criminal case. Control of the training procedure and its documentation ensures that the pros are able to make positive statements when they testify in court and back them up with their training records. The trouble with dogs is that they are too good. You are free of these constraints because you are teaching tricks.

The Scent Cone

The behavior of a wind-borne scent is such that it will spread out in a cone-shaped configuration from the scent-emitting (decoy) object. The dog depends on the wind to carry the scent toward him. Dogs that learn to use their noses will develop their own way of working a scent cone. This technique is called scouting. Wind speed and the distance from the quarry dictate the width of a scent cone. The faster the wind, the narrower the scent cone. The greater the distance from the decoy (quarry), the wider the scent cone. Vegetation, terrain and buildings also have an effect on the cone's characteristics. The strongest odor is in the center of the scent cone, and most dogs prefer working its center. Occasionally a dog will work the edge of the cone. An integral part of working the scent cone in this fashion is a faster but not as positive method of working. The interpretation of the dog's behavior, or reading the dog, depends on a well-trained, observant handler. When working a dog, you have to be aware of the wind direction and how it is shifting. Search areas should be marked off so that a search can be conducted in a logical fashion. Ideally, your dog should "cut" the wind. In other words, ideally the wind (and it might be quite slight) should be at a right angle to the direction in which you and your dog are working the area. Under normal conditions, a minimally trained dog should be able to pick up someone at seventy-five yards. A well-trained dog should get a 150- to 200-yard pickup. Again, vegetation has a bearing. In dense jungle, a pickup of twenty-five yards is about as well as a dog will be able to do.

The Bar Bet Trick

"GET!"

1. Toss a bill from your wallet on the floor and send Holmes to retrieve it. Do this three or four times.
2. Now get a friend to toss another bill on the floor; then you throw the previously used bill down again.
3. Make sure that it doesn't touch the new bill and is between the new bill and Holmes. The denomination of the bill doesn't matter at this point. Holmes will invariably go for the bill with his saliva and your odor on it.
4. Be alert to the million-to-one possibility that he goes for the other bill. If he acknowledges the fresher bill at all, give him a cautionary "No."
5. Keep running these tests, ultimately rearranging the positions of the bills so that Holmes has to pass *over* the new bill to reach yours.
6. At this point you can change the bill: Your bill is laden with scent from both Holmes and you handling it.
7. You can do this a dozen times and more, building up the scent on all the bills you might use for the trick. The actual training time will be minutes, but the tricks will be performed rapidly.
8. A lot of verbal praise and petting should be given as Holmes brings home the bacon. If you are really turned on to clickers, you can use one here, but as you will see, praise and petting are much easier to use than the clicker. A couple, three or four rapid sessions will get you up to speed. Up to this

point we haven't used a command. The command you give will be *"Get!"* but slur some words after the get. Later, you may want to pretend that there is more to the command than just "get." Periodically, work Holmes with bills from other family members.

PRESENTATION: Now here is where the bar bet comes in.

1. Take Holmes to your favorite watering hole. If they won't let Holmes in the bar, you can claim that he is the designated driver! Holmes is going to be a conversation piece without you saying one word. Start bragging about how smart he is. Claim that he can read numbers. Then insist he can read numbers. Insist *with determination* that he can read numbers. Offer to prove this ability. Now you spring your trap.
2. Make sure you have a five, ten, twenty, fifty and hundred dollar bill. They don't make bills higher than $100.
3. Ask that anyone put down whatever denomination bill they want.
4. You put down a higher denomination bill and tell the dog to retrieve the bill with the higher value. Offer four-to-one odds, or the winner gets to keep both bills.
5. If someone puts down a five, you put down a twenty and tell Holmes, *"Get!* the twenty!" Should someone put down a twenty, tell him you *generously* will put down a hundred. You just cannot cover anything higher than a twenty, and I doubt if you will find anyone that adventurous.

Note: Do not use this scam more than twice. Say Holmes has to go home and prepare dinner. People do not like to lose, and if you win more than twice, they will start to insist on restrictions and adjustments to the way you perform the trick. Hey, there are a lot of other bars in town, and if the place is a real dive, you may have to fight your way out. Let's hope your "drinking buddy" is a Neapolitan Mastiff or a Dobe.

Finding Things for Fun and Profit:

GOLF-BALL RETRIEVAL
"GOLF BALL!"

Now, what can Holmes find that will produce some revenue for the two of you? Need a new part-time job? Finding lost golf balls at your local course is a great one! Your business will increase in direct proportion to the incompetence of the golfers. By now I hope I have convinced you of your dog's keen sense of smell. He certainly can tell the difference between golf and tennis balls. The way to teach Holmes this difference is to just start having him retrieve golf balls and reward the heck out of him when he brings one back to you.

1. The command is *"Golf Ball!"* You may want to take him to the tennis court, but there aren't enough lost tennis balls to make that a good business.
2. Keep throwing golf balls for him to retrieve.
3. Introduce some other kinds of balls as a distraction.
4. He'll keep going to the golf balls.
5. Take him out to the course and watch him clean up. There is nothing complex here.

PRESENTATION: Getting your dog on the course is going to be the hard job. I'd suggest working at night when the course is closed, but you need the golf course's permission. The ownership of the balls is a sticky wicket. Bringing in buckets of balls for resale may upset someone, so be careful how you operate your new business.

Finding Other Things

There are all sorts of things a dog can be taught to find that can turn a profit. If you're going into this to make a lot of money, I suggest you keep your day job. It is enjoyable work, but generally hard and often done under adverse conditions. If you want to do it as a hobby, on a part-time basis or as a trick, fine. Do not attempt to compete with the pros for obvious reasons.

Lost People/Children

"SCOUT!"

There are all sorts of search-and-rescue organizations, and I would suggest you join one of these organizations to take advantage of their training programs. There are so many aspects to this work you can spend a lifetime learning it. Pros in this field find it deeply rewarding. I remember I had Lt. Lionel Hetu of the Rhode Island State Police speak on their Bloodhounds at the Dog Fanciers Club in NYC. He finished up with a story about being called out on Thanksgiving Day to find a lost child. He missed his Thanksgiving dinner but found the child. He explained that the sacrifice was worth it. There wasn't a dry eye in the house.

Here we will give the quick trick approach, which is a very simple way of teaching the dog. The motivation is the dog's instinct to pursue moving objects. You can enlist the help of a child for this work. The dog's work uniform consists of a harness with an attached leash. As you go through the ritual of putting the harness on Holmes, he will know that he is getting ready to work.

INSTRUCTION FOR THE YOUNG DECOY

The child (or adult, even) needs some preliminary instruction before you start using him as a decoy. Explain as much as you can to him. The child's age will dictate his level of understanding.

1. Tell the child to hide out of the dog's view but with the wind blowing from him to the dog. He should be out of sight but should keep his eyes open for Holmes's approach.
2. When going to the hiding place, the child should approach it from the rear. The reason for approaching from the rear is to make sure that Holmes doesn't start to track the child's (decoy's) previous steps instead of scouting as he should.
3. When the dog is close, but not too close, you will tell the

decoy "Break!" and he will take off and run, with Holmes following behind.

4. A young child should be told to start running to one side or the other. I would suggest, again depending on the child's age, pointing in one direction or the other when instructing the child, because a child may (or may not) have the ability to tell right from left.

5. The child should run a short distance, then, when you tell him, break off to one side and hide again so the dog loses sight of him. Tell the child Holmes is going to veer off in the opposite direction.

"INSTRUCTION" FOR THE DOG

1. Start from about twenty-five feet away, and tell Holmes *"Scout!"* As he enters the scent cone and begins to register the child, encourage Holmes and tell the child to take off and run.

2. When you tell the child to break, he will veer off to the left or right. You will veer off the opposite way and praise and pet Holmes for a job well done.

3. It is your job to make sure that Holmes continues on in that different direction after the decoy breaks contact.

4. Do this a half-dozen times and Holmes will get the picture. If you have the time to work on this full time, you will develop a deep understanding of your dog. You will be able to "read" to the highest degree what he is smelling. A good military scout-dog handler and dog can tell how many people's scents are being picked up and the approximate distance, shoot an azimuth (a compass point) to the enemy/decoy(s) and identify their activity. To be that good will have your behind dragging. Don't kill yourself.

PRESENTATION: The presentation is training for your dog. The kids in the neighborhood will love to play hide-and-seek with him. *Be sure you clear it with the parents before working* *with the children,* and please let the children know this is all in good fun. Praise the kids as well as Holmes.

Lost Dogs and Decoy Dogs

"LOST DOG!"

Now here is an area where there is a real need. Every so often someone desperately calls me looking for a dog trained to find lost dogs. I refer them to someone who can help them. After you train your dog to find lost dogs, let me know and I will be happy to refer these callers to you. The technique used in finding lost dogs is similar to the one for finding lost people. We are going to cover the training of the decoy dog first. If you feel the decoy dog training is too difficult or time consuming, you can put a person out with the dog. This is not my recommendation, because what you will be teaching the dog is to find a dog *and* a person at the same time. Take the extra time and train that decoy dog.

TRAINING THE DECOY DOG
"Down!" "Stay!" "Voraus!" "Right!" "Left!" "Stop!" "Break Right!" "Break Left!"

The decoy dog should be completely obedience trained and, hopefully, have learned a number of the commands from chapters 12, 14 and 21.

1. Take the decoy dog out in the field and give him a down-stay behind some shrubbery.
2. Move away about a hundred yards and then return to the hidden dog.
3. When you are five yards from him, give him a sharp *"Voraus!"* (See chapter 21 for the Send-Away or Voraus trick.) This command will send the decoy dog away from his hiding place.
4. Chase the decoy dog fifteen or twenty feet and give him a directional command *("Right!"* or *"Left!"),* followed by the *"Down-Stay!"* command.

5. Reward the decoy dog and place him at a different location in a down-stay position. At this point we are training the decoy dog to be pursued by the scouting dog. You do not even need the scouting dog in the initial stages of training.

6. Repeat as above, only this time when you are ready to halt the dog you are going to say *"Stay!"* You are trying to teach the decoy dog to mimic the actions of the previously mentioned human (child) decoy.

7. You are going to gradually drop the *"Stay!"* command and switch to *"Stop!"* There is a reason for the gradual changing of commands: The new commands make for a better presentation. For example, the *"Right!"* and *"Left!"* will be changed to *"Break Right!"* and *"Break Left!"* Repeat the sequence about a half-dozen more times and quit for the day. The next day out in the field you will start with the previously mentioned *"Right!"* and *"Left!"* commands, which the decoy dog already knows. The new command will be *"Break Right!"* or *"Break Left!"* The *"Stop!"* command is the next to last command given in this series. The last command will be *"Down!"* to make sure the decoy dog is out of sight. You'll find that the decoy dog will anticipate the *"Down!"* command permitting you to eliminate that final command. Please note that up to this point you have not chased the decoy dog with the scout dog. We are working on the decoy dog's commands, not the new scout dog's (Holmes's) commands, though these commands will spill over onto Holmes's training. Now we have the decoy dog well trained and it is time to train Holmes.

PRESENTATION: Rather than a presentation, this is training for the decoy dog to be a—well, decoy. The reason for the training is to make the decoy dog your assistant. Granted, you could demonstrate the decoy dog by himself, but you are better off presenting the decoy dog first by himself, then explaining the purpose of the training, then following this up by actually having Holmes out there finding the decoy dog. Each presentation is a training session. Here you are working two dogs simultaneously. You are killing two birds with one stone.

TRAINING THE DOG-SCOUTING DOG

Training your dog to scout (find) other dogs is the same as training him to find lost people. A couple of important points: Scouting is different from tracking (trailing), and a dog can be trained to follow another dog by giving the trained dog the lost dog's scent. Does this mean that you can teach a dog to find people *and* dogs? Yes, you can, but I would recommend, if you were a full-time professional training dogs for detection purposes, that you train the dogs as specialists—to find either dogs or people, but not both. Since you are doing this as a trick, I will go along with the cross training. Put the type of decoy/quarry on command. In other words, if you are looking for a dog say, *"Lost Dog!"* and if it is a person, say, *"Lost Person!"*

1. "Suit up" the dog you are training in his harness. It is his work outfit just as it is the outfit for the dog that finds lost people. After you work with Holmes on this new trick a few times, he will know what is expected of him, and it will not even be necessary to use the *"Lost Dog!"* command.
2. Put your decoy dog out in the field, hide him behind some vegetation and tell him, *"Down-Stay!"*
3. A word of caution: When placing the decoy dog, go *around* to the area in which you are placing the decoy rather than directly to it. If you follow a direct line, the ever-clever Holmes will start to follow your trail over the ground you just covered rather than scouting for the decoy. You can be fooled by the dog. Be consistently aware of the dog's attempts at changing the rules. It is not a matter of the dog outsmarting you. He just decides he wants to play a different game.
4. Approaching the hiding place from the rear, you must realize that it will look different from the front. You must know where you are hiding the decoy so that you can tell

him to take off as you approach his hiding place with the scout dog in training.

5. When you get into close proximity of the decoy dog, and Holmes has indicated that he has already picked up his scent, tell the decoy dog, *"Voraus!"* and have Holmes chase.

6. Let Holmes enjoy chasing the decoy for a short distance. When you tell the decoy dog, *"Break Right!"* veer off to the left side and give Holmes all sorts of enthusiastic rewards, pats, praises and applause.

7. Holmes will pick this up very rapidly and will enjoy it. You may even get some joyful barking. I should point out that military scout dogs are not permitted to bark—*ever*—but it is not necessary for you to forbid barking, because you are not going into combat against an armed enemy. Let's hope.

8. As the training progresses you will introduce the *"Stop!"* *"Break Left!"* and *"Break Right!"* *"Stop!"* will be introduced in conjunction with the *"Stay!"* command. Holmes already knows the *"Stay!"* command, which will slow him down.

9. If you then say, *"Stop!"* Holmes will recognize that as the end of an exercise and turn to look at you. With the clicker-trained dog you have some time before giving a further reward.

10. Be aware that *both* dogs are hearing these commands at the same time. Try to shorten the decoy dog's command to simply *"Break,"* and have him choose right or left. Realize the breaking direction is different for each dog, and we don't want to confuse Holmes on his right and left.

PRESENTATION: Rather than giving a presentation, do it for real! Dogs get lost all the time. Be wary of showing Holmes off, because your friends will probably want him to "find" their dogs. Naturally, their dogs will not be as well trained as your decoy dog, so you will have to have the owners hide out with their dogs. A couple of caveats: If you work Holmes in finding one particular dog all the time, he will be looking for *that* dog and not *any* dog that is out there. If you work him against a dog with his owner all the time, he may start looking for people and dogs together. I point this out to show you how careful you have to be in this type of work, and to encourage you to bear this in mind and make the necessary adjustments in training.

Another important thing to remember is that if you actually are called out to find a lost dog, you may be able to find him, but not necessarily to catch him. The lost dog is generally frightened and confused. These jobs often run for many days and the best way to secure the dog is to have someone the dog knows extremely well immediately available. Let me throw in an old coon hunter's trick for recovering lost dogs. Lay the dog owner's well-worn jacket out alongside food and water dishes. Hopefully that will draw the dog into an area where you may be able to catch up with him.

Let me know when your dogs, including the decoy dog, are trained. I have people asking me about dogs that can find lost dogs all the time. The time to do the training is *before* a dog is lost.

18
TRICKS FOR THE SHOWBIZ DOG

There are show-business tricks that will make your dog "Kate" a star! Remember that *all* the tricks in this book have a show-business application. For more complete coverage of this subject, read my book *How to Get Your Pet into Show Business.*

Some of the tricks given here are needed on a regular basis—others may be required on short notice, without giving you enough training time. The following short-notice, no-training-time jobs can become your dog's entrée into show business.

Hitting a Mark

"MARK!"

This trick *will not* get Kate a job, but it certainly will get you a lot of future work once you're in the business. You'll look like a true pro and be ahead of 80 percent of the other showbiz dogs.

A mark is a spot onstage or on the set where an actor stands and does a piece of business. Piece of business means *shtick* which means—well, shtick is a Yiddish word, and Yiddish is the second language of show business. Shtick is little things that people do. Part of George Burns's shtick was taking a drag on his cigar immediately after delivering a punch line. Now back to a mark, which is a spot on the floor, generally indicated with tape, and unseen by the camera or the audience. The mark can be troublesome for actors to hit because they can't look down to see where it is. If an actor can't hit his mark, it creates a lot of unhappy people. When you tell them to put down the mark for Kate, they're going to be astonished because no one has ever asked for a mark for a dog. But you've done your homework and the both of you are prepared.

1. To teach this trick, give Kate a sit-stay, move forward, and stretch a piece of ribbon between two points at about her chest height to act as a tape barrier.
2. The tape will stop Kate's forward motion, and you can call her forward and say *"Mark!"* as she reaches the ribbon.
3. Encourage her to watch you.
4. Call Kate when you are on the other side of the tape, and as she approaches, tell her *"Mark"* and *"Stand-Stay!"*
5. Do not tell her *"Sit!"* or *"Down!"* You want her to stand and wait for you to give her the appropriate follow-up command.
6. You also want to reinforce the stand. (I know you had Kate obedience trained, but too few trainers work on the *"Stand!"* command. I'm describing this trick under the assumption that Kate already knows the stand.)
7. Do this three or four times, repositioning Kate each time.
8. Now take three paces back from the tape and repeat as above three or four times.
9. Then go out and buy a roll of half-inch masking tape. (In subsequent sessions you'll use the masking tape because you just stick it onto objects rather than tying it.)
10. Lower the chest tape until you are sticking it on the floor. The word "mark" is not *exactly* a command, it's more for informational purposes. Every time you work on this exercise, tap the tape and say *"Mark!"*

Normal tape marking consists of a pattern that is T-shaped, seen from Kate's POV—meaning "point of view." (Oh boy, the showbiz stuff you learn here!) Initially, you should practice indoors in a quiet place. Once Kate is rock steady, take her outside. A film set may be a quiet, romantic living room scene, but off camera it's pure bedlam, with fifty people milling around, working, smoking, supervising, etc., etc.

PRESENTATION: Get as far away from Kate as you can. You can't be in the frame when the camera rolls. Find out what position (stand, sit or down) the director wants Kate to be in when she hits her mark. There will be time available to rehearse on the actual set. Use it! As they are adjusting lights, positioning cameras, etc., you and Kate can rehearse. Always ask permission to use the set, and stay out of everyone's way. The purpose of this presentation is to show off your professional skills. The cast and crew are your audience. Don't be surprised if, after the director says "Cut," there's a round of applause for Kate. Not you, but Kate.

Tug

"TUG!" "STOP!" (OR "STAY!") AND "OUT!"

Kate may have already started teaching *you* this exercise. Has she grabbed her leash and tried to pull it out of your hands? Put that on command and you have a great new trick that is *really* handy for the theatrical dog.

If there is a nearby fancy-coffee shop that sells in bulk, try to get your hands on one of the burlap bags in which their coffee beans were shipped. An alternative is to go to a fabric shop and buy a couple of yards of burlap. It won't be as heavy and hardy as the coffee bags, but it will do.

In this trick, the work is the reward. Kate enjoys tugging on that sack.

1. Entice her as you give the command *"Tug!"*
2. Pull and twist the sack so she gets pleasure from it. (Be care-

ful how much you twist her head and neck. You don't want to injure her.)

3. When you're ready to stop, command her to *"Stop!"* at which point you "will" Kate to continue to pull on the sack but not to twist and turn.

4. Pause and wait until Kate calms down before you tell her *"Out!"* which means to let go. She probably will be reluctant to do this, but if she does, give her a treat and simultaneously click.

5. The offer of the treat will cause her to release the burlap in order to eat.

6. The food reward is *really* important here. If she's slow to release, force her mouth open, gently remove the sack and *then* give the food reward.

PRESENTATION: This trick can be used to get Kate to pull a child out of the path of an oncoming vehicle, pull a wagon, drag a jacket or do any one of several dozen other scenes in a film. The *"Stay!"* command is used for print jobs (photographs). Moving pictures are *moving* pictures. Still shots or print jobs freeze a split second of time in space. Some still shots photograph action and some still shots capture what *appears* to be action. You *cannot* photograph a dog pulling on a pair of trousers by simply putting the trouser leg in the dog's mouth. There has to be pulling, otherwise it will look fake. In film work, shooting a wide shot of the dog charging in from camera left at the trouser leg, grabbing and pulling it, is dramatic. A still shot of a close-up of the dog's mouth grabbing a trouser leg must freeze that second in time. Too much movement makes shooting the still shot difficult. Not enough movement makes shooting the motion picture difficult. Kate can handle either shot, and you will show her off for the crew.

Here is an excellent example of a showbiz dog in action. In a takeoff on the old Coppertone ads, Muffin, a Golden Retriever owned by dog trainer Babette Haggerty, tugs on the model's pants. Either the Tug command or a pad-trained dog could handle this job.

The Pad Dog

"PAD!"

Really astute showbiz dog handler/trainers always have a few good pad dogs around. What's a pad dog? One that will go energetically after a five-inch-square burlap pad that is two-inches thick, with heavy strings attached to each corner. Showbiz trainers always have these pads available because they may be necessary when least expected.

The showbiz dog has to be able to do many different things, and the well-trained pad dog can handle them. Rescue someone who is drowning? Put the pad under the actor's clothes at the back of his neck. Pull a child out of the path of an oncoming car? The pad goes into the seat of the child's pants. Grab the postman's trousers? Strap the pad to his leg under the trousers. A little touch of squalene will increase the dog's interest in the pad. The odor is important, because the dog is being cued to the pad as well as to the individual pad's odor.

A good natural retriever will learn this trick rapidly. Use it! You want Kate to go bonkers when she sees the pad. Remember the advantages of frustration in training, and do not let her get hold of it. This is a variation of the Tug trick just described. The difference is that you want to create ultimate frustration and the desire to secure the pad. In the Tug trick, you want control—in the Pad trick, boundless energy and lust.

Playing with the pad will intensify Kate's interest in it, but it is *not* to be a constant toy; just give it to her periodically. When you show the pad, she should become completely energized. You want her rockets-in-her-rear hot to trot, and ready to *explode* to get ahold of the pad. Toss it and send Kate to get it.

If you want a show-business career for Kate, this is one important exercise. It will solve problems before they arise. On a film set, the director will tell you, "The dog doesn't have to do too much. All she has to do is to scale that wooden fence, go into the burning building through this window and drag the fifteen-pound baby from the crib and exit via this door. Then she should lick the baby's face and go down to the corner and pull the fire alarm. We want to do that all in one continuous shot. Make sure she is gentle with the baby."

I'll tell you what the director will say if you tell him, "They didn't tell me any of this!" He'll say, "Isn't Kate a trained dog?" Welcome to Show Business!

The pad work will solve one of the problems. No, not dragging the baby out of the burning house, but dragging a dummy that *looks* like the baby out of the fire.

PRESENTATION: An understanding of camera work and shooting sequences will help you choreograph dog action. Use a lot of exaggerated moves and motions when you're setting Kate up for her big scene. This way, the crew will think that your exaggerated moves are being played to your dog, when in fact, you're really playing to the crew. Rent or buy the movie *There's Something About Mary.* It will help you understand how a stuffed dummy dog can be used interchangeably with a live Border Terrier. Watch the movie more than once. Run it in slow motion. It shows you how action is edited. Good stuff!

Lift Leg on a Fire Hydrant

"PEE!" "RIGHT PEE!" "LEFT PEE!"

This trick is called "Lift Leg on a Fire Hydrant," even though your dog often will be required to lift his leg on a person. Also we're working with Kate, who doesn't lift her leg at all. Don't worry if your dog is a female. Movie people aren't *that* concerned with details.

1. With Kate in the stand position, put your hand right below her knee (stifle) and gently bend it up and pull slightly out to the side.
2. Tell Kate *"Pee!"* as you scratch her gently between her leg and stomach.
3. Don't do it for more than thirty seconds the first time. Cut it off sooner if she seems bored or uninterested. You want her attitude to be calm and relaxed while enjoying your scratching.
4. Gradually extend the period of time that she elevates her leg in the appropriate position. If you don't know what that is, stop by some fire hydrants and watch.
5. Next, move your hand from under the leg and onto the root of the tail. Kate has to learn to stand there without your hand under her leg. You'll know you are getting results when you approach her side and say *"Pee!"* and she starts to lift her leg without feeling your hand on her leg.

6. Work on one side initially, and after she has that down pat, switch legs. Start teaching her *"Right Pee!"* and *"Left Pee!"* Eventually work her up to three minutes of keeping her leg up.

PRESENTATION: When you're asked to set up the shot, ask, "Which leg?" It won't matter to them unless she can only lift one leg. In which case they'll want the other one. The reason you ask which leg is to show what a pro you are. The crew is your audience.

Walk Slowly

"STEADY!" "SLOW!" "TAKE TIME!" OR "EASY!"

It's important to have your dog able to walk at various speeds on command while on a movie set. Any actor, after a hard battle, or fighting a raging river, moves slowly and stiffly, not rapidly. This training takes place in your day-to-day life. If Kate pulls on the leash, say *"Steady!"* or *"Slow!"* or *"Take Time"* or *"Easy!"* Anytime you need to slow her down, apply a slight pressure on her leash. (One technique that is used for slowing a dog down, particularly in livestock herding, is to "drop" or "down" the dog.) These commands *should not* be used with the show-business dog. We want to keep the show-business dog in the stand position. That is the best initial position from which to move a dog into different positions. The sequence in show business is to slow Kate down, and then say *"Down!"* rather than having her go directly into the down position. A subtle point, but Kate may need to remain standing or sitting at that point in the script rather than lying down. If you teach her using *"Down!"* she may later automatically go into that position without being told.

PRESENTATION: The presentation is the handling. Kate has a lot of training. To get the desired speed, use as many of these commands as possible. The first part of your presentation is for you to ask the question, "Can we shoot this MOS?" they'll know they're dealing with a pro. You're speaking their language. MOS is "without sound." It goes back to the German film directors of the thirties who said, "Mit out sound." If you're shooting MOS, you can make all the sounds in the world—nothing's being recorded. In that case, carry on a conversation with Kate, using your voice tones and commands to bring her in at the appropriate speed. A variety of commands delivered at the right time might be, *"Steady!" "Slow!" "Easy!" "Stay!" "Stop!" "Come!" "No!"* and anything else that will control her movement. That ongoing conversation, with Kate responding, is going to be impressive to the film crew.

Walk Fast

Here's an exercise that should be performed in a brisk fashion. The standard recall command calls for a *"Fast Walk!"* Now, if Kate is coming slowly, you may have done something wrong in the initial training. If she was coming too fast, don't sweat it. Better too fast than too slow. A cardinal rule in theatrical dog training is that it's easier to slow dogs down than to speed them up. Too exuberant is better than too calm. *Do not* slow Kate down too rapidly; do it gradually, otherwise it becomes difficult to speed her up.

PRESENTATION: The presentation follows the same guidelines as those in getting Kate to move slowly. Your up-sounding voice encourages her to speed up.

Running

Everything you've read earlier in this chapter should be taken into consideration. You're dealing with a *handling* rather than a *training* situation.

PRESENTATION: It's the handling that pulls together all the earlier training to make it appear that Kate is doing something that she may not *really* be doing. My rule of thumb on the set is to have one handler for each dog. On a multidog job, I usually add one extra. In other words, three dogs will arrive with four handlers/trainers. As a matter of fact, one dog often will require two handlers to do the job right. (To get Kate to run, the assistant handler holds her in the stand position. You don't use a crew member to hold her. They're not qualified handlers and lack the feel or the touch, no matter how many dogs they've owned.) The assistant will hold Kate back as you call her. He'll keep one hand on her chest/throat area and the other restraining her hindquarters. She'll be geared up to move out. When released, she'll charge toward you.

Digging

"DIG!"

Digging can be a trick of opportunity. If you see Kate digging, say *"Dig!"* and click if you have a clicker handy. One occasion that may cause Kate to dig is when her water or food bowl is empty. You are more likely to see it on the water bowl because she knows that when her food is gone, it's *all gone*. (There should always be water in her water bowl.) If you know when she'll dig, it becomes a trick of opportunity. Seize it!

1. If you don't have the opportunity dropped into your lap, start off with a small empty plastic jar with a screw-on top.
2. Sit down in front of Kate (be very close), take out one or two tidbits and offer them individually, clicking every time.
3. Let Kate see you put two more treats into the jar, then toss it about ten feet away. Without being told, she'll rush over to it.
4. The next step is to stick the jar into some soft dirt, with half of it exposed.
5. When Kate brings it to you, give her the treats.
6. Now cover the jar completely.
7. Tell Kate *"Dig!"* and click at the same time.
8. Keep saying *"Dig!"* until she unearths the jar.
9. Reward her along with a click.

10. Graduate to burying the jar deeper and tamping the earth down. Point to where it's buried.
11. Now eliminate the jar. Point at the ground, then treat and click as soon as she starts to dig. Make her dig for longer and longer periods of time; treat after you tell her to stop.

PRESENTATION: When the director wants your dog to dig, you ask "Where?" Give her a sit-stay and point to the designated area and tell her to *"Dig!"* The director will love it. (If the dirt has to be replaced to do the shot over, it's not your job. Union films or commercials have more than enough people to prepare the set, even if this means replacing dirt!)

Scratch

"SCRATCH!"

There's a call for this trick every two-and-a-half years. Be aware that it cannot be taught overnight if you want Kate to have it on her résumé.

Scratching on cue is an excellent trick for the showbiz dog. Here Jordan Heppner's Belgian Malinois Hobo performs.

Learn the location of Kate's tickle point (which is different from her pleasure point). The tickle point is that spot—or spots—that, when scratched, cause her reflexes to move her hindquarter in a quick scratching motion. This is a "conditioned reflex" rather than training.

What you're doing with most of these tricks is training Kate to do what she is commanded to do. A conditioned reflex is somewhat different. It's a response Kate has no control over. The first scientist who identified the conditioned reflex experimented with dogs. Ivan Pavlov would ring a bell and then feed his dogs. He reached a point where he would ring the bell and the dogs would salivate regardless of whether or not they were fed. Were they trained? No, conditioned. The dogs had no control over salivating.

1. You'll condition Kate by zeroing in on her tickle point and tickling it while saying *"Scratch!"* The best positions for her at the start of this conditioning are On Your Back, Dead Dog or as in the Comedy Dead-Dog Trick. The tickle point can be used to keep Kate in position and concurrently work on the scratch conditioned reflex. The tickle point causes the leg to move in a scratching motion.

2. When the reflex occurs, say *"Scratch!"* and reinforce, using the clicker and treat. The behavior actually is self-reinforcing because it is a reflex. This is concurrent training.

3. The actual training takes place when Kate is in the sit position and you scratch the area around the breastbone, causing the conditioned reflex.

4. At this point (if you haven't run out of hands) use food and the clicker. Also try to catch the behavior.

5. The hand signal for this exercise is scratching your side. Keep your eye on Kate and be ready to give her the command *"Scratch!"* when she has an urge to scratch. Dogs sit down to scratch. (Rarely will they stand and scratch, and if they do, it's usually the sign of an impending skin problem.) This is a rather prolonged training program, but by doing it as outlined, it will take a minimum of actual sustained work.

PRESENTATION: This is a cute trick that can be performed anywhere. It adds humor to films and commercials. I remember one commercial done by the late Mug-Z. The political commercial was disparaging one political figure because of his associates. The theme was if you lie down with dogs, you get up with fleas, at which point Mug-Z scratched.

Sneeze

"AHHH-CHOO!"

Sneezing is another caught behavior, and like the Scratch trick, is a little tough to initiate. There are similarities between the two tricks, as you shall see. You want to "catch" every sneeze, but how can you initiate one? This should be done in short sessions because you're working with a conditioned reflex.

What causes a dog to sneeze? Something that's irritating. For that reason any of the following provocations should only be used once or twice each time you practice.

1. Rubbing your hand gently over your dog's nose.
2. Tickling the nose with a feather.
3. Blowing in her nose.
4. Making her excited.
5. Continual barking, particularly when you're teaching her to start barking (speak) on command.
6. A whiff of perfume
7. Dog grooming spray.

Use these sneeze-producing irritants judiciously. Don't use sneeze powder. It can be harmful; the above methods are kinder. The signal for "sneeze" is to move your head in a big exaggerated upward movement and rapidly lower it on the "choo" part. The verbal command is, *"Ahhh-Choo!"* complete with head movements.

PRESENTATION: Don't make Kate sneeze to excess. When on the set, give the command only when they're ready to shoot.

Remember that you're not on the set only to show off, but to do a job. The successful way to handle the sneeze is to keep repetition to a minimum so you don't "wear out" Kate's ability to sneeze. Try not to do more than three sneezes per session.

Put Your Head Down, Close Your Eyes, Raise Your Head Up

"HEAD DOWN!" OR "PLOTZ!"
"CLOSE EYES!" AND "HEAD UP!"

1. With Kate in the down position, gently press her head down between her outstretched paws and say *"Head Down!"* This is also referred to as the plotz position.
2. As soon as her head is in the correct position, gently scratch between her eyes. The scratching reward must be delivered in a calm and relaxing manner.
3. As Kate relaxes and closes her eyes, say *"Close Eyes!"*
4. As the training progresses, you want her eyes closed for longer and longer periods of time. You can accomplish this by giving the command as you *pretend* to stick your fingers in her eyes.
5. Alternate this exercise with the command *"Head Up!"* which will be delivered as you show a tidbit.
6. As soon as her head pops up and she's looking at the food, click and put the tidbit in her mouth. The reason you're putting the food in her mouth is that anything else may cause Kate to break from the down position.
7. After you do this a number of times you can toss, click and say *"Catch!"* at the same time, knowing she will remain down as she catches the tidbit. Don't rush it. Kate should focus on the food treat.

There are two different moods with each exercise. The "head down" is soft and calm, the "head up" has a bit more pizzazz, but not so much as to make her break. These mood shifts present no problem. They give you the opportunity to have more control over Kate and will help you learn how to adjust to and with her.

PRESENTATION: These two exercises can be used to have Kate demonstrate certain moods on a film set. Kate's head down with eyes closed is exhaustion. Her head down with eyes rolled up shows devotion. Her head popping up shows Kate reacting to any of many different things. That's why you want her focusing on the food. It enables you to get her to appear to react to whatever the director wants.

Plotz is a variation of the down position. Here we have Hobo Heppner, a Belgian Malinois of Winnipeg, Canada, performing.

Salute, Be Shy, Wipe Your Mouth, Wipe Your Nose, Wave, High Five, Who Do You Love? Who Is the World's Greatest_____?

We'll begin this trick at a point that will illustrate how you can change a trick and its command slightly to produce new and exciting tricks. Take a peek at chapter 24 and read the Patty-Cake trick so you can understand how to expand on this trick even more.

The High Five is cute and prepares the dog for other exercises. Kathy Ahearn of Tom's River, NJ, trained this dog.

The Salute trick is a versatile one that can be manipulated to create different moods in a film or on TV. There are a number of different positions that Kate's paw can be put into. Targeting and the clicker can be used successfully here.

Kate's right paw high over her right eye is the traditional position for the Salute trick. The paw is dropped down a little, to the eye, for the Be Shy trick. With the paw moving farther downward still, it becomes the Wipe Your Mouth or Wipe Your Nose trick. With the forequarter straight up in the air it becomes Wave, then High Five, which is completed when you slap her paw with your palm.

Here is a variation of the High Five, with the hand making contact. The Shetland Sheepdog is Hillary, owned by trainer Susan Zaretsky of Newburgh, NY.

Why not ask "Who Do You Love?" or "Who Is the World's Greatest_____?" Of course the answer is "You" no matter what the question.

Here's the perfect sequence of tricks, using the techniques of marking and the target stick. Don't teach these tricks one after another, though, because this can cause confusion to Kate. Teach one or two *other* tricks in between each pair of these changing leg positions. Be *very* specific as to the location of Kate's paw for each one of these different tricks. Put the target stick in the appropriate position and have her target in on it. This is really the most efficient way of teaching the precision needed for these tricks.

Wipe Your Mouth is a useful showbiz trick. Here the Shetland Sheepdog Puddleduck waits for the command.

On getting the command from her trainer, Susan Zaretsky, Puddleduck moves into action.

Puddleduck completes the Wipe Your Mouth exercise.

Kate will be picking up on all sorts of cues at this level of training. You are teaching with the target stick, but phase it out before presenting these tricks—although the temptation will be there to keep it nearby. Actually, the presence of the target stick, even if you don't use it, will tip Kate off to the fact that you'll be working on targeting. Your body language, always a constant and subtle cue, will further tip her off. You won't even realize that you're giving these subliminal sensory cues to her. High-level competition training dictates that your performance be devoid of all these cues, but you aren't working on competitive training.

PRESENTATION: The presentations on this are endless. Let your imagination go wild! My daughter, Babette, trained Jack Nicklaus's Golden Retriever, Tali. When asked, "Who is the world's greatest golfer?" Tali immediately pointed at her owner and barked "Yooo!" Now, you know that Tali wouldn't lie.

Hold Your Breath

"HOLD!"

This is an important trick for showbiz Kate. Print jobs will often call for a close-up of Kate that's shot under hot lights, which cause panting, with her tongue lolling out of her mouth— not a pretty picture. For this trick most of the training takes place on the set rather than beforehand.

1. If Kate's tongue is hanging out, just before the photo is to be taken, you, the competent handler/trainer, tell her *"Hold!"*
2. Then you'll attempt to grab her tongue, which she will immediately pull back into her mouth. You may feel this is a handling trick rather than a training trick, and you're certainly correct. Basically you're working against a conditioned reflex (panting) and replacing it with another conditioned reflex (pulling her tongue in) that is put on the command *"Hold!"*

PRESENTATION: You'll want to time your *"Hold!"* command to the split second before the photographer is ready to shoot. How do you know when that is? By following the tempo set by the photographer. A photographer generally shoots a sequence of shots at a fixed tempo. By paying attention to when the flash goes off and Kate's mood, you will be able to produce a dog with no tongue hanging out in all the photos. Most photographers are unaware that the you, the handler, are doing such an efficient job. They just realize the shoot went well. Oh well, you can't get credit all the time.

Take a Bow

"BOW!"

"That's a wrap!" is what you'll hear when you finish your showbiz job. There is no better way to wrap up your performance than with a bow, referred to as a "play bow" because Kate is in a playful mood. This can easily be a caught behavior if you have the clicker handy during one of Kate's happy moods.

But here's the more labor-intensive approach with a number of variations.

1. After the clicker (see above), with Kate beside you in the heel position, give her the command to *"Stand!"*
2. This is followed by extending your left forearm under her tuck-up as you say, *"Down!"* If you have a toy-sized dog, put your index and middle fingers together and slide them under her tuck-up. (When you view the dog from the side, the underside section between her chest and hindquarters— the stomach—is tucked up, and that's the tuck-up.)
3. Your forearm will stop Kate from lowering her hindquarters as she lowers her front into the bow position.
4. Keep Kate calm by scratching her stop, and have her hold the position for several seconds.
5. Release her with applause and an explosion of pats and praises.
6. Gradually extend the period of time for the bow, and move farther away from her when giving the command.

ALTERNATE APPROACH: The root of the tail is a prime pleasure point, so take advantage of it.

1. Instead of having Kate start from the stand position, place her in the down position and pin the leash with the ball of your foot as you start to scratch the root of her tail.
2. As Kate gets interested, lift your fingers slightly so she must elevate her rump to continue being scratched.
3. Should Kate attempt to get up, the leash will restrain her.
4. The scratching will not immediately bring her rump up into the full position. Improvement will come an inch at a time. In three or four short sessions, you will have Kate raising her behind into the bow position.

PRESENTATION: This is the grand finale. It's the end of Kate's performance on the movie set, the end of a series of tricks. In other words, it's a wrap!

19
USEFUL TRICKS

Retrieve the TV Remote

This is the world's most useful trick. Do you female readers know how to get your husbands to exercise? Hide his TV remote!

In this useful trick, your dog "Pup" is going to use his nose to find that elusive channel changer. It has a characteristic odor to your dog's knowing nose. (This is a variation on retrieving toys by name found in chapter 16.)

1. Before starting to train, remove the battery from the remote so the TV doesn't go crazy.
2. Follow the procedure outlined in chapter 16 for learning the names of toys.
3. Start practicing by "hiding" the remote in plain sight.
4. Then hide it under a table, followed by hiding it under an armchair.
5. Start hiding the remote under the covers and under the cushions in the couch.
6. The dog will have the time of his life with this new game.

PRESENTATION: You do not want to show anyone this trick. They'll kidnap your dog and not even send you a ransom note.

Naming Names

"GO TO LUCY!"

Teaching your dog the names of family members is the foundation for a series of useful tricks. In the two-member household, this is easy. Your dog probably has learned the names of both members through invisible training. He has even learned the pet names you have for one another. In larger households name recognition can easily be taught anytime the majority of your family is playing with the dog. Puppyhood is a great time to start. When your dog is a pup, more members of the family will be likely to join together for puppy playtime.

1. Begin this game with the family in a loose circle.
2. Start off by giving "Pup" a good rubbing down; face him toward Lucy as she calls "Pup!"
3. Give Pup a gentle shove toward "Lucy" and say her name. *"Lucy!"*
4. As Pup wiggles up to Lucy, she gives him a happy rub-a-dub.
5. It is back to you again, with Lucy saying your name and following the same procedure.
6. You can precede the name with *"Go to_____!"*
7. Start sending Pup to different family members, each time emphasizing the person's name. This will also reinforce the dog's coming when called. Once Pup has an idea as to what you want, it will not be necessary for the other family members to call him.

PRESENTATION: The important part of this exercise is the individual name. Pup will know that you want him to go to that person. The "Go to" part is to set him up for a series of variations on this trick. Pup will initially know what is expected of him from the context in which the command is delivered. At this point it is more of a game than a presentation, so continue on with the training by sending Pup to people when they are in other rooms. Should a neighbor stop by, you can show off Pup going from one family member to another.

Take Daddy His Slippers

Some pieces are coming together. You've developed the more grown-up Pup into a reliable retriever, after having taught him Daddy's name.

1. Put Dad's slippers in Pup's mouth and tell him, *"Take Daddy His Slippers!"* The emphasis in the command is on "Daddy."
2. Daddy calls Pup and praises him lavishly, and in that short session, Pup gets a grasp on the idea.
3. It still requires additional work and fine-tuning, but the context of putting the slippers in his mouth and emphasizing Daddy's name has sent Pup into action. On the other end, Daddy must praise and pet Pup. It's that simple to marry two tricks.

PRESENTATION: In your presentation, have Pup deliver one slipper at a time. Are you concerned that you are doubling his work? Not to worry, he has nothing better to do, but more important, you're getting in twice the practice. Pup also can be used for carrying messages back and forth.

Wake Lucy Up

The preceding trick was preparing you for a couple of variations like this one. You probably need help in waking the kids to get them ready for school. Tell them you're going to play a game.

1. Put either butter or squalene on their faces as they lie quietly and not moving on their beds.

2. Send Pup into their bedrooms to wake each one by name, e.g., *"Wake Lucy Up!"* and nature will take its course.
3. Pup will be attracted to the smell of the squalene or butter and start licking their faces.
4. Even though you remind the children that they must lie still, once Pup is licking their faces, they'll laugh. Remind them to remain still because this is part of the game, even though they will not stay still for long. Pup loves the kids and the kids love Pup. In three repetitions you will have set the pattern. If you use this trick every morning, very quickly it will become a deeply ingrained performance. The synergy created between the dog and the children every morning will be self-reinforcing. By the third day you can eliminate the squalene or butter on the face. The children's enthusiasm will be reinforcement enough!

Be aware that the children may not want to play this game every morning, not because they don't want to play, but because they don't want to get up. Make sure Pup goes to the person you've named. If he heads in the wrong direction, a cautionary "No" is in order, followed by repeating the command and sending him to the right family member.

PRESENTATION: This is easy to demonstrate. When you pridefully show off your children to visitors, they hate it! But the family, especially your children, is going to love showing off Pup. Have the kids lie on top of the covers on their beds, and send Pup after them one at a time. Your visitors will want to borrow Pup. Tell him that they can't have him, but they can buy this book.

TUCK LUCY IN

"PULL COVER!" "UNCOVER!" "DROP IT!"

Here are some "growing" tricks in which the previously learned tricks build into the next one. Your attitudes of waking up and going to sleep are different; you first must create the mood that exists when you tuck someone in. You're going to readjust the previously learned tricks, using retrieving and targeting, which means that teaching this trick will take more time and skill than the tricks taught earlier in this chapter.

1. Start without the children.
2. Fold back the covers on their beds and put a full laundry bag on the bottom sheet.
3. Call Pup in and, using targeting techniques, teach him to retrieve the edge of the top sheet and *"Pull Cover!"* over the laundry bag.
4. Then tell him *"Drop It!"* Don't worry about tucking in at this point.
5. Do this about six times, then start to teach Pup to *"Uncover!"*
6. Pup now grabs the sheet and pulls it the other way. (We haven't finished yet.)
7. Now that Pup is covering, add the children to the trick. (The purpose of teaching the uncovering first is to make it easier on your back while training Pup. Let him do the bending instead of you!) Another reason for teaching the uncover is to expand your waking-up trick. Don't worry about the tucking in yet. Have Pup practice covering the children in short sessions over the next two weeks.
8. Now it's back to the laundry bag. After Pup covers the bag, get him to use his paws on the space between the mattress and the side of the box spring or bed frame. Use the *"Paw!"* or *"Touch!"* command, which you've used in marking training with the clicker (see chapter 7). The *"Paw!"* or *"Touch!"* command is to be changed to *"Tuck!"* for presentation purposes. Do not worry about changed commands confusing Pup. It is just an additional command that he'll learn. *"Paw!"* and *"Touch!"* are specific commands for use with the clicker, and you can whip out your clicker to get Pup going. Some clicker trainers want to use the clicker for everything. The approach of this book is to use *what-*

ever it takes. Although we are looking for the most efficient methods, and clickers are efficient, they are not the answer to all the world's training problems.

9. Gradually you want to change the command to *"Tuck!"* Now, the initial command was *"Tuck Lucy In!"* although Pup was not yet tucking her in. Not to worry! Pup was learning what to do in the context of the situation.

LEARNING PATTERN FOR "WAKE LUCY UP!" AND "TUCK LUCY IN!"

1. Pup learned everyone's name.
2. Pup went to the room of the person he was told to wake (Lucy) and saw her lying on the bed with a delectable taste on her face—a great taste reward!
3. Pup didn't learn how to wake Lucy up, but he learned to lick her face. It produced the desired result.
4. The interaction between Lucy and Pup further reinforced the trick.
5. The command emphasis was on the "Lucy" as the training started.
6. Pup was taught to cover and uncover properly without the presence of a child in the bed. Concurrently Pup learned two additional commands, Drop It and Tuck.
7. The training was put to daily use for a few weeks with the children in their beds.
8. Pup was then taught to tuck the laundry bag in.
9. Next, the children were added.
10. The commands were phased and changed as the training progressed.

The purpose of the above is to help you understand how training develops. It shows the advantage of viewing training as an art, rather than a science. It's free-flowing, rapid and beautiful. Portions of this were also available for almost immediate use rather than only after tedious, long, drawn-out training over a period of many, many weeks.

PRESENTATION: The help Pup gives you every day is all the presentation that you need. Don't hide your light under a bushel. You'll have guests who will be tickled silly with this trick.

Seek Back

"SEARCH!" "TAKE IT!"

This was an old-time AKC obedience exercise that was, unfortunately, discontinued. You will seldom *need* it, but the minute you do, you'll kick yourself in the pants for not teaching it.

You've left the house with Pup. You've locked your door and are sure that you had your keys up to this point. Where did they go? You had the keys when you left, but now, at your car, you can't find them. Check all your pockets. Still no luck? If you have taught Pup every trick in the book up to this point, it will take no time to teach him this.

1. *"Search!"* you tell Pup and he backtracks to the house, using his nose. He can "see" better with his nose than you can with your eyes. And this isn't restricted to finding keys. He can be taught to find anything, even your contact lens case.
2. Pup picks up on two things: your scent, and the hottest scent. Not only does Pup find the keys, but, with a little training, he puts them in your hand! You can use this trick in the house when you do not want to get out of the chair or bend over when you drop something. Be as lazy as possible. It is good training for Pup.

The method?

1. Throw something out there and tell him, *"Take It!"*
2. Do that three or four times followed by rambunctious praise when he obeys. Why praise and not a click? In everyday life

you'd probably not be prepared for this and wouldn't have your clicker with you. If you do have it, then click.

3. When going from point A to point B with Pup, surreptitiously drop your keys.

4. Travel a little bit and come to a halt.

5. Face about and tell Pup to heel.

6. As you turn, he will sit at your left side.

7. Cup your left hand over his nose so he can take your scent, even though he has smelled you often enough.

8. With your left hand sliding alongside Pup's head, point in the direction you just came from and say *"Search!"*

9. It doesn't matter if Pup sees the keys the first time. In subsequent sessions you will make them harder to find. "Harder to find" means dropping your keys or glasses case in tall grass or someplace else where Pup will be forced to use his nose.

10. Once he uses his nose, you're home free. You don't have to worry about anything you misplace.

11. Pup will find it. Just a few short sessions will teach your dog this wonderfully handy task. Pup is locating the object with the hottest odor on it. The one you last handled.

Get a Tissue When I Sneeze

"AHHH-CHOO!" "TAKE IT!" "OUT!"

This is another easy one if Pup—and you—are well trained as outlined in the previous trick!

1. Put a single tissue on top of your coffee table.

2. Make an exaggerated sneeze, motion Pup toward the table and tell him to *"Take It!"*

3. He already knows this trick and will rapidly pick up the tissue and return it to your hand.

4. Tell him *"Out!"* as he returns it to you.

5. Toss the tissue on the table again a few times, make your big *"Ahhh-choo!"* and he'll start going on the sneeze. A snap!

6. Next, get one of those pop-up tissue boxes and affix it to the table with double-sided tape. You can now ahhh-choo to your heart's content. Every sneeze will bring a new tissue. If you have a hay-fever attack, Pup will hop between you and the tissue box. (I wonder if you can get some money from your health-care plan for Pup?)

PRESENTATION: The command makes the trick. Exaggerate that sneeze. You can't make it too big. That double-sided tape will permit you to put the box just about anywhere without Pup knocking it over.

Hold the Dustpan

"DUSTPAN!"

Have you ever noticed how hard it is to sweep the floor and hold the dustpan at the same time? Why not have your dog do the hard part? This is a variation on the retrieving trick, and you'll want to thank Jo Ann Hise of Roswell, New Mexico, for it.

1. Use a plastic dustpan. The concept is a little bit different from the retrieving trick because we have Pup not only holding the dustpan by its handle, but also resting the pan on the floor. The unbalanced weight of the dustpan will cause Pup to lay the edge on the floor, which is fine.
2. Gently pet and caress Pup's head and say *"Dustpan!"*
3. You can click and praise.
4. You want Pup to put the edge of the pan on the floor wherever you indicate by pointing while saying *"Dustpan!"*
5. Pup has to remain steady when the dust is swept into the pan, so, from the beginning, make sure that you go through the motions of sweeping in front of the pan-holding dog.
6. When actually sweeping the dust into the pan, water the floor to keep the dust down. Don't sweep dust directly into Pup's face.

7. Sweep at right angles to him, and when it is time to sweep into the pan, sprinkle more water on the dust.
8. Sweep slowly into the pan. Just because you have hay fever is no reason to make Pup sneeze.

PRESENTATION: I know you don't clean the house when company is there, so rather than showing off, you'll just enjoy the helping hand . . . paw . . . mouth. A warning: If, by accident, you do push the dust in the direction of Pup's nose, he'll sneeze. Put it on command and work on it as a variation of the sneeze trick.

Cute Tricks are appropriate after Useful Tricks. The kids will love these tricks.

Peek

"PEEK!"

Getting "Buttercup" to peek out from under a tablecloth is simple and cute.

1. Start with a rectangular table covered by an overlarge table-cloth. The shape of the rectangular table means that the tablecloth will hang with an "opening" at the table's corner.
2. With Buttercup in a stand-stay under the corner of the table and hidden from view, click, and as she sticks her head out, treat. (Remember, she's been trained to the clicker and knows a reward is forthcoming.)
3. Repeat two or three times. Up to this point this is *pure* clicker training.
4. Now introduce the command *"Peek!"*
5. The sequence is *"Peek!"* Click. Treat. Control Buttercup's forward motion with the placement of the treat.

6. Do not let her stick her whole head out from under the tablecloth—just her muzzle and one eye should peek out.

PRESENTATION: The location of the dog under the tablecloth is all-important. Too far forward or too far back isn't cute. You can practice with Buttercup during dinner every day.

Paws Up

This is a handy trick to build on.

1. Find a good steady table that's the right height for Buttercup.
2. She sits in front of the table.
3. You tap it and say, *"Paws Up!"*
4. As soon as she puts her paws on the table, slip her a tidbit.
5. Six or eight repetitions are sufficient the first time out. (Remember that Buttercup is not permitted to put her paws up unless you tell her to do so.)

PRESENTATION: Keep using the same table in the initial phases of training. Somewhere along the line you'll want Buttercup to learn paws up on tables of different heights, as you'll see in the next trick.

Say Your Prayers

"Say Your Prayers!" is the next logical step and flows from paws up. At this point you should have shifted to different tables in different locations. These tables are of varying heights. Now it is time to use different objects. You can never tell where you'll be asked to perform.

1. To make things easier for yourself (less bending), practice this exercise on the dining-room table first.
2. If Buttercup is too small to reach the table, have her get up on a chair or some other object.

3. Use a lure and reward to draw Buttercup's nose down between her paws, which are resting close together (in her prayer position) on the table.
4. Lure her head downward with the food in one hand and pass the food to your other hand, which you have positioned between Buttercup's paws.
5. Make Buttercup work for that tidbit. Hold it between your fingers and have her mouth the piece of food.
6. You want to extend the period of time she says her prayers.
7. Use the command *"Stay!"* to keep her in position for longer and longer periods of time.
8. You'll wean Buttercup from the luring technique as you have her hold her position until you release her.
9. When you release her from the position, shower her with praise.

PRESENTATION: Say Your Prayers on a table is an easy, vest-pocket trick, one you can do just about anywhere. Also, the action taking place is high enough so that people can see what is happening, their vision unobscured. If you want to get into more of a "production" trick, then I suggest getting a miniature human-type bed, with four legs, a head- and footboard. Once you start adding minature beds and fancy props though, you are changing a simple trick into a production. Buttercup will be lower and tougher to see, but if you are getting into a "production," it's time to have the trick done on a raised stage.

Shake, Rattle 'n' Roll

This is a trick that can be caught or taught. The broad-backed breeds (Pit Bulls, Bull Terriers and French Bulldogs) do a better job with this trick than the narrower backed breeds (Salukis, Whippets and Afghans). Again, a caught behavior always works better if your dog is clicker trained.

You want your dog to be in a happy, upbeat mood.

1. Start off with Buttercup twisting and turning on her back, feet up in the air.
2. Read the Giggle Gaggle trick in chapter 9.
3. Hold your hand open, fingers extended and bent in a claw-like fashion, much as if you were tickling a little child on the stomach.
4. This is what you're going to do with Buttercup, except you are trying to touch as many tickle points as possible. The emphasis is on the tickle points, but if you have also hit a pleasure point or two, that's fine. When in an elated mood, some dogs will do the "Shake, Rattle 'n' Roll" for several seconds.
5. Your "claw" becomes the hand signal for the trick.
6. It's your job to increase the time to thirty seconds, which may seem quite a short period to you, but it is more than long enough for this trick.
7. Buttercup should keep twisting and turning as long as you tell her to *"Shake, Rattle 'n' Roll!"*

PRESENTATION: This is one trick that really is enhanced by a little tape deck with rock and roll music. I suggest "Shake, Rattle 'n' Roll." You have to judge the best length of time to continue this trick from a theatrical point of view.

Comedy Dead Dog

"STRETCH!" "DEAD DOG!"

1. Here is another trick that begins with the On-Your-Back/Flea-Check position (see chapter 22). Buttercup is squarely on her back, even if it is necessary for her to bend her spine to maintain that position. Her legs are up but not extended.
2. When all four legs are extended straight up in the air you have a really funny dead-dog position. The normal dead-dog position is with the dog on her side. The secret to getting her legs extended is finding the correct pleasure points.

3. Start with the forequarters as you work with one leg at a time. The pleasure point on the forequarter is up in her "armpit."
4. Use one finger, gently scratching and searching until Buttercup extends her forequarter.
5. Tell her *"Stretch!"* in a drawled-out tone of voice. (You can see that the mood and attitude for this trick are the exact reverse from the Shake, Rattle 'n' Roll trick just described.
6. You want Buttercup to be calm and controlled and enjoying herself.
7. With the first forequarter extended, caress the extended paw, then bring the other paw up as you gently caress the two paws together.
8. Then scratch the second armpit in the same manner and repeat *"Stretch!"*
9. Once her two forequarters are extended, work on her hindquarters. The pleasure point to work is her Achilles tendon, which extends from the tarsus, or tip of the hock joint, on up to the rear of the hindquarter.

A little comparative anatomy here will help you better understand what I'm talking about. Unlike humans, all dogs are toe-walkers. In their hindquarters, the "heel" does not touch the ground. It's the tip of the hock that is equivalent to the heel. Now you can visualize the Achilles tendon. You want to massage the flesh between the tendon and the hindquarter, occasionally slipping over to the tendon itself. Remember to work on one leg at a time and give the *"Stretch!"* command to get the leg extended.

PRESENTATION: This is a stationary trick, and steadiness is important. There's not too much action involved in doing it, but you can add some by getting Buttercup to sail into the room and do a quick flip onto her back, followed by the *"Dead-Dog!"* command adds a lot of pizzazz.

Stick Out Your Tongue

This is another one of those tricks that are made for clicker training. Use squalene to encourage Buttercup to put her tongue out.

1. Put a drop of squalene on your right index finger and offer it as a target to Buttercup.
2. As her tongue flicks out, click. The squalene reward is delivered a little earlier than usual in clicker training. (Normally, the clicker serves as the secondary reinforcer, marking the end of the exercise. Here it's becoming a primary reinforcer and marks the *beginning* of the exercise.)
3. You'll slowly change that approach to the raised finger being the primary reinforcer, with the clicker moving down to its normal "position."
4. Have Buttercup respond six to eight times, then move to a variable reinforcement schedule with the squalene.
5. Load up a cotton puff with squalene and hold it in your right hand between your fourth finger and the heel of your hand.
6. Before each attempt at eliciting the behavior, move your index finger down to the cotton. (Sometimes you will touch the cotton with the index finger and sometimes you will not, thereby making the reinforcement variable.)
7. Buttercup will stick out her tongue each time.
8. You will also make her extend her tongue by holding that finger farther away. The distance away that you hold your finger is critical. Its purpose is to have Buttercup extend her tongue, not have her stretch her neck forward.
9. As her tongue is extended forward, increase the period of time that it is kept out.
10. Gradually increase the period of time from when the tongue is first extended until the click is sounded. Increase slowly but surely, by tenths of a second.

PRESENTATION: Ask Buttercup to comment on any unpopular question. The funny response is the tongue stuck out.

Balance and Catch Blindfolded

This trick is divided into two parts. The assumption is that Buttercup has already learned the Balance and Catch trick (see chapter 15), which is the first part of this trick. The second part is teaching Buttercup to wear a blindfold. If she has worn sunglasses, hats and clothes, it's a little easier to acclimate her to wearing a blindfold. Realize that you are now obscuring Buttercup's vision, and that puts her at a disadvantage.

1. Tie the blindfold very loosely around the eyes, bringing it under the ears and behind the head.
2. In the beginning, leave one of her eyes uncovered. (Every dog develops their own "method" for flipping tidbits into the air and catching them and will follow the same pattern when blindfolded.)
3. Is Buttercup going to be 100 percent accurate in catching the tidbit? No, but she'll probably catch it at least 80 percent of the time. On top of that, Buttercup earns an A for effort.

PRESENTATION: Start off by doing the trick with the blindfold obviously covering just one eye. After a round of laughs, someone will point out that only one eye is covered. Follow this up with both eyes covered for a (probably) successful performance of the trick.

21
SENDING AND MARKING TRICKS

A number of handy, dandy tricks are covered here. You've started to work on parts of some of them already.

The Send-Away

"GO OUT!" "VORAUS!"
The purpose of the send-away is to send "Gomer" out in front of you and have him wait for an additional command. This is distance control. All dog owners want their dog to come when called. In reality what they want is distance control. The lazy man's way to teach the send-away requires no additional work at all. You're here, and you want your dog Gomer there. A simple request and not unreasonable. No need to go through a long, drawn-out training program: Gomer knows the rudiments of this advanced exercise already.

1. With Gomer sitting at your left-hand side in the heel position, move your left hand forward in the direction you want him to go and give the *"Voraus!"* or *"Go Out!"* command. *Voraus,* pronounced "for-AWS," is from the German, meaning go out.

2. Gomer moves fifty feet away, turns and looks for further instruction.

3. Tell him to *"Stay!"* At this point you can give him another command, such as *"Sit!"* or *"Down!"* or keep him in the stand position.

4. If you walk your dog off leash, one drill that should be built into that walk is having Gomer sit before crossing a street. The ideal street would have a big empty field on the other side. (Now, the city dweller may discover that it's difficult to find that sort of street and may have to settle for a nice fire hydrant across the street.)

5. Automatically sitting at the curb ensures Gomer doesn't break and cross the street without being told. In traffic you need all the insurance you can get.

6. When Gomer is told to *"Sit!"* he knows what's coming next and wants to cross that street. You, of course, want to make sure there is no car coming. Previously you had released Gomer with *"Release!"* or *"Okay!"* I'm suggesting changing the command because you want to change the *context* of the command. Rather than a release, it's a command to go forward. Brimming with enthusiasm, Gomer waits for your *"Release!"* command to cross the street by himself.

7. Instead, you are going to change that *"Release!"* to the command *"Go Out!"* or the German *"Voraus!"* I prefer *"Voraus!"* for the onomatopoeia—it's a word that sounds like what I want Gomer to do. Switching commands is no problem. You will use different commands for slightly different situations. Notice the subtle difference here. A release means that Gomer can do what he wants (cross the street). A command to go out is telling him to move forward. A change in context, but an easy approach to teaching this trick.

PRESENTATION: The charging enthusiasm that you let build up in Gomer is what *really* makes this trick shine. You can vary this when you are walking along with him in the heel position. Tell him to *"Voraus!"* He'll go shooting forward and look over his shoulder as if to say, "What now, boss?"

Go to Place

This handy trick directs Gomer to go to a certain place in your house. Pick a central location to send him to when guests appear at your doorstep or if you just want him out of the way. This is a good example of adapting previously learned tricks to serve a different purpose (see "The Ultimate Emergency" in chapter 13).

1. First, place a mat in the spot you have picked for Gomer to go to.
2. Stand three feet away from the mat, use an extended target stick and move it in the direction of the mat.
3. As Gomer moves toward the tip of the stick, click and treat.
4. Gomer moves toward the mat, and you click and treat. You're looking for even *minor* moves in the right direction. You're not looking to have him grab the gold ring, just move *toward* it!
5. Seven to ten clicks for minor moves toward the mat are enough for a short session.
6. If he hasn't gotten close to the mat, start again in five minutes. Otherwise, if you feel like it, you can wait until the next day. You aren't in a rush.

Don't worry about what Gomer is going to do when he reaches the mat. The sit, stand and down positions all are correct. You want Gomer to relax. Later you'll introduce the commands for what he is to do once he gets to the mat. As he starts to go to the mat consistently, add the command, *"Go to Place!"* Ultimately you will be able to tell Gomer to get into different positions after he arrives at the mat.

PRESENTATION: Visitors are impressed when, rather than jumping on them, a dog goes to a designated spot in the house—on command.

Get Up on the Chair

"GET UP!"

I know, I know, you don't want Gomer to get up on the chair. He isn't allowed on chairs—unless you tell him. This exercise doesn't have to involve a chair. It can be any object you want him to get up on. *"Go to Place!"* and *"Paws Up!"* have prepared Gomer for this trick. Building on tricks is invaluable in teaching new tricks. Guide Gomer over to the object you want him to get up on and tell him to *"Get Up!"* Because of his previous training, he'll get the message in three or four attempts. Undoubtedly you'll be sending him up onto different objects, so don't just train him on one particular piece of furniture. The more you do this (on different objects), the more versatile Gomer becomes.

PRESENTATION: This is a natural for the show-business dog that has to get up on whichever object the script says. But it's a trick that can be shown off just about anywhere.

90-Degree Turn

"TURN!" "LEFT TURN!" "RIGHT TURN!" "FACE FRONT!"

Now the difference here from the tricks in chapter 14 is CONTROL. In teaching tricks you want to be able to slow down the trick your dog does. Your dog's rapid performance of one trick after another obscures many tricks. Do *not* let your dog do this. Slow the performance with controlled individual performances.

1. Start out by facing Gomer. In previous chapters we have explained a number of different ways to teach your dog right from left. Teaching Gomer to turn 90-degrees is not the same thing as having him spin to the right or left. Gomer is to turn to the left or right and wait.

2. Use the target stick to guide his head to his left, click and treat.

3. Introduce the command *"Turn!"* then click and treat. Now, this is not pure clicker training, because we are introducing the command before Gomer knows what you want him to do. You will be working left and right.

4. A turn to the left *("Left Turn!")* prepares him for a turn to the right *("Right Turn!")*.

5. He's learning to turn, but he will develop a preference for going to the left, so you want to begin alternating directions by the second session. Gomer's learning curve will depend on the training that has gone before. That includes responding to the target stick and knowing right from left.

6. Phase out the target stick as soon as possible. While working on left and right turns, Gomer can wind up turning 360 degrees (in a circle), or you can introduce a new command.

7. *"Face Front!"* means that Gomer must turn to face you.

8. Visualize a clock with Gomer facing in one of four different directions: twelve, three, six or nine o'clock. Gomer starts out at six o'clock facing you.

9. Two right (or two left) turns will face Gomer away from you as he faces twelve o'clock. (Don't forget that if *Gomer is facing you,* your right and left are not Gomer's right and left, they are the opposite!)

10. Adding the command *"Face Front!"* adds another dimension to the trick with a minimum amount of effort.

PRESENTATION: People will be amazed when they see Gomer facing in different directions on command. This trick can be done anywhere.

Spinning

"RIGHT SPIN!" "LEFT SPIN!"

Some dogs love to spin because it gets the endorphins going. It's lots of fun and a great energy release.

1. Use the target stick and get Gomer to follow it as you guide him in a circular motion. In the beginning, don't expect a long chase.
2. As you click and reward, you should increase the speed and length of time of spinning.
3. Start off with a half-dozen left spins.
4. Then introduce the right spin twice, then go back to the left spin.
5. Pay attention to Gomer's attitude. He has to develop endurance for this trick, which he'll learn to love. Also, it's a way to exercise him with a minimum amount of effort.
6. Eliminate the target stick as soon as possible, but keep that clicker handy.

PRESENTATION: As your dog turns into a whirlwind, he will impress all who behold him. This trick can be performed anywhere. Rapidly changing the dog's direction will cause spectators eyes to pop.

22
HEALTHFUL TRICKS

Healthful tricks are, well—healthful, and can be enjoyable for both you and your dog. Their purpose is to make the care and maintenance of your dog "Casey" easy. Some dogs are very sensitive when they are being examined by a veterinarian and fight these needed exams. Using these tricks desensitizes Casey to being examined. For now, you will not be examining Casey. You will be petting and caressing him. Later you can examine! A few big secrets to lessen the stress of examinations:

1. Put your dog on command.
2. Train with empathy.
3. Make exams a regular routine.
4. Make exams fun, and turn them into tricks.

On Your Back

"ON YOUR BACK!"/"FLEA CHECK!"
This is a fun trick for Casey. He rolls on his back and gets his tummy rubbed.

1. Start with him on his side, in the normal dead-dog position (see chapter 20).

2. He should lie on his left side with his legs pointed toward you.
3. Kneel with Casey to your left.
4. Brush your left hand over his shoulder, and *gently* roll him away from you, beginning to slowly roll him over on to his back.
5. Scratch his chest or tummy as soon as he rolls over even a little bit.

This exercise is done in a slow, gentle, deliberate fashion. You're not trying to win a race. The command is *"On Your Back!"* but is said as one word, *"Onyaback!"* To get Casey out of the OYB position, tell him to do a down or sit. Repeat a number of times.

Occasionally you'll get some resistance. There are two ways to deal with this:

1. With the dog lying on his side with his body to your left, you put his chin in the palm of your right hand (if Casey is a tiny toy dog, put his chin on your index and middle fingers), then gently rotate his head in a clockwise direction. You won't have to make a complete circle to get him on his back.
2. The other method is to use your right hand to grasp the ankle of his left front leg and slowly pull it toward you in a slightly upward, rotating motion. Finish with a tummy rub or a rib-cage scratch at Casey's tickle point.

PRESENTATION: Your choice of command can add spice to this trick. *"Flea Check!"* is a good choice. In the U.S. Army I used a female German Shepherd when I gave classes. The rather lengthy command I gave her brought down the house. I'd ask her, "What are you going to do when your boyfriend comes home on leave?"

Examination of Ears

"EAR CHECK!"

Your dog's ears should be checked (and cleaned) weekly. Most owners wait until there's a problem before checking the ears. Then their dog develops an aversion to having his ears checked. It's much more intelligent to train Casey beforehand and make the ear check a *pleasurable* experience.

1. Give the command *"Ear Check!"* and gently massage below the ear at the mastoid notch. That is the place directly below the cartilage base of the ear where's there's a small notch. Observe Casey and you'll learn exactly where he enjoys being massaged the most.
2. Spend more time massaging than poking and prodding—that can take place later when it's time to clean out those ears.
3. The next spot that you gently rub is the ear leather, the part that hangs over the opening of the ear channel in flopeared dogs.
4. You can further refine *"Ear Check!"* by adding *"Left Ear!"* and *"Right Ear!"* The dog will start offering the correct ear to you. At this point in the training, Casey knows his left from the right and will rapidly understand what he's to do.

PRESENTATION: You can show off this trick just about anywhere. All you are asking Casey to do is to stand and be petted. The training will certainly impress your veterinarian when you explain to him how to check your dog's ears.

Examination of Paws

"PAW CHECK!"

This can be taught in conjunction with *"On Your Back/Flea Check!"* and is a matter of getting Casey desensitized to having his paws rubbed and caressed. Some dogs initially object to this because of unpleasant experiences (usually the cutting of toenails) during examination of their feet and toes. You want to overcome that problem and have your dog willingly offer his paws for examination. With him on his back, gently rub and press each paw.

PRESENTATION: This is more of a private trick between you and Casey. It is designed to make both your lives easier.

Examination of Teeth and Gums

"TOOTH CHECK!" "SMILE!"

1. Start off with Casey in the flea-check position and gently massage him.
2. As he relaxes, move your hands to his face and scratch his stop (the space between the eyes) and gently caress his muzzle.
3. Slide a finger under his lip and massage his upper gums as you say *"Tooth Check!"*
4. Lift the upper lip so you can see his gums and massage them. Some dogs will actually smile when they're in the flea-check position. (Golden Retrievers are well known for this smile.) It's a smile of contentment—just as you smile when you're happy. The appearance is of a drawing back of the corner of the lips in a straight line (rather than upturned as in a human smile). If drawn back far enough, the upper lip will lift slightly. Occasionally some dogs, when extremely happy, will come up with a full-blown smile that looks like a snarl but isn't.
5. Start to use the *"Smile!"* command when offered this smile, and click as Casey performs.
6. If Casey is well trained to the clicker, hold off the delivery of your tidbit. Attempt to get as long a smile as possible. You need to practice this dozens of times with him on his back to get him to respond to the command when he is standing.

Not only is this exercise useful for examining your dogs gums, but think of all the different tricks you can turn this into simply by changing the command from *"Tooth Check!"* to *"Smile!"* to *"Watch 'Em!"* Tommy Butler, a Collie X Shepherd, trained by Susan Zaretsky of Newburgh, NY.

PRESENTATION: The smile makes a cute trick because the dog looks like he is snarling. The incongruous command is what produces the laughs. Add another command, *"Say Cheese!"*

23
JUMPING TRICKS

The Flying Dog

I enjoy watching different breeds jump. Australian Cattle Dogs sail over jumps with just a millimeter to spare. The stocky Staffordshire Bull Terrier springs up on all four feet at once and pounces over the jump. The Belgian Sheepdog gracefully arcs over the jump. You can jump an Italian Greyhound at twenty inches all day long (I'm speaking rhetorically here). You'll be amazed at the style and grace that this fine-boned beauty demonstrates as he clears the jump by a fraction of an inch. Lower that jump to twelve inches, and again he'll clear the jump by a fraction of an inch. All dogs, regardless of breed, do no more than they need to, to accomplish the task at hand.

There are tricks that can be slightly modified and shifted to appear to be entirely new tricks. When a dog jumps over an obedience jump, he isn't doing anything very impressive, however, jumping through a hoop is WOW! It's all in the presentation. Jumping tricks can make something fairly simple look spectacular.

Regarding jump paraphernalia: Obedience jumps consist of a solid high jump, an open jump and a broad jump—fairly standard. Check out the agility obstacles if you want some ideas about jumps. They'll give you food for thought and perhaps some good ideas. The goal for jumps is that they be light, portable and mobile. The obedience buff has the entire back of his car crammed with jumps for use in practice in strange and different places. You really have to see the obstacles in action to appreciate and understand what they are used to accomplish. These jumps, while good, can be replaced with more easily portable items. If you know someone with jumps, borrow them instead of purchasing your own. Two dynamic jumps that together cost less than a five-dollar bill are an old broom (from the back of the closet) and a hula hoop. In fact, you can pick up a hula hoop on sale for a buck, so your total cost is one dollar.

High Jumping, Phase One

"HUP!"

1. To keep it simple, begin with a standard obedience high jump. It doesn't matter how small your dog "Jack" is, simply put the narrowest board in the bottom slot of the jump. (More boards can be added to the jump later to make it higher.)
2. With Jack on a leash, at heel, get him to step over the board as you say *"Hup!"*
3. Praise Jack profusely. *"Hup!"* is the universal command for jumping up, down, over and even scaling (climbing) a wall. After a half-dozen walkovers, it's time to add an additional board, *if Jack's in a playful mood.*

It's useful to draw a parallel with horse jumping. The rider *must* help the half-ton horse over the jump. The "good hands" that a jumper has enable him to help "lift" the horse over the jump. Same thing with dogs. You have to help "lift" your dog over the jump. Ultimately he'll sail over without your help, but in the initial phases you have to supply that boost. Think about giving Jack that extra lift with the leash as he clears the jump. Don't just stand there like a bump on the log, allowing Jack to leap into the air, hit the end of the static leash and crash down on the jump. That's a disaster! It will take a great deal of time to desensitize Jack and remove his fear of jumping before you can resume training. Don't concentrate on lifting him, instead, focus on *helping* and *encouraging* him up and over the jump (even if it is just one board). Your body English will follow naturally as you assist Jack up and over. You and Jack will work as a team in much the same manner as a steeplechase horse and rider.

Every successful jump gains applause and exuberant congratulations. This is a hobby Jack will enjoy. It's also an excellent way to exercise him with minimum effort on your part (see chapter 14). In one or two days you'll be able to show Jack off.

A word of caution about the height of the jumps: Make sure Jack is in good health and shape. Jumping involves exertion, and a checkup with a veterinarian is to be recommended. A safe height for any dog to jump is his own height at the shoulder, if he is a very heavy or short-legged dog; one-and-a-half times his shoulder height for other dogs. These are *supersafe* heights. You can increase the height, but don't overexert your dog.

High Jumping, Phase Two

Start training for this trick using an open jump with the bar at a low level. You're starting from scratch again, but Jack will progress rapidly because he already knows what's expected of him. He also knows that it's easier to *walk* under the bar than to *jump* over it. Get him into the enjoyment of jumping over the bar jump, and then he'll be prepared for learning more and more tricks.

PRESENTATION: Now you can increase the areas in which you can show off. Use the fences in the park, in your neighborhood, in any and all places when you travel. In these new locations the trick automatically becomes more impressive. Also, this prepares Jack to work in different locations should you want to take your act on the road.

Stick Jumping, Phase One

"HUP!"

This is not candy-assed stick jumping, it's world-class stick jumping. (Would you expect anything else from this book?) Cut the bristles off that old broom, and you have a tool for a great trick.

So how do you get Jack to jump over the stick?

1. Go back to the solid jump and extend the stick out just below the top of the jump and have him do two or three jumps. At this point you shouldn't need the leash.
2. Now move the stick just over the top of the solid jump and have him do three or four jumps.
3. Then raise it a little bit higher.
4. Now you're ready to start Jack on the stick alone. Hold the stick out to your side. Don't start off at a particularly great height.
5. Elevate the stick slightly, and Jack will leap over it gleefully.
6. Do this over and over, but don't wear him out. Just have him enjoy himself. This is self-rewarding training. The reward is in the doing. Dogs enjoy working. You can continue to elevate the stick gradually.

Follow these next steps exactly, now that Jack is happily working off leash.

1. Give a sit-stay.
2. Sit down on the ground facing him, spreading your legs wide into a V.
3. Hold the stick, one hand on each end, over your head and bend your head down as low as possible. (Let me caution you. This will not work if Jack is a Chihuahua.)
4. Give the *"Hup!"* command, and Jack will sail over your head.
5. Really jackpot him at this point.
6. He's just done the greatest trick in the world. Let him know.

7. Work on this for short sessions and gradually raise the stick higher, ultimately holding it as high as Jack can jump.

8. Next, *kneel* with the stick held above you. *Do not* hold it higher than Jack can jump.

9. Position Jack behind you and have him jump forward. Start him jumping over you from the rear, then add having him jump from the front. There are two reasons for this. One reason is that if he will jump from both the front and rear, you can accomplish more jumps in each practice session. You remain in place, and Jack jumps back and forth. The other reason is for the presentation. Now that you have Jack hitting a high point, extend the stick in your right hand as you face him. Hold the stick at the greatest height he can jump, and *after* he clears the stick, raise it even more. (Thus, you make it look as if *he* jumped even higher.)

Stick Jumping, Phase Two

1. Once you have established the height that Jack can jump, have him do it over and over. Don't bore him, but make sure he gets it right. This then becomes a trick for a maximum amount of exercise with a minimum amount of work on your part.

2. As you are learning what Jack's highest jump is, you'll start holding the stick at that height as second nature.

3. Now turn your back to Jack and hold the stick at the appropriate height.

4. If it's necessary to lower the stick, place one leg in front of you, bending at the knee. Stretch your trailing leg out.

5. Get Jack to successfully jump over you from the rear to the front at least a dozen times.

6. You will tell Jack to sit and stay, do an about-face and have him jump in the reverse direction, but still rear to front. There are two reasons for the rear to front jump: One, it makes for a better picture; and two, you will be better able to see when to *elevate* the stick after Jack clears it. Keep reading and you will see how this follows.

Now it's time to train *you*. You have to learn some fancy footwork. Without Jack being present, stand up, extending your right hand, and imagine you are facing him. Pivot on your right foot and take a wide step to your left, positioning yourself *under* the stick, grasping it on each end. It's your job to practice—at least a dozen times, in three sequences, or until you can get that height *exactly* right. Remember that bending your legs helps to lower the stick.

Time to reintroduce Jack to stick jumping.

1. Through a lot of practice, Jack will understand that your moving under the stick is his command to jump. That is exactly what you want.
2. Begin by facing Jack with the stick in your extended right hand. You gracefully spin 180 degrees and move under the stick as Jack sails over you and the stick just after you've completed your turn.

PRESENTATION: This is show business! If you're bending your legs, do it gracefully. Rather than doing a deep knee bend, lead with your right leg bent at the knee. The foot of your trailing leg is perpendicular to the ground and bent at the toes. You can also raise and lower the height of the stick by the closeness of your hands. The closer together the hands, the higher the stick. Conversely, the wider apart the hands, the lower the stick.

The clincher here is to, immediately after Jack clears the stick, stand up to your full height. The audience will swear that Jack leapt much higher than he did. Do not do this more than twice, or people will figure out what you are doing. Add a little bit of tricky footwork for a really impressive finale.

Arm Jumping

"HUP!"

This is a variation on stick jumping. Not on the grand-finale stick jumping, but on the initial trick, where you extend the stick out to your side. The easiest way to transfer Jack over to arm jumping is to use shorter and shorter sticks. Rather than chopping up every broom in the neighborhood, simply slide the stick up to your armpit and behind your back. *Slide* it shorter rather than *making* it shorter.

PRESENTATION: By keeping the cut-off broomstick in the trunk of your car, you and Jack become a self-contained flying-dog unit. You can go anyplace and do a variety of tricks together.

Jump Through a Hoop

"HUP!"

Introduce the hula hoop into your playtime with Jack. Let him see and smell the hoop; then slowly place it over him.

1. Go back to the solid jump, and let Jack do a few jumps back and forth.
2. Now put the hoop right up to the solid jump, with the bottom third below the top of the jump.
3. Send Jack back and forth a half-dozen times while slowly raising the hoop's bottom to the top of the jump.
4. After Jack jumps back and forth another six times, move away from the solid jump. The purpose of the solid jump was, one, to have Jack jump over something he knew, and two, to stop him from walking under the hoop.
5. Have Jack jump back and forth through the hoop.

PRESENTATION: You can keep a hoop in the trunk of your car to show Jack off whenever someone starts bragging about their dog! And, as Jack keeps getting better and better, reduce the circumference of the hoop. You'll be amazed at how small a hoop Jack can jump through. (Make sure you point out to the audience how narrow the hoop is.) Using two different-sized hoops can add to this trick! Raising the hoop after Jack goes through it, as discussed in stick jumping, adds to the presentation as well.

Jump Through a Closed Hoop

Attach some paper streamers to the top of the hoop; then keep adding more and more. What this does visually is make the hoop appear "closed" to Jack. Don't be afraid of having Jack jump through the streamer hoop too often. He'll love it. You've taught him a new game, and Jack loves new games.

Now you're ready for the solid hoop. First, paste two pieces of newspaper, one to either side of the hoop, with six inches of space between them. Make sure that space is dead center in the hoop. We've changed the game slightly here. We want that open space so that Jack doesn't experience difficulty breaking through the paper. It should be dead center so that he targets the center of the hoop. As Jack progresses, close up that space between the newspapers.

PRESENTATION: As a grand opening *or* finale, you can use paper on the hoop with both of your names printed on it. Use lightweight tissue paper that tears easily. It is always a good idea to slit or score the spot in the paper where Jack is going to jump through. Jack should jump dead center, but be sure. Videotaping his performance will help you determine his pattern. He'll jump through the same spot consistently. In height he won't be dead center. He'll only just clear the bottom of the hoop.

Jump Rope

"SPRING!" OR "JUMP!"

This is a great trick for Jack Russell Terriers, Fox Terriers and other breeds with springs in all four feet. However, this doesn't mean that only these breeds are good at jumping rope.

Jumping rope is a trick that is best done with two people, and if you've found such a coworker, you're in Fat City. However, my initial explanation will tell you how to do it by yourself—in case nobody else seems as excited by this as you.

This is a trick ideally suited for the clicker. All dogs at one time or another will jump up with all feet off the ground. It can be one of those serendipitous caught behaviors. Click and treat! Monitor Jack's moods. (You should be doing that continually anyhow.) When he's in a good, bouncy mood, use the clicker.

The verbal command is *"Spring!"* or *"Jump!"* and that's only part of the job. You have the hardest part—working with the rope. Clothesline is best because it rotates and spins easily. Your job is to learn how to turn the rope and be consistent in your rotating speed and arc.

1. First locate a post and tie off one end of the rope, three to four feet off the ground.
2. Practice rotating the rope without Jack.
3. Develop a feel for it. A single rotation and jump with the click is a good starting point for Jack. Remember that part of the advantage of using the clicker is the delayed reward.
4. Once you get Jack jumping you can escalate the number of jumps done in one session. Twenty jumps is too many at first. One or possibly two jumps in the beginning is great. With practice you can increase the number of jumps (and Jack's stamina). Jumping is hard work for Jack, although he will appear to be taking it in his stride. The fun doesn't negate his fatigue. Your goal is to increase the number of jumps, but be practical and reasonable about it. (Even if Jack *can* jump that rope a hundred times, it becomes boring.) Work toward at least six jumps each time.

Enlist the assistant's aid any time you can. Work together to develop the right tempo and rotation of the rope. Practice rotating the rope with your partner and without Jack. The rope must be ready to pass under him when he's in the air. It is your job to get the rope rotating at the right speed. Jack will learn to respond to the rope, but *first* you have to respond to him.

PRESENTATION: This is a real crowd pleaser. It is also a good exercise for Jack.

Jumping into Your Arms

"JACK, COME HUP!"

If you're five feet tall, weigh a hundred pounds and own a Great Dane, don't attempt to teach this trick.

The best way to start is when Jack is a wiggly-waggly puppy. Little Jack, as a puppy, would try to climb into your lap whenever you were squatting down—and that's actually the first step to this trick. Even if you were late in starting to teach this trick and now have a grown dog, your best bet is to begin by squatting.

1. First, you get him to leap into your arms, and then you slowly shift into a standing position.
2. This is going to take a lot of short sessions, with no more than two or three attempts per session, because you need enthusiasm to make this work.
3. A good way to work on this is to have Jack stand behind a closed door.
4. Call his name and get him excited; he needs to be animated to learn this trick.
5. Open the door and have Jack jump enthusiastically into your arms—regardless of whether you're squatting or standing.

PRESENTATION: This is an excellent final exercise for wrapping up a performance. Onstage, tell Jack to stay on one side of the stage and then call him. As he jumps into your arms, bow and walk off with him, very dramatic indeed!

Back Flip

"HUP!"

Here's some heavy-duty trick training. This trick is usually done by a smaller dog, but there is no reason why a larger dog can't be taught to do it. However, the giant breeds lack the required agility, speed and high energy level, so if your dog doesn't have what it takes, forgeddaboutit. Fox Terriers and Jack Russell Terriers are great for this trick.

1. Begin work when Jack is in a happy mood. Use a clicker and treat. As Jack bounces off an object, such as a wall, handle this as a caught behavior, and click every time he does it. It is likely that a dog doing this will do so over and over again. Concentrate on the click rather than the treat. Treating will cause the behavior to stop, and you want Jack to jump and flip a number of times.
2. Select other inanimate objects for Jack to bounce off, a wooden telephone pole, for example. Now you can practice just about anywhere! It also gives you the chance to show off as you do the training, and this is a great motivator for *you*, while the applause will motivate Jack.
3. When Jack is responding to the command, and the click, extend your forearm and hand, palm open, horizontally above the spot on the wall that he is bouncing off.
4. Now hold your forearm *below* the spot he is hitting.
5. Nudge your forearm and hand upward just as Jack hits the wall, so that he feels the pressure, and gradually move farther and farther away from the wall. Note that smaller dogs will receive the upward thrust from the palm or wrist, while larger dogs receive it from the forearm.
6. Continue to click, while gradually applying more and more upward thrust with your arm, while continuing to move away from the wall.
7. The goal is to have Jack hit either your arm, wrist or palm. At this point the trick will be self-rewarding and you can eliminate the clicker. Give lots of praise, or an occasional treat, at the completion of a series of jumps (which are not yet *full* back flips).
8. Gradually put more spin on your arm to get Jack to approach a *complete* back flip. Move your arm back over Jack's head as you push upward.
9. As Jack completes a back flip, start to reduce the upward and backward movement of your arm, as well as the thrust.

10. Start to pull your arm away every third time just before Jack hits it.
11. Then every other time until you phase out use of your arm altogether.

Now you are a real trick dog trainer. You have developed the rapport and understanding of one another that makes dog ownership a truly rewarding experience. Send me a picture of the two of you doing this trick, and I'll put it up on my Web site.

PRESENTATION: An interesting rule of thumb about trick presentations: the easier a trick is to teach a dog, the more impressed the audience. Conversely, the more difficult, the less impressed. The back flip is an excellent example of that. Part of the problem with the back flip is that it is a quickie. You must enhance the trick with appropriate changing commands. "I'm head over heels in love!" "What do you think about your new collar?" To keep the trick *au courant*, change "new collar" to your favorite political candidate's name. Should you want to use this trick throughout your act, punch up the routine following an old teaching axiom. Let the audience know what Jack is going to do, have him do it and tell them what he did. An example would be to say: "You know, I'm head over heels in love with her!" Cue Jack and, after he does his back flip, turn to the audience and tell them, "Even my dog knows I'm head over heels in love with her." Put your hand to your mouth and, in a stage whisper, say, "Don't let Jack know I love her more than him."

Scaling

"HUP!"

Scaling is different from jumping. In scaling, Jack actually has to climb the wall instead of jumping over it. In terms of the height of the wall, a breed such as the German Shepherd or Doberman Pinscher can successfully be trained to scale six feet straight up!

1. Start with an A-frame wall.
2. An A-frame wall is flat on both sides, so Jack can climb up one side and down the other.
3. An adjustable chain forms the crossbar of the A-frame. Shorten the chain to bring the two sides of the A-frame closer together to make the climb steeper, higher and more difficult.
4. Start off by modeling Jack over the A-frame in its stretched-out position, sides well apart.
5. With Jack on the leash, guide him over the A-frame about a dozen times. The next session, make the A-frame steeper by bringing its sides closer together. Encouragement and the challenge of climbing are Jack's reward. As Jack's enjoyment increases, you can remove the leash and have him soar by himself. A bit of history about obstacle training: At one time in advanced training there was a straight-up-and-down wall referred to as a "palisade" wall. It was six feet tall—sometimes even taller. Because of apprehension over the dog injuring himself when he jumped down from the top of the wall, the A-frame was introduced. Then there was no crashing down on the other side, because the dog could "walk" down the reverse slope.

PRESENTATION: The A-frame makes for an impressive presentation. It is somewhat difficult to transport, and usually needs at least two people to carry it. I would save this for a full-scale demonstration rather than carrying it in your trunk, as you would a broomstick or a hoop.

24
TRICKS WITH KIDS

Want to have "Skippy" help pick up tossed-around toys? Or maybe Skippy can even help with baby-sitting! How? You, the parent, teach these tricks, and the entertainment value of some of them will keep the children busy as bees on a rainy day!

Putting Skippy together with your children requires that you use common sense. Realize that something the children love to do may become boring to Skippy. Also, don't ever leave child and dog together unattended. Realize that no matter how good Skippy is with the kids, and how bright and caring your children are, they could hurt or annoy the dog, which could lead to unpleasant behavior on the dog's part (like biting)—which of course isn't good. Should you not listen to this advice and leave Skippy in full charge of the baby-sitting, make sure you leave him a number where you can be reached.

Pirouette

"STAND HIGH!" "PIROUETTE!"

What can be classier than a French ballet trick? How can you get Skippy to pirouette *on his toes?* Pirouette is simply spinning on the toes. Actually, dogs already walk on their toes, which have become their feet. A dog pirouette is this: The dog stands on his hindquarters and spins around. For a little background on this type of training you might want to reread the Tour the Mall trick in chapter 11. We do not need that high a level of training to teach the pirouette trick. However, you will use a lure-and-reward method of teaching the trick. The clicker aficionados can use their clickers here, but pure lure and reward works just as well.

1. Hold a tidbit over Skippy's head and encourage him to stand up on his hindquarters as you say, *"Stand High!"* You need a feel for Skippy's mood to lure him up on his hindquarters.
2. Once you have him standing up, treat. He'll stand high for only a second or two, but that is enough as a start.
3. If Skippy is standing on his hindquarters for a period of time, you'll get a slight one-quarter spin. Encourage and lead that slight spin.
4. Lead the spin *in very small circles,* and increase the spin as you say, *"Pirouette!"*
5. Gradually increase the period of time that Skippy pirouettes to three minutes.

PRESENTATION: This is another one of those vest-pocket tricks that can be performed anywhere. Working it in with appropriate music and other dance steps starts you and your dog on the way to developing a real routine.

Shake

"SHAKE!" "LEFT PAW!" "RIGHT PAW!" "THE OTHER PAW!"

Here is a shortcut to the most traditional of dog tricks. Rather than you simply taking the dog's paw and repeating *"Shake!"* over and over again, the approach here is to cause the dog's shifting his weight and raising the paw. I have been using this approach for years, but this is the first time that you will see this time-saving technique in print.

1. Sit facing Skippy. The simple extension of your right hand may cause him to extend his left paw.
2. If not, simply exert a slight steady pull on the right side of his collar. That slight pull to Skippy's right will cause him to attempt to maintain his balance by elevating his left paw. We're talking about Skippy's left and right here.
3. Shake the paw and praise him. He's got it! It won't take too many trials to get him working. Introduce the *"Paw!"* and *"Shake!"* commands here. We want Skippy to walk on either command.
4. If you've gotten this far, you might just as well add the right paw. But first, get Skippy to give you that left paw consistently. Be aware that your sides are reversed (mirrored) when you face him.
5. Introduce *"The Other Paw!"* You will be extending your left hand, leaving your right hand free to grasp the collar.
6. Gently pull the collar to Skippy's left, and his right paw will rise.
7. Intersperse *"The Other Paw!"* with the actual *"Left Paw!"* and *"Right Paw!"* commands. He'll learn this faster than you might imagine.

PRESENTATION: This simple standard trick can be expanded by alternating paws, calling for the left, then the right. Asking for the "other paw" takes no more time to teach and adds panache to the trick. People are amazed that a dog can learn left from the right—since there are people out there who can't.

Patty-Cake

You know the game. You played it when you were a young sprat—unless that was before 1889 when patty-cake first appeared. It's easier to teach this to Skippy than you might imagine. The trick is an outgrowth of the High Five trick, which is an outgrowth of Shake or Wave. It starts off with Skippy sitting facing you. The command is *"Patty-Cake!"* but Skippy will be responding more to the hand motion than the command.

The reason this trick works so well is motivation! The reward for Shake is the tactile stimulation of you touching Skippy's paw. In the High Five trick, the touch is not as rewarding because it is a contact with the pads of his feet. The sense of touch is much more highly developed in your fingers than on the callused, toughened soles of your feet. The same applies to the dog's pads.

1. With Skippy in the high five or wave position, tap his paw with the palm of your hand.
2. Have your fingers pointed at the sky. You have to work with Skippy, and the faster and more frequently you work, the easier it is for the fingers to move skyward. Your hand movement will become as much a signal to Skippy as any command you use.
3. Initially, give him a lot of praise and food rewards—which you'll phase out, because both hands are needed with Patty-Cake.
4. Keep up a cheerful conversation with Skippy. Short and frequent happy sessions are the order of the day.
5. Work on one paw six or seven times. Observe how Skippy's body weight shifts slightly to the side opposite the raised paw.
6. Now *you* shift your body.
7. After you shift your body and weight, settle down.
8. Watch Skippy. As he settles, it should be on the same (mirror) side as you. If not, don't worry.
9. Slowly raise your other hand—the one Skippy wasn't hitting before.
10. Shift, settle, then pause. Do this three or four times. He'll pick up from your body language.
11. Alternate back and forth between paws.
12. Gradually pick up speed while excitedly praising.

Skippy will grasp this concept and reach out for your raised and extended palm. Be sure that you do some cross–patty-caking. It isn't necessary to develop a pattern, but it will help marginally. You really want Skippy to work off the raised palm, rather than in a set routine, so that any child can step up and play with him.

PRESENTATION: *"Patty Cake!"* is a natural command for this exercise. Reciting the entire nursery rhyme also adds to the trick. Turn the kids loose on this one. They'll love it! Make sure that Skippy does this only under your direct supervision. Children will patty-cake him to death if unattended. Music can also be added. If you stick with one song, Skippy will cue to that music.

Do the Hokeypokey, Phase One

Cairn, Irish, Kerry Blue, Sealyham and Fox Terriers will do exceedingly well learning this trick. They have an extremely high energy level, which of course is the good news and the bad news. Channeling their energy in the direction you want it to go is the difficult part. It takes a special type of person to own any of these breeds (which I'm sure you are), so you should have the energy to teach both the Hokeypokey, Phase One and Phase Two, as well as the Advanced Hokeypokey. You're an Advanced Hokeypokey type of guy.

> *Put your right foot in,*
> *Take your right foot out,*
> *Put your left foot in,*
> *Take your left foot out,*
> *Put your four feet in and turn them all about.*
> *You do the hokeypokey*
> *And turn yourself around,*
> *That's what it is all about.*

This is the formula. What does it mean and how do you execute it?

1. Make a chalk circle on the floor.
2. Face the standing Skippy toward both you and the circle.

3. Skippy will learn to put his right foot in and pull it out of the circle.
4. This is followed by his left foot in the circle, then pulled out.

Before going into the step-by-step procedure let's review what you have already taught Skippy. Skippy should be well up on his targeting at this point. You've just read about teaching Right and Left Paw. At this point in the training, Skippy should know his left from his right. As early as chapter 12 you started teaching "left" and "right," and you've refined it with the Left Paw–Right Paw trick just covered. The purpose of this review is to motivate you to work Skippy briefly on the tricks already learned. If it has been a period of time since you worked Skippy on these tricks, you should bring him up to speed. Let me again remind you to be aware that when Skippy is facing you, his right paw is on your left side. You *must* keep the left and right straight.

Now on to the training procedure you will follow to teach Skippy this trick. You want him to touch the target stick with his right *forequarter*. Moving toward the target stick with his right forequarter will cause his right hindquarter to move in that direction, but that is not what we are working on. Concentrate on the forequarters.

1. Tell him *"Right Touch!"* as you use the target stick to guide the right paw into the center of the circle.
2. He'll be a little confused at first, but on the first indication of his moving in toward the target stick, click and treat.
3. After he puts the paw in and you have clicked and treated, start guiding Skippy into taking that same paw out.
4. Do it four times, then it is time to change paws.
5. Tell Skippy, *"Left Touch!"* Do not click if he offers his right paw. If he offers the wrong paw, say, "Wrong!" in a flat tone of voice.
6. Click and reward only on the correct paw.
7. You want Skippy to put each paw in and pull it out of the circle.

8. When the paws are going in and out smoothly, it is time to start changing the commands to *"Right In!"* and *"Right Out!"* along with *"Left In!"* and *"Left Out!* These commands will start to match the words of the little ditty you are singing. While it will not be a perfect match, you can emphasize the command words as you sing. That is all you will do for the first five training sessions, which should last about eight minutes each.

Now, you have a completed trick if you just sing "Put your right foot in, take your right foot out, put your left foot in, take your left foot out." It is just the first phase of the Hokeypokey trick, but you have a trick you can do. You want to coordinate the tempo of the song with Skippy's foot movements. You also want to coordinate the words in the song with the level of Skippy's training.

In clicker training you settle for approximations. Even an approximation will get the correct foot moving, which is your goal. Don't worry about the "turning all about" at this point. That comes after you have taught Skippy how to "Put your right foot in, take your right foot out, put your left foot in, take your left foot out." Thanks for this trick go to Karla Clinch and Danny Thomson.

Do the Hokeypokey, Phase Two

The first phase of the trick is a trick unto itself. Now we want to match the trick to our revised Hokeypokey ditty. If you read and add the Spin trick, which is in chapter 21, you have done your job. You can revise the song, depending on the spin results you get with Skippy—from, "Put your *four* feet in and turn them all about" to "Put your *both* feet in and turn them all about." Once you put both tricks together you will be ready to practice the entire sequence in every session.

PRESENTATION: The circle on the floor is not necessary in order to do the trick. The circle can add to the trick, but if you are doing it in a living room with wall-to-wall carpet, bypass the chalk circle. Adding music always helps the presentation of this trick, but is not necessary when entertaining children. It's important to monitor the children when they are doing the Hokeypokey with Skippy. If you are doing this on a stage, the audience will not even see the circle.

The Advanced Hokeypokey

I don't want you to even *start* on this trick until you have the previous trick down pat *and* Skippy is doing the Tour the Mall trick in chapter 11 like a champ. He has to be able to walk at least five minutes on his hindquarters. You *must* build up Skippy's endurance. It would be very healthful if you jogged five miles a day before breakfast, but waking up tomorrow morning and jogging five miles the first time out would probably kill you. You, as Skippy, have to build up your endurance slowly. It is a question of endurance and conditioning rather than training. Toy and small dogs are best suited for this trick. Toy and Miniature Poodles, Bichon Frisés, Papillons, Chihuahuas, Miniature Pinschers and Pekingese are good candidates for this trick.

Before even starting a training session, I want you to have Skippy able to walk on his hindquarters for at least two minutes to warm him up.

1. Have Skippy walk up (on his hindquarters) to the circle.
2. With Skippy facing both you and the circle, extend the target stick in front of his right hindquarter and say *"Right Touch!"* You have the idea. Proceed as in Phase One.
3. As soon as Skippy gets the idea, start alternating between right and left hindquarters. This may take a few sessions, so stay at it.

Once your dog has been putting his right and left hindquarter in during seven sessions, it is time to add the Pirouette. Get forward motion on the hindquarters to bring him to the center of the circle before he spins. He has to "Put both feet in."

A word of caution about overexertion. At this point you should know how long Skippy can comfortably stand on his hindquarters. Quit long before he is fatigued so that you leave him wanting more. This is supposed to be fun for both you and your dog—remember?

PRESENTATION: Now we are getting into some really fancy tricks. This can still be done just about anywhere, but I do think it's time for you to put a dog act together.

Conga Line

"PAWS UP!"

Let's start off with *"Conga Line!"*

1. Mom or Dad (you) give Skippy the *"Paws Up!"* command, with Skippy standing behind the child.
2. Skippy's paws should rest on the child's back as the child walks slowly forward for two steps, then stops while you praise Skippy. The location of the paws on the child's back depends on the size of Skippy and your child.
3. Don't have Skippy get down. Keep him up there until the child goes forward four steps. It becomes one quick, free-flowing game.
4. Repeat about a half-dozen times and take a break. Time permitting, come back to this a few times later in the day. You have to watch out for bored dancers.
5. The context in which this is done will alert Skippy as to what is happening. You may never need to say *"Conga Line!"* especially if you use the same music every time.

Our goals may seem contradictory here. One idea is to keep your child busy (and perhaps a bit tired) to give you a break. You can give your child (and Skippy) a tiring workout by increasing their activity. As you use this diversion over and over, the length of the dance will increase. Bring in the neighborhood kids to join the line and the fun. Adding music will further dictate the tempo of the trick. Use the same song consistently so that the children and Skippy will know what's coming. A tired child and dog are a good child and dog.

Bunny Hop

"PAWS UP!" "BACK HOP!"

Hold off on the Bunny Hop until Skippy has done the Conga Line at least a dozen times. Not the Conga Line in training. The real-life Conga Line on rainy days with the neighborhood kids. The reason for this is that the sequence for the Bunny Hop has a backward hop too! Skippy has to learn how to handle that backward hop. You, the parent, will teach the backward hop. Skippy, if he weighs at least sixty pounds, will be given the *"Paws Up!"* on the parent. If he weighs less than that, a child will have to be used because of the location of the paws on the back. We do not want Skippy stepped on.

1. The first step is to work on the back hop. The parent who is teaching the back hop will gently put both hands on Skippy's paws. If Skippy is a smaller dog, then the parent puts one hand on the dog's paws and the child's back.
2. The other hand is placed on the child's stomach to control the child's backward movement.
3. The command *"Back Hop!"* is given each time there is backward movement. Initially a *really high* jump and a one-inch backward movement accompany the command.
4. Do five one-inch back hops in succession.
5. Take a fifteen-minute break and repeat the back hop, but now you'll make a two-inch back hop. You will work on *just* the back hop.
6. Take another fifteen-minute break, and then go for a three-inch back hop. A three-inch back hop is all that you are going to work on. Do not hop more than three inches.
7. The next day's practice will consist of one forward hop followed by one backward hop. You will do three five-minute

sessions of the front and back hop—you will do this for three days. Each backward movement is preceded and punctuated with the *"Back Hop!"* command.

The Bunny Hop routine is one hop forward, one hop backward, repeated three times at a moderate speed, then three quick forward hops. It is time to initiate the whole routine, but it *must* be accompanied by the music, and the movements must follow that tempo. This music cue will help Skippy avoid being stepped on.

PRESENTATION: This is great for a bunch of kids. The Bunny Hope or the Conga Line can occupy every child in the neighborhood. Skippy is on the end of the line, and all the kids will want to be next to last. You can rotate the children's position in the line. This suggestion from Susan Muick of Southington, Connecticut, deserves your rainy-day thanks.

Hide-and-Seek

This is a natural. Send Skippy to find one of your children by name as described in the Go to Lucy trick in chapter 19. He's going to use his nose, and that means if the child is in your house, it's almost impossible for her to remain undiscovered. At this point in the training, Skippy knows household members by name, so just send him to find them one at a time. This is great fun for kids on rainy days!

Now, not only must Skippy find the kids, but they have to find him! The children are not allowed to call him or use his name. Put Skippy in a closet or some out-of-the-way spot. Give him a down-stay. The assumption is that he can do a really long down-stay, because the kids will not find him as fast as he finds them.

PRESENTATION: Skippy's rapid locating of individual household members is the ultimate presentation. True, it can be shown off, but look at it as fun for the kids (and Skippy too).

Read a Book

The first two tricks I ever taught a dog were Read a Book and Tell Me a Secret. I won't tell you how long ago that was, but I was about seven or eight years old. I didn't have the advantage of a great book on tricks like this one. Regardless, I devised simple systems that worked—and still do.

1. Put small pieces of crunchy food between the pages of a book.
2. Then open the book in front of Skippy and tell him *"Read!"*
3. You have to handle the book and turn the pages so that the food doesn't scatter around.
4. As the trick progresses, lay the book on a steady, flat surface as you turn the pages.
5. Next, phase out the food reward. Use a lightweight book, not one the size of *War and Peace*. That's too long a read. We will not teach Skippy to turn the pages. He might be too rough and rip a page or two. I have too much respect for books to permit that.

PRESENTATION: Let the kids teach this trick. Skippy will appear to be reading although he is really just searching the food out.

Tell Me a Secret or Whisper

This is even easier to teach. Put a piece of food in your right ear. It should fit in rather snuggly. Let Skippy have a whiff as you say *"Tell Me a Secret!"* or *"Whisper!"* This simple routine gets him licking your right ear. As I said, I was about eight when I first devised and taught a dog this trick, so your children in that age range should be able to handle teaching it as well. Parents: Supervise your children. Read the next warning before you are tempted to let them try this unsupervised. *Warning!* Make sure that the piece of food is big enough not to get forced back into the ear canal. Make sure that the ear is washed cleaned (not by Skippy, but by you) after the trick.

PRESENTATION: Letting kids teach this trick is great, but pay attention and ensure that the food is not being pressed back into the ear canal.

Training Your Children

Review the tricks in other sections of this book, and you'll have enough fun and games to keep both children and Skippy in a constant state of exhaustion! Take another look at chapter 16, where your dog learns to pick up items by name; this also can be used to help you explain to children how they should pick up after themselves. The Pick Up the Room trick in chapter 11 certainly teaches the children a good lesson. If your dog can set the example for your children to pick up and put their things away, not only will you have the best-trained dog around, but also the best-trained children. Should you decide to home-school your children, why not turn their entire education over to Skippy?

25
MAGIC TRICKS

Are you ready to receive the magician's oath? I'm serious! As a magician myself, I only can reveal how a trick is done to another magician. So, raise your right hand and say, "I solemnly swear that I will reveal these magic tricks only to other magicians." You are now sworn in, and I can tell you how to do some tricks that will amuse and amaze everyone. They'll be broken down into three general areas: numbers, mentalism and sleight of paw!

Shake Your Head No

"SHAKE NO!"

Any mentalist dog has to be able to communicate. Shaking his head no is a step in the right direction. There are mentalist questions that can be asked requiring a yes or no answer. Before you begin, *stop, sit and think about this,* and your first time out, do it just once. There are two approaches to training your dog "Merlin." One involves tickling Merlin's ear with a long feather; the other, blowing in his ear. You're going to use the clicker and a treat here.

1. Either gently tickle the inside of Merlin's ear or blow into it as you say, *"Shake No!"*
2. Click and treat as Merlin shakes his head no.
3. Take a break of at least a half hour.
4. Repeat this twice in a row during the next three training sessions.
5. At this point Merlin should be getting the message and start to shake his head as you get into position to tickle or blow into his ear. Your body language is the subtle cue that you are going to use when you want him to shake his head no. Don't worry about it at this point. It will come naturally, with time, even without you worrying about it.

Nod Your Head Yes

"NOD!"

Nodding is different from shaking. Nodding stands for "yes" and shaking for "no."

1. With Merlin in front of you, wait for any slight downward head-tilt; click, which will bring the head upward, and toss a treat.
2. Wait and you will be offered the nod again.
3. Knock off training once you've gotten four nods. Next time, wait for the nod, then click and treat. The next nod gets a click but no treat. You're going into variable reinforcement now, but if you are offered two nods at one time, make sure you treat. You're going to start getting a lot of nods. The command that you use is *"Nod!"* but again you'll be giving subliminal cues for this. A slight downward (quarter-inch) motion of your head is something that you might unconsciously use when you ask a question requiring a positive answer. Your dog will pick these subliminal sensory cues before you do.

PRESENTATION: You can ask questions requiring a "Yes," "No," "Yes," "No" sequence of answers, or you can cue Merlin as to what to "say." An example of questions requiring a sequence of yes and no answers would be:

"Isn't this a great audience?"
"Do you think that yesterday's audience was as good as this one?"
"Would you like to perform before this audience again?"
"Do you want to go home?"
"In other words you are having a great time here?"
At this point you can say, "Isn't that great! How about a big round of applause?"
The real presentation is when you develop a mentalist act.

The Numbers Trick

Dogs make great mediums and assistants for a variety of reasons. One is that they work cheap. Also, they aid in "misdirection"—a magician's term for drawing the audience's attention away from that which the magician wishes to go unnoticed. And what could be more attention riveting than a dog as magician?

The purpose of the Numbers trick is to have Merlin answer a math question or a question with a numerical answer. There are two variations to this trick. One is where he barks the answer, and the other is where he picks the correct number out of a circle of the ten digits, each written on a cardboard placard.

If you want him to spell out a word, substitute letters for digits. However, this trick is often not practical because it is too cumbersome. A more practical approach to spelling out answers is assigning the letters numerical values. A dog that does math is impressive, but one that reads minds knocks people's socks off.

Use a simple math question such as "How much is four plus two?" (in case you don't know, the answer is six), and have Merlin bark six times. An alternate version of this is to have Merlin go around a circle of cardboard placards, each with a number on it, and pick up the number six. How does Merlin know? You tell him.

In the barking variation, *"Good Boy!"* is the signal for Merlin to stop barking. (As you perform this trick you'll find that the audience applause will *also* stop his barking.) In the picking-up-the-right-card trick, how do you let him know when he has reached the right card? Your patter will contain a cue word that tells him when to stop and pick up the placard. You ultimately will develop more than one cue to stop the barking or pick the placard.

Patter is the ongoing talk (hopefully occasionally punctuated by jokes) that you carry on for the audience's benefit. The cue can be *"Keep Looking!"* Use that contradictory phrase when it is time for Merlin to pick up the placard.

An example of ongoing patter: "Circle to the right. Look for the right card. I know you have a lot of choices out there, but you know the answer. Don't you see the right card? I'm going to have to have your eyes checked. Maybe you need glasses."

As Merlin reaches the correct card say, *"Keep Looking!"* and continue your patter until after he retrieves it.

The impression conveyed is that Merlin the Magician knows the answer. *You* have to know the answer. It is not Merlin's job to know the answer, sorry. But always give him the credit. Work on simple math before going into mentalism routines. It will sharpen both you and Merlin in preparation for the more difficult mind reading. Crawl before you walk and walk before you run. You have time.

Pick the Right Placard

You will have to refer to previously covered training methods to teach this trick.

1. You have laid out a circle of placards, and you want Merlin to go around them.
2. Tell Merlin to *"Circle Left!"* and slide the back of your left hand alongside Merlin's right cheek.
3. Read chapter 12 dealing with moving livestock by circling

the dog around the stock. Be able to tell Merlin to circle to the left or right.

4. In the training period you initially tell Merlin *"Take It!"* (see chapter 16). This is training for both you and Merlin. You have to judge distance and Merlin's reaction time to get him to select the correct placard.

5. You will later phase out this *"Take It!"* command and substitute *"Keep Looking!"* The cue will not be delivered as a command. It will be emphasized in the patter when you want Merlin to pick up the card. It is a subliminal (to the audience) sensory cue.

PRESENTATION: Your presentation will improve the more often you do it. You will come up with more subtle cues than you will ever need as Merlin progresses. You'll also find that the audience will unconsciously cue him. When one dog I had was performing for a bunch of kids, often a child would want to try the trick. The enthusiasm of the children negated my need to cue this dog. She picked up on the kids' reactions. Should your dog reach this level of training, there is one caution that I would give you. Make sure the questions the children ask are ones a child their age could answer. Excited children will often ask questions to which they *do not* know the answer and are therefore incapable of reacting at the correct time to cue your dog.

"How Much Is_____?"

Go all the way back to chapter 1 to find out how to get Merlin barking. The barks should be single, individual barks that are not run together. Merlin has been trained to bark on the *"Speak!"* command, but now you're changing that command to *"How Much Is_____?"* You stop the sequence of barks by saying *"Good dog!"* and tossing a treat. As you improve your technique, you'll gradually develop more and more subtle cues.

PRESENTATION: Work on the simple math tricks before going on to the more complex mentalist routines. Your performances are training sessions. Perform enough and you really will become a world-class performer.

Long Division: The Master Mathematician

1. With a chalkboard facing an audience, choose an audience member to write a twenty-digit number.
2. Merlin sits calmly, and you turn to him and ask, "Is this number divisible by four?" to which Merlin shakes his head no.
3. "Can I add something to the end of that string of numbers to make it divisible by four?" Merlin nods his head yes.
4. "What do I add?" Merlin barks twice so you write the number two to the end of the string of numbers.
5. "Is that it, Merlin?" He shakes his head no.
6. "What do I add?" and Merlin barks eight times.
7. You write the number eight while asking, "Is that it, Merlin?"
8. Merlin nods his head yes, and then you tell your audience to check it out. The truth of the matter is that if you add twenty-eight to a string of numbers, it becomes divisible by four. Both you and Merlin know that. The audience will be busy dividing this long number by four to see if Merlin was right long after he has made his pronouncement.

PRESENTATION: Don't jump right into this routine. There are all sorts of lower-level variations of this trick that will give both of you fun-filled practice sessions. When actually doing the trick, rap the blackboard with your knuckle to get Merlin's attention when asking him the questions. His quick glance and answer "prove" his intelligence.

Sleight-of-Paw Tricks

Sleight of paw is easy. Sleight of hand is more difficult. If you, the human, are to become involved in it, make sure that you get it right. It takes a lot of practice. Merlin and his movement can and should be used in the misdirection of attention whenever possible. In the Jiffy Coin trick, you'll see how Merlin and the accompanying patter keep the audience's eyes away from the action. For more sleight-of-hand tricks, see Edwin Sachs's *Sleight of Hand,* and *Dog Tricks,* by Captain Arthur Haggerty and Carol Benjamin.

JIFFY COIN TRICK

This trick works extremely well with an audience filled with children. It uses a relatively inexpensive device available at magic supply stores that ties in with dog tricks very nicely. The device consists of a coin chute, one end of which is inserted in the neck of a tiny sack, secured with a rubber band, the sack itself inside several successively larger canisters, also secured with rubber bands. The coin passes down the chute into the sack. The chute is then removed, making it appear that the coin has found its way into the sack by magic. Merlin must be able to retrieve an object. That is the sum total of his mastery in this trick.

1. Ask someone in the audience for a quarter, and have one of the children scratch the coin with a key in order to mark it.
2. Take the quarter, hold it up in your hand and toss it on the ground for Merlin to retrieve and return to you.
3. Put your right hand in Merlin's mouth, searching for the coin, and indicate that you can't find it. (At this point you've already palmed the coin.)
4. Stand up and extend your left hand (misdirection) toward Merlin and say, "Merlin swallowed the quarter!"
5. Your right hand is in your pocket, putting the coin down the coin chute.
6. Remove the chute as you continue speaking to the child, saying, "I'm sorry you lost your quarter. My dog swallowed it."
7. Pull the canister (which now contains the quarter) from your pocket, and toss it out for Merlin to retrieve.
8. As he brings it to you, take it from his mouth and have the child who marked the coin open the canister. First, the child will remove three rubber bands from the outside of the can-

ister. Inside is a similar, but smaller container, also secured with three rubber bands. The child removes these, and inside is a small leatherette sack with a rubber band securing the top. The child removes the final rubber band and pulls the marked coin out of the sack. Ask the child to check to be sure it's the marked quarter. Magic!

There are all sorts of tricks that can be purchased from magic stores. Don't rush out and buy them. Develop a feel for magic and what you can do with your dog first.

PRESENTATION: Develop your patter as you develop the trick. Try to bring in as much humor as possible. Do not repeat tricks, no matter how well they go over. Each time you repeat a trick it becomes less impressive and increases your chance of exposure. When using props, as in the Jiffy Coin trick, make sure you have empty pockets. You do not want to wade through a pocketful of junk.

More Magic

There are numerous variations of mentalism and magic tricks besides the couple of examples given here. If you really want to become more involved with magic, there are good books available. All you have to do is adapt other tricks into a magic routine for your dog. See the previously mentioned *Dog Tricks*, by Haggerty and Benjamin; Karl Fulves's *Self-Working Mental Magic* and *Bill Severn's Magic in Mind.*

26
TRICKS FOR THE MULTIDOG FAMILY

How many dogs do you have? If you have several, I suggest teaching *all of them* tricks. Why not let everyone have fun? It takes less time, per dog, to train three dogs than it does to train one. Honoring, the first trick, is an excellent example of that synergistic training.

Honoring

This is not a revolutionary training procedure. As a matter of fact, it's been used in all sorts of testing programs. Simply stated, one dog honoring another in a position (sit-stay for example) as you compete the other dog. For example, in United Kennel Club obedience trials, one dog does a down-stay with the handler out of sight. The next dog in competition concurrently does his exercises. The same procedure is followed in SchutzHund trials. You actually can have two (or more) dogs doing different tricks at the same time. There are some tricks you can do simultaneously. Training more than one dog at a time is a valuable advantage in the multidog household. A great time-saver!

HONORING IN TRAINING

Here's an extension of the training aspects of honoring. It takes some skill and forethought, but can be easily developed.

1. Start off with two dogs.
2. Put Dog A in a sit-stay position as you teach Dog B to balance a book on his head.
3. Give Dog B a stay with the book on his head.
4. Turn your back on Dog B, move over to Dog A and tell him *"Down!"*
5. Say *"Stay!"* to Dog B as you turn your attention back to Dog A.

In two short minutes you've accomplished a number of things. Both dogs have had their stays reinforced and lengthened during a time when distractions were occurring. In other words, you're training in the *real* world. Also, you've been doing twice the work in half the time. It takes practice to do this, so start off slowly. You have to work on your powers of concentration, focusing on one dog while still paying attention to the other. Dog B is put in a simple sit-stay or down-stay position. Both these positions are very steady, and there is little chance of a well-trained dog breaking or moving from his position. Should a dog do something wrong, the answer is to correct him. But be aware that we are not trying to make your dog make a mistake. The term "proofing" in dog training means to test the dog to make sure that he performs. Contrary to popular belief it is not necessary to "trick" a dog into making a mistake just in order to correct him. Let him do it *right* over and over again. That will also proof the dog, without correcting. Of course, if he should make a mistake, you have to be prepared to make the correction for any error that he makes. Honoring is made for this training. Maximum training with a minimum effort.

Work on this simple, straightforward process *before* going on to the next step. You must have good control over two dogs before expanding to teach two dogs two tricks at the same time.

Dog A is working well on balancing that book on his head in

the sit position. Next you're going to work on his sit high while balancing the book.

1. Place Dog B in the down position and then in the OYB (on your back) position with a stay.
2. Go back to Dog A (while still watching Dog B), who is balancing the book on his head, and begin to work with the sit-high position.
3. Give the *"Stay!"* command.
4. Start working Dog B on the comedy-dead-dog position from OYB. Concurrently working these tricks requires constant attention and readjustment of the dogs involved. It will rapidly expand your dog-handling skills as well as your powers of concentration, while all the turning and bending will slim down your waistline. *Do not* jump into this advanced work. Work into it gradually and slowly as your ability increases. When you get really good you can progress to three dogs.

What about rewarding dogs in multiple-dog training? Use anything you like, but my recommendation is primarily verbal praise augmented with tactile reward. Your rapid movement back and forth restricts the use of other methods. A major consideration (and problem) is making sure that each dog knows it is being rewarded. This is a bit of a problem with audible rewards, but can be overcome by using your body to shield the sound as you direct your praise toward the correct dog.

Clean Ears

This can be a little gross but is a "handy" trick. A word of caution: Don't rely on your dog to take full charge of your other dog's ear care. On command, you want one dog to lick the other's ears clean. You want this trick to be done on command only because some dogs can become obsessed with ear cleaning, which can produce too much moisture in the ear and turn it into a hothouse for fungus and mold.

1. Begin by putting a dab of squalene on a cotton swab.
2. Gently touch the inside of the dog's ear with the swab and tell the other dog "*Clean Ears!*" It's that simple! You may have to point to each individual ear.

PRESENTATION: This is yucky! You do not want to show this to your friends and neighbors. Please don't tell anyone where you learned this trick.

The Three Monkeys

Hear no evil, see no evil, speak no evil. You know the story of the three monkeys? Think about your three dogs in the sit-high position, covering their ears, eyes and mouth. Sorry! They can't do that. For biomechanical reasons, dogs cannot sit high and reach their ears at the same time. You have to teach these tricks from the plotz position (see chapter 18). Should you decide to undertake this task, read the next trick before starting on this one. It will give you some food for thought.

Two approaches, modeling and shaping, are used in teaching this trick. Modeling will be discussed first because of the stretching required for some of these configurations. Now, stretching is not bad. Can you bend over and touch your toes? If not, you can work on that and gradually stretch your ligaments so that you not only can touch your toes, but also can place the palms of your hands on the floor. Stretching is possible and isn't hard on your dogs if done intelligently.

There are three different exercises, all starting from the plotz position, that make up this trick. All require "unusual" positions for the dog. Getting a single paw up in any one of those positions is not difficult. Two paws up requires a certain body suppleness. In Speak No Evil the paws should be alongside the mouth rather than over the nose. It doesn't require very much stretching. With the dog in the plotz position, head between the forequarters, gently position one paw and then the other alongside the muzzle while repeating "Speak no evil" in a quiet, relaxed, calm tone of voice. Scratch between your dog's eyes as he lies there with his paws in the correct position.

See No Evil requires more stretching because the paws have to be placed right on top of the forehead in order to cover the dog's eyes.

1. Start with one paw at a time. You want the same calm demeanor as with the first dog.
2. Scratch between the eyes as a gentle reward.

Hear No Evil, with the paws covering the ears, presents a problem. This is the most difficult trick because it requires the most stretching.

Begin by working with the dogs individually. You will have to put in the greatest amount of time and effort on the Hear No Evil trick.

As the training progresses, consider working more than one dog at a time. In the modeling approach, it's possible to work two or three dogs simultaneously. (Expert professional dog trainers always look for ways to work more than one dog at a time.) Here's a situation where it can be handily done. There are additional benefits when working more than one dog at a time. The stays are steadier and of longer duration. You're getting the dogs to work together as you move from dog to dog. (Make sure you have enough space between the dogs so that you can step over them and move about freely.)

Shaping the behavior has the decided advantage of actually having the dog place his paws into the right position. This technique is slower than the modeling approach—particularly since you can work only one dog at a time. In shaping, you work on slight improvements and click the improvement, no matter how slight. You'll be able to work *only* one paw at a time. Should you get a movement with two paws in the right direction, click and jackpot. A two-paw movement can become a quantum leap forward in the appropriate placement of the paws. Keep clicking and treating as the dog moves his paws into position. When going from one dog to the other, make sure you are clear about what you want from that individual dog. Moving from one dog and trick to another can throw you off.

ABOUT STRETCHING THOSE LIGAMENTS

In stretching your dogs' ligaments, do not go for extreme, bizarre stretching. A moderate amount of stretching will work.

PRESENTATION: This is a striking and impressive trick. Do it anytime and anywhere and you'll draw crowds.

The Three Monkeys from the Sit-High, Stand-High and Walk-Tall Positions

With sufficient time and effort, you may be able to progress to the sit-high position. The stand-high position has the same challenges as the sit-high. The most difficult trick to do from the sit-high position is covering the ears, followed by covering the eyes; the easiest is covering the mouth. Most important is the overall conformation and suppleness of each individual dog. Before starting, decide which one of your three dogs is the most supple and has the best conformation for stretching out into the desired positions. Working from the plotz position will carry over to the sit-high and stand-high positions. Needless to say, your dogs should be well grounded in both those positions before even attempting them.

Remember in the initial explanation of the Speak No Evil trick, paws *alongside* the muzzle was discussed? In these other two positions the paws can and should be partially resting on the top of the muzzle to assist the dog. Because the overall position has changed, you have to change the position of the paws.

PRESENTATION: The sit-high position makes for a better picture than the stand-high position. By picture, I mean what you might set up for a photographer or an audience. The image of the sit high is centered and static while that of the stand high or walk tall is diffused. You'll lose your audience with too much movement.

Take Off Blindfold

"TAKE IT!" "TUG!" "TASSELS!" "PULL!"

This is a variation on retrieving exercises. With one dog blindfolded and in the sit-stay position, another dog, on command, pulls the blindfold off the first dog. The secret is to have the blindfold tied with a bow behind the blindfolded dog's head. Removal can be facilitated through the use of tassels on either end of the blindfold. Train the second dog to grab the tassel and pull.

1. Pretrain the second dog to pull on the tassel before even putting the blindfold on the other dog. This is done by offering the second dog the tasseled end of the blindfold and saying *"Take It!"* When he does, say *"Tug!"* (see chapter 10).

2. You'll later change the command to *"Tassel!"* Your pretraining blindfold should have a tassel on one end only, and the dog will only grab the tasseled end.

3. After working the dog on grabbing the tassel two dozen times, offer both ends. Should the dog attempt to go toward the plain end, give a cautionary "No!" If he succeeds in grabbing it, give him a sharp *"No!"* You've been telling him what he is doing right for twenty-six chapters. You have to tell him when he is doing something wrong too. The work blindfold will have tassels on both ends. In the actual blindfolding, as long as the dog grabs either tassel, the bow will open. The pretraining's purpose is to make sure the dog doesn't grab the bow rather than the end. After the actual removal of the blindfold, click and treat.

PRESENTATION: This blends beautifully into the Balance and Catch Blindfolded trick (see chapter 15). The tassels add élan to the trick in addition to helping the dog grab the blindfold in the right spot.

Crawl Under

See chapters 8 and 10 to review the crawl before starting on this impressive trick.

In this trick, one dog is put in the stand position and the second dog is told to crawl underneath the first dog. The second dog should be a crawling fool; but even if he is, this takes a bit of training. The bulk of the training has already taken place with both dogs.

1. Put the standing dog in position and have the other dog crawl around without elevating his rump, gradually coming closer to the standing dog. If the standing dog shies, knock off for the day. You need a rock-steady stay on the standing dog's part, and if it takes a few days to get this, so be it. No crawling under until the dog is steady.
2. The first run-through has the standing dog between you and the crawling dog. The crawling dog, in the down position, is told to crawl toward you. Don't spook the standing dog. Slow and steady wins the race, once again.

PRESENTATION: The size of each dog in relation to the other is important. You can't have a Saint Bernard crawl under a Chihuahua, but you can have the Chihuahua crawl under the Saint. This trick is too precious for words. The downside is that it looks easy because of the contrast in size. A larger crawling dog makes it look harder, particularly if the crawling dog brushes against the standing dog's underside. Of course, that requires a higher standard of training for the standing dog.

AN ASIDE

Now, the assumption in this book is that your dog is already obedience trained. Remember our deal? The well-trained dog will be doing a rock-steady stay. If your dog is not, here's a tip. There is a product called Happy Legs. It consists of four stilts, steadied by industrial-strength magnets. Getting these dogs up on these short stilts will steady the stays. The dog's inability (or discomfort) to step on one of the stilts passively teaches him to remain steady.

Jump Over

"JUMP!" OR "HUP!"

This trick requires that you have one dog that can do a rock-solid stand-stay and one that knows how to jump. The introduction to training is to work the dogs around one another and to put up a jump for the jumper. Rather than moving the jump closer to the standing dog, gradually reposition him closer to the jump.

The jumping dog knows how to jump over jumps. Now we want to train the jumping dog to jump over another dog.

1. Have the jumping dog go back and forth over the jump, and bring the stationary dog into the area.
2. Have the stationary dog do a stand-stay in the vicinity of the jump as the other dog jumps.
3. Position the stationary dog in front of the jump and tell the jumping dog to *"Jump!"* over the dog and the jump.
4. Do that three or four times, then stand the stationary dog behind the jump.
5. The step before graduation is to set up a jump of at least the same height as the standing dog, but preferably a smidgen higher, and with the jump between the standing dog and the jumping dog, give the command to *"Jump!"* or *"Hup!"* Click and treat.
6. After the jumping dog clears the jump (and the dog), heel the jumper back to the starting position and repeat a half-dozen times.
7. Have the jumper go back and forth from one side to the other in effect reversing the jump. Do that a dozen times. That's enough for now. Next time you'll still have the jump on one side of the standing dog, and the jumper will jump back and forth a dozen times.
8. Finally, remove the jump and have the jumper do four com-

plete round trips, back and forth. Knock off for the day. Both dogs have graduated.

PRESENTATION: An advantage of this trick is that you have 100 percent mobile props with you and can therefore perform the trick anywhere and anytime.

To me, the beauty of a dog act is that it's 100 percent mobile—
until you add props that increase your transportation and labor
problems. But these can also add great enjoyment too! While
most of the previous tricks called for few or no props, this
chapter brings you into the heavy-duty stuff.

Operate the Computer

"COMPUTER!" "TYPE!" "PRINT OUT!"
"TAKE IT!" "DELIVER!"

More and more people are becoming computer literate, so
here's a trick for the twenty-first century. Much of this routine
uses tricks previously covered. Securing props is a no-brainer:
outdated equipment abounds. If you want to spend a couple of
bucks on really lightweight props that will help save your back,
contact Props by IDM at www.propsbyidm.com. The *"Computer!"* command is a variation of the *"Paws Up!"* command.
Use a lure-and-reward technique, augmented by the clicker.

1. Lure the front paws to the keyboard.
2. Present your hand as for the shake signal, but don't take the
   paw.

3. Let the paw hit the keyboard, say *"Type!"* then click and treat. Movement of the paws on the keyboard can be obtained by the *"Left Paw!" "Right Paw!"* commands. You can develop a nice quick tempo with the paws on the board. See "Front Legs Prancing" in chapter 29.

Sven Brooks types on his computer before sending a post to his friends Lassie and Benji. Sven, owned by Los Angeles dog trainer Steve Brooks, can speak and say, "I love you."

The *"Print Out!"* command is a variation of the *"Bump!"* command. (See chapter 9.) Your message is already preprinted, so your dog "Roy" can hit almost any key. Using the appropriate commands, tell Roy to take the preprinted sheet of paper *("Take It!")* and either deliver it to the audience or show it to the audience.

PRESENTATION: You don't need the smoke and mirrors or lights and bells that the real equipment has, because the monitor will be facing *away* from the audience—they won't know if it is functioning or not. The equipment can be functional, but this multiplies your problems, because it generally needs outlets. A flickering light on the monitor, powered by a dry-cell battery, can add that touch of realism. A standard piece of paper with a birthday greeting on it can be retrieved, or you can use a much larger piece of paper to make a sign suggesting APPLAUSE. If you use a sign, make sure it's printed on both sides. Should Roy hold the sign upside down, simply take it from his mouth and reposition it while explaining to him, in a calm tone of voice, that he should hold it so the audience can read it. Then explain to the audience that Roy always positions the paper that way so *he* can read it.

Get on the Internet

"INTERNET!" "WHAT'S ON THE INTERNET?"

For those dogs that washed out in chapters 1 through 3, there is hope. Here's a variation on the Talk trick to help those mumbling and grumbling dogs who didn't stay in school long enough to perfect the King's English. A variation on the *"Computer!"* command is *"Internet!"* Same trick, different command—to show off your smart dog. The "What's on the Internet?" question probably will take more work on your part. Again, the question makes the trick. Settle for simple barks, speaking, but a mixed bag or grumbles, growls and barking makes an even better response. Review chapters 1 through 3 to expand on this one.

PRESENTATION: This trick can be milked for laughs by interrupting with a series of questions, such as, "What did she say?" "Oh, he said that on the Internet?" "What was your answer?" If you do this, be aware of your audience, and don't let it go on for more than a minute and a half.

Play the Piano

"PAWS UP!" "PLAY!"

Here's an area where Roy can be training you, serving as a manipulator. (Some are offended by the notion that their dog would or could control the situation. It's the Disney effect—the most perfect of God's creatures would *never* manipulate. Well, they will, believe me!) My general recommendation is that Roy usually should not control the situation—you should. But if Roy manipulates you and it becomes a great trick, why not? Ultimately you will control the situation. I will cover several approaches to teaching this trick: modeling, lure and reward, target stick, click and treat and play and treat. Naturally, you need a piano for Roy to play. If his playing is discordant, don't worry about it. Be sure you have some funny patter regarding his playing.

Here Sven Brooks plays the piano and accompanies himself singing. Trained by Steve Brooks of Los Angeles.

1. Start off with the *"Paws Up!"* command. Now we have to get him pawing the keys. You can manually get him to hit the keys (modeling).
2. You can, with Roy's paws on the keys, lure him back and forth over the keys and reward him. You can use a target stick to have him *"Touch!"* the keys. You can also use a click-and-treat method to get him to "play" the keys. My favorite method is one I developed called play and treat. This is a gas! Use any of the previously mentioned methods to get Roy to hit a key.
3. When he hits the key for the first time, you will treat. The quizzical look Roy gives you is priceless. He is doing the playing, and you are delivering the treat. Watch how quickly he picks this up. The command in all cases is *"Play!"*

PRESENTATION: If you are opening in Vegas, you'll need a snappy comeback for someone who says he can play the piano better than Roy. Hope and pray for that wise guy to show up. You'll be ready! "Let's see how good a pianist you are," you respond as you whip out a pair of mittens with the thumb sewed down. When your heckler protests and asks what they're for, explain that Roy is playing without fingers, and you're simply creating a level playing field. The mittens should look like dog paws, with nails and paw pads on the palms. And remember, *always* take those mittens with you!

Ride a Skateboard

"SKATEBOARD!" "PUSH!" "RIDE YOUR SKATEBOARD!"

I love dogs who gravitate to the skateboard. They're generally the bigger dogs and are fascinated with this moving object. If Roy grabs hold of the skateboard and tosses it around, your job is half done. Encourage him with the command *"Skateboard!"* Use the word to help develop his enthusiasm. Use that old encouraging tone of voice—"Where's your skateboard?"—to get him up.

This shows a good use of props and building on tricks with Paws Up. These dogs are owned by Jordan Heppner of Winnipeg, Canada.

Don't give him constant use of the board: control and monitor it. All good things come from you, and the skateboard is one of these things. It's not a chew toy, it's a prop. You have

275

seen the enjoyment he gets from the board. Encourage his free play with it. Applaud as he gets worked up.

The clicker comes into play when he first puts a forequarter on the board. Watch him carefully—your timing is important here. This is a self-rewarding game. Use the clicker judiciously. You don't want Roy changing his concentration from the skateboard to the reward. The click is an occasional reward, not immediately followed by a treat. The praise, applause and excitement as Roy uses the board are the reward. That excitement is intensified by your control of the board and his access to it.

You'll find that he'll enjoy putting one forequarter on the board. At this point introduce the command *"Push!"*

1. Your task now is to get him to put both forequarters on the board.
2. When he does, jackpot Roy with petting, rubbing, applause, praise and an abundance of treats. The clicker will precede the treats.
3. Don't be disappointed if he puts only one forequarter on the board at first. His pushing is the important ingredient here.
4. Back to work while he's energetic. Watch that energy and enthusiasm. You want to finish with Roy wanting more. Don't run him into the ground.
5. Now you have Roy pushing the skateboard with two and hopefully three paws on the board. The third paw is Roy's option, not yours.
6. At this point in his skateboard training, start to have him do a sit-stay on the skateboard. It's not the steadiest of platforms. Pet and encourage him to sit steadily and then you move the board forward one foot.
7. Praise, click, treat, and have him sit without moving until he is relaxed and enjoying himself.
8. The next step is moving the skateboard two feet, followed by the reward.
9. Work him up to four feet and knock off for the day.

10. Build Roy up to a rolling trip of six feet in a week's time, then go back to square one and start him standing on the board.
11. Go a little more slowly in this phase of the training, with the same goal as in the sit-stay ride.
12. As you take him on that ride, gradually increasing the distance, he will start by putting all four feet on the board for just a second or two. Build up the amount of time that all four feet are on the board. That fourth foot is a rarity and we must depend on Roy deciding to do it.

This trick has two phases. One where he pushes the board and one where he rides the board.

PRESENTATION: You can show off as you develop this trick, from the time Roy has one forequarter on the board and has learned to push. It isn't necessary for him to have all four feet on the board. (As a matter of a fact, even a human skateboarder only has one foot on the board most of the time.) Bring Roy out in front of the audience, riding on the skateboard in the sit or stand position. Roy will know what comes next, but use the *"Ride Your Skateboard!"* command to enhance the trick. At this point, Roy will start pushing the skateboard with one, two, or three feet on the ground. We take what we can get! That pushing and forward motion makes the trick.

Ride a Motorcycle

"HUP!" "SIT!" "STAY!" "SEAT!" "RIDE!"

Here comes the heavy prop work. This trick is simpler from the dog-training point of view than it is from the prop-making point of view. Get your motorcycle-riding dog "Evil Knievel" used to the motorcycle sound by periodically turning on the motor when he's around. Be aware that, although motorcycles have kickstands, you can't depend on them when teaching Evil to get up on the seat. So make sure the bike is braced on both sides with training wheels before starting to teach this trick.

1. Call Evil over and tell him *"Hup!"* He'll look at you in wonder.
2. Pick him up and sit him on the bike the first few times.
3. This is modeling and the fastest approach.
4. Later, put him on the leash and guide him onto the motorcycle. You can use lure and reward and clickers here if you like, but it will take considerably longer.
5. Once you have him sitting, put his front paws on the handlebars. Give the command *"Seat!"*
6. Calm him down by talking to him and gently petting.
7. Have Evil sit there for at least five minutes. Don't stand over him, watching him. Attend to some other business while keeping an eye on him. Eventually you want him sitting with paws on the handlebars for a longer period of time. Give him a stay for a half hour.
8. Once Evil has gotten used to sitting on the bike, slowly push it with its front wheel locked in position. Give the command *"Ride!"* The front wheel is locked with two metal braces, one on either side of the wheel (see "Presentation," below). When the bike is moving, sit and stay become the hard parts. Do not put the bike in gear. The power and direction will come from you. *Slowly* circle around the stage. You are standing by to rescue Evil from any nervous attempt he makes to terminate the trick. Later you can use the commands *"Seat!"* and *"Ride!"* to get Evil to ride his motorcycle.

PRESENTATION: I'm a Harley man myself, but you might be better off using a "rice burner" because of its lighter weight. Another consideration is the way you rig the motorcycle to turn in a continuous circle. A good handyman-welder can make an adjustable wheel lock. You have to figure out the size of the circular route the bike will take on the stage. It must fit within the area available. That is the reason for the ajustable wheel lock; adjustable for different stages. Also have a gear shift lock to keep the motorcycle in neutral. You want the motor running for additional effect.

Sven Brooks takes the family vehicle for a jaunt to the dog park.

Ride a Scooter

"PAWS UP!" "STAY!" "PUSH!"

Here, you will need a child's scooter with the front wheel locked in place as described in the previous trick. Make sure to add training wheels to the scooter if they are not there already. Skateboarding dogs will adjust to this trick, and if you start with this trick instead of the skateboarding trick, the latter will be easier to teach—and Evil will have an even easier time riding the skateboard with three feet on the board. The scooter has to be high enough that he can extend his body upward, but not so high that he can't reach the handlebars. Now the question may be raised, why not teach the scooter first? Well, there are two reasons: (1) skateboards are more readily available than

279

scooters, and (2) they require no additional equipment on them before they are ready to go.

1. Start with the *"Paws Up!"* command to get Evil's paws on the handlebars. If you have to hold the scooter steady, you will not be as able to assist Evil. Both of his hind feet should be on the ground, not on the scooter.
2. Tell Evil to *"Stay!"* in that position, gradually working up to five minutes.
3. Now position his right hindquarter on the scooter with his front paws still up on the handlebars. Work toward that five-minute goal again.
4. Once Evil's good and steady in this position, it's time to move the scooter a step as you tell him to *"Push!"*
5. Keep him in the paws up position, scratch and praise. This should be calming praise, not excited praise.
6. Take another step forward, and the dog will be forced to move his left rear paw. Repeat this a half-dozen times. Gradually, and slowly, increase the distance. Evil will start moving his left foot repeatedly. Don't let him get too excited, because if he falls or knocks over the scooter, it will set back training considerably. That is why, even with the use of training wheels, you have to be close by to make sure that nothing goes amiss. Regarding the training wheels— wait for a while before removing them. Better to wait too long than to remove them too soon.

PRESENTATION: This is an impressive trick no matter how you slice it. You can show off even with the training wheels on. And besides, once he's gotten the hang of it, it's loads of fun for the dog!

Ride a Tricycle

"HUP!" "SIT!" "STAY!" "RIDE!"

Training wheels are not needed on a tricycle, but a front wheel lock is. A larger seat may be necessary depending on the size of Evil.

Start off with the *"Hup!"* command to get him up on the seat. Make sure he's sitting and facing forward, as you develop his steadiness and confidence on the trike. He's not going to pump the pedals, because he will be unable to reach them. All Evil has to do is remain steady as you push the tricycle and tell him *"Ride."*

PRESENTATION: This is a great starting point for any of these prop-riding tricks. It can be taught rapidly to any dog with a good foundation in training. If you have gotten this far in the book, your dog has that foundation. You haven't just been reading, have you? You must have done *some* training.

Ride a Horse

"HUP!" "SIT!" "STAY!" "RIDE YOUR PONY!"

In showbiz speak, a horse is a prop. My recommendation, depending on the size of Evil, would be to use a miniature horse or pony. Give some advance thought to the saddle you are going to make, because it has to be longer and flatter than saddles for human use to provide the broad base that is necessary for your dog. Don't dwell on the riding part of this horse trick. Think about the variations you will create on this impressive presentation.

The hard part of the trick is getting Evil to jump on the horse and remain in position on its back. A "step" that's positioned just below the saddle will help him mount on the left side. Keep in mind that Evil is not a jockey who will be riding in a steeplechase—a gentle trot around the ring a couple of times is sufficient.

Here are three animals from Timbo the Clown and Welch's Sheltie Circus getting into the act. Not only do we have Frosty, a Bichon Frisé, riding Crackerjack the pony, but Bailey, a Shetland Sheepdog, is leading them. Trainer Tim Welch of Thompson, PA, owns all these animals.

You already have the foundation for this trick. The commands you'll use are *"Hup!" "Sit!"* and *"Stay!"* followed by the unnecessary but impressive-sounding command to *"Ride Your Pony!"*

First, Evil has to be acquainted/familiarized with, desensitized to the pony. He has to be helped up (modeled) on the horse's back initially, and taught to sit and stay there as the horse takes a few steps. Don't rush through this trick, but also don't be surprised by how rapidly Evil picks up on what he has done previously. Again, slow and steady wins the race. The dog will go wherever the *horse* wants to go. This is a book on dog, not pony, training. Have a well-broken pony for your dog. Forevermore you will refer to the pony as Evil's pony.

PRESENTATION: You're going to take advantage of previously taught tricks to come up with a socko grand finale. It's time to reintroduce a couple of old favorites, such as Sit High and Jump Through a Hoop when Evil is riding the pony.

When you first taught those tricks, you might have thought they were pretty tame. Combining sit high and hoop jumping with riding on the pony's back will give them a rebirth.

Ride a Rubber Raft

"HUP!" "SIT!" "STAY!" "STAND!" "RIDE YOUR RUBBER RAFT!"

A rubber raft can be a portable prop—providing there is always a pool nearby. There is a small advantage to having your dog get used to the raft on terra firma, so start training outside the pool. If your dog is your constant swimming companion, train him to ride in a raft with you! Teach Evil to get into the raft in the shallow end of the pool, where you can wedge the raft into the corner and even prop up the middle with some submerged pool furniture. If he was a balancing fool before you embarked on this trick, you're ahead of the game. Some dogs work their hearts out for their owners, and if they've done a lot of climbing and balancing, they'll attempt to do this balancing act also. (You may think that there is no balancing here—

nothing could be further from the truth.) Breeds that will work well on this trick are the Bichon Frisé (originally bred as a circus performer), the Standard Poodle (originally a water dog) and just about any of the retrievers.

PRESENTATION: Don't bother trying to put this into your act, but it will be a great diversion at pool parties, especially with the *"Ride Your Rubber Raft!"* command.

Get the Cellular Phone/Get the Cordless Phone

"CORDLESS!" "CELLULAR!"

We have Jo Ann Hise of Roswell, New Mexico, to thank for these two tricks. (I'd be afraid *not* to give anyone from Roswell credit. I might be kidnapped by aliens or alien dogs.) The two are variations on some previous tricks. They may seem like the same trick, but they're not. In both cases, your dog is taught to sniff out the characteristic odors of the cellular phone and the cordless phone. Believe me, he knows the difference! It doesn't matter which phone you start with, unless you have a tiny Maltese, in which case, start with the lightest weight cellular. If he can't fetch the cordless, have him bring you your cellular.

Besides your spoken command, another cue to retrieve the cordless phone will be its ringing. When your dog proudly brings you the cordless, tell him, "I'm not taking calls now. Take a message." If he can't use his nose to find the cordless, use your cellular to call your cordless. Ahhh, modern technology. As advanced as technology is, it can't equal the flexibility of our four-footed pals. Reread chapter 16 to bring you up to speed on retrieving.

PRESENTATION: Guests will be really impressed when the cordless phone rings and your dog brings it to you.

28
AN OPEN-AND-SHUT CASE

Not only will your dog learn to open and shut a "case," but now he will learn to open and shut doors, drawers, cabinets and just about anything you want him to. This is another skill that allows you to expand your repertoire! Previously covered retrieving tricks (chapter 16) have taught most of the pulling, and clicker training (chapters 7 and 9) will have developed the touching and bumping tricks.

A quick comment about the nature of doorknobs and dogs. Do you want your dog to twist doorknobs? Give that some thought before teaching this trick. After all, the two reasons dogs have not taken over the world are that they don't have an opposable thumb, and they cannot open doors. Do you want to change that?

Touch and Bump

Use the target stick in shaping your dog "Tucker" to touch or bump. (Other devices can be used for targeting.) The difference between touching and bumping is that touch uses the paws and bump uses the nose.

To review what was covered in chapter 7, every movement

toward the goal is rewarded. The movement doesn't have to be perfect, just approximately right. Improvement is always sought.

1. With the target stick in your left hand, wait for a movement toward a piece of tape on the end.
2. As Tucker moves toward the tape, use the clicker (also in your left hand), then treat with the food in your right hand. The hand in which to hold these tools is not set in stone. Do whatever feels most comfortable for you.
3. When Tucker's nose touches the stick, simultaneously click and say, *"Bump!"* and then treat.
4. Should his paw touch the stick say, *"Touch!"* Purists say that you should only teach one thing at a time. Hey, there are 150 tricks in this book for you to teach to your dog. You don't have time to teach them one at a time.
5. Either *"Touch!"* or *"Bump!"* can be used to have certain items closed. Which one depends on what the item is. A heavy refrigerator door needs a strong, continuous push with the nose rather than a light pat with the paw.

Open the Drawer

"TUG!" "OPEN!" "DRAWER!" "DRAWER OPEN!"

Start by teaching Tucker to grab and tug on a rope, as explained in chapter 18, using the command *"Tug!"* Immediately after a tug session, attach a rope to the handle of a lightweight kitchen drawer with internal rollers. Lead Tucker to the rope and say *"Open!"* When he pulls on the rope and the drawer slides open, give him a ton of praise, clicks, applause, treats, toys and anything else you can think of to celebrate this wondrous accomplishment. There is a difference between tugging as a game and pulling on a sometimes-stationary object (the drawer). He has to feel his way through this, and it's your job to encourage, reward and praise him throughout.

You may think that he's wonderful for having learned the *"Open!"* command so rapidly. That is not what has happened. Tucker knew you wanted him to tug the rope, and he wanted to do that as well. It was a combination of the environment, training that had occurred previously, the rope, you and your mood that produced the results. Tucker hasn't learned the command yet. What he has learned is what pleases you and pleases him under that set of circumstances.

Let me contradict myself. I said that you would teach more than one thing at a time because you have so much to teach your dog. You're now teaching Tucker to open the drawer. Do you want to work on closing the drawer at the same time? (It has to be closed before it is opened again, and that would save time.) The answer is a resounding *no!*

If Tucker already knows how to close the drawer, then you can have him open and close it. Otherwise, after he opens the drawer, rapidly close it yourself and repeat the *"Open!"* command. Tucker will grasp this concept very rapidly because he has been grounded in the Tug trick and has developed a penchant for learning new tricks.

The term that refers to how a dog learns to perform a job in all circumstances and environments is "generalization." Having similar equipment and props help in generalization. It is reasonable to assume that you will teach this exercise in the quiet and privacy of your own home. How will this affect generalization? It shouldn't present a problem if you have practiced sufficiently. If you're invited to someone else's house with Tucker, for the express purpose of showing off your prized canine to twenty dinner guests, practice in the host's house at least two or three times before the guests arrive.

Once Tucker is working on the *"Open!"* command, introduce the *"Drawer!"* command. Tap on the drawer and say *"Drawer."* He quickly will learn the name of the object to be opened. Start working on distance by sending Tucker from one room to the other with the *"Drawer Open!"* command. He'll know what you want him to do because of:

1. The command.
2. The rope hanging from the drawer handle.
3. Generalization.

4. The fact that you have been doing the exercise frequently; sort of the flip side of generalization. This is the most important reason for the response.

Later you can have Tucker retrieve something from inside the drawer.

PRESENTATION: This is an iron-clad rule for any occasion where you are showing Tucker off or working on a film set: Practice two or three times in the actual area where he is to perform. If it's a film set, it is always a good idea to tell them that you are going to use the set. When you tell them, do it in a requesting fashion to avoid hurting the assistant director's feelings. If there's a sign designating it a "hot set" you must positively ask.

Open the Cabinet

"OPEN CABINET!"

You don't have to use the *"Tug!"* command here since the previous trick taught the *"Open!"* command. Cabinets generally require less of a pull to open them than drawers, but there's another consideration. Tucker has to get out of the way of the swinging door. Have no fear, he'll figure this out quite rapidly! Another consideration on the cabinet/drawer is that when you wean Tucker away from the rope, he'll have to change his jaw positioning in order to grab the handle.

To teach this trick, follow the same procedure as for the last one, but you'll progress even more rapidly than before. The *"Cabinet!"* part of the command is the last thing that you'll teach Tucker.

PRESENTATION: Visitors will enjoy this trick, and you can take it anywhere. All you need is a little rope and a house with some cabinets.

Close the Drawer

"DRAWER!" "BUMP!" "CLOSE!" "CLOSE DRAWER!"

Tucker knows the *"Bump!"* command from previous training. Pick the right spot on the drawer to bump. Play around with the drawer to see where to hit it to make it slide the easiest. We want to mark that spot on the drawer, but first, look at the size of Tucker in relationship to the height of the drawer. This will have a bearing on the line of thrust of his nose. In most cases he will be thrusting upward. Straight-on and downward are other possibilities. This will have a bearing on how much pressure Tucker will have to exert and where he should place it. Simply stick some tape or glue a poker chip in the best spot on the drawer for him to bump. Empty the drawer so that it slides easier. Change the *"Bump!"* command to *"Close!"*

PRESENTATION: Opening and closing drawers are tricks all by themselves. Add impact to the trick by specifying items to be taken out of the drawer and returned.

Close the Cabinet

"BUMP!" "CLOSE CABINET!" "PULL!"

As before, this works with the *"Bump!"* command. Have Tucker bump where the handle is located. This is a good spot to pull and bump, but it requires a bit more guidance and encouragement in closing cabinets. Gently push and pull on the door to find the best place for your dog to bump. Your job is to select the best spot to bump the cabinet closed and the easiest way to open it. A downward pull will not do the job. Now a *slightly* downward pull may be necessary because of the knob's height in relationship to the dog. The dog must pull away as much as possible with or without using a rope. As the dog's enthusiasm and vigor increases you can shorten and eliminate the rope. Use the *"Pull!"* command.

PRESENTATION: There are more exciting items to retrieve from a cabinet than from a drawer. If Tucker is really soft mouthed, try having him retrieve a fine china cup or some heavy crystal (after he's practiced with plastic). This adds class to the trick.

A Switch on Opening Drawers and Cabinets

You've been using rope on the handles of both cabinets and drawers. Now that Tucker is doing well, wrap a small towel around the handle. In this way he will learn to use a more "normal" knob or handle (one without a rope attached to it). Your next step is to remove the towel and have Tucker go "au naturel."

PRESENTATION: The presentation can now be accomplished anytime, anywhere.

Opening French Doors

"PAWS UP!" "DOOR!" "OPEN DOOR!"

Think! Think twice! Think a third time! Do you really want your dog to open doors? Well, okay. Just remember, I warned you. This one is a piece of cake, and I would be concerned with a dog that didn't learn it by accident. Call Tucker over to the door and tell him *"Paws Up!"* right in front of the door handle. In an excited tone of voice repeat *"Door!"* a few times, and encourage him to hit the handle. It doesn't matter if the door opens in or out, just encourage Tucker to go through once he's opened the door. As I've mentioned earlier (and often) any dog's Second Commandment is, "If a door opens, go through it." They spend their lives looking for doors to go through. This, in itself, is reward enough, but you will keep moving away from the door and rubbing, petting, applauding and praising Tucker. "Hooray! I went through a door," thinks your dog as you turn around and return to the now closed door. Repeat for a half-dozen round trips, using the command *"Open Door!"* and the subject has been learned. Keep your eye on Tucker for the next couple of days. If you see him making a lunch and packing an overnight bag, lock the door. And remember, I warned you.

Opening Doors with Doorknobs

"TAKE IT!" "PULL!" "TURN!" "OPEN DOOR!"

Read the caveat for the preceding trick twice. Teaching your dog to open doors with doorknobs is harder than teaching them to open French doors, but equally dangerous. After you teach this trick, lock *all* your doors.

Here is an opportunity to use frustration to get Tucker to turn the doorknob.

1. Start with a door that opens inward. Tape the latch open with duct tape. Wrap two washcloths around the doorknob. Secure with duct tape.
2. Tell Tucker to *"Take It!"* indicating the doorknob. As soon as he grabs the knob, tell him *"Pull!"* and make a big fuss as he pulls the door open. Do this a half-dozen times while building up his enthusiasm through praise.
3. Remove the tape from the latch but keep the washcloths on the knob. Tell Tucker *"Take It!"* and *"Pull!"* He'll be unsuccessful and start to become frustrated. Encourage that frustration and use the tips of your fingers to help turn the knob. Introduce the command *"Turn!"*
4. Next time, leave the door unlatched and tell him to take it and pull.
5. Slam the door so that it latches shut. Now tell Tucker to take it and pull. The frustration factor will kick in. Tell him *"Turn!"* and help him turn the knob. Watch out for your fingers. Once he has his mouth on the knob, you should be safe. Even so, get your fingers in and out of there as fast as possible, before the teeth slip off the knob. When Tucker opens the door, shower him with praise. Alternate between latching the door and keeping the door ajar.
6. Start latching the door more frequently. Pay attention to

Tucker's frustration factor. You want to frustrate him until he gets the idea that he must *turn* the knob. Use short, frequent sessions. Don't forget the praise, and don't remove the washcloths too soon.

7. Introduce a door that opens out. The command sequence is *"Take It!" "Turn!" "Open!"*

PRESENTATION: This trick can be done anywhere. If you are visiting someone not particularly fond of dogs, this will endear Tucker to them. Tell him *"Door!" "Open!"* Then leave Tucker in the house alone when you all go out for dinner. If you return to the house and find the silver missing, your hosts will blame Tucker for letting in the thief.

Flip-Top Garbage and Trash Cans

"BUMP!" "OUT!" OR "DROP IT!" "TRASH!"

Much of this has been covered in previous chapters, particularly in chapters 7 and 9. Get Tucker, holding a trash bag in his mouth, to bump a spot low on the flip top of the trash can and tell him *"Out!"* or *"Drop It!"* so he deposits the trash in the bin. Seven times in one session, and you have it under control. Change the *"Bump!"* command to *"Trash!"* and you have it all together. These instructions are for the swinging-top trash cans.

PRESENTATION: Trash sounds more genteel than garbage. This is the way to make your dog a welcome houseguest. He can help you gather up the trash during the cleanup after a rowdy party and then deposit it in the can.

Lights On / Lights Off

"PAWS UP!" "BUMP!" "TOUCH!"
"LIGHTS ON!" "LIGHTS OFF!"

Modern technology has developed all sorts of light switches. Here the actual method of switching a light on or off depends on what you have on your wall. If Tucker is at least 26 inches at the shoulder, he'll have the height to reach the switch. A simple, single-push-button light switch that you push for either ON and OFF is a piece of cake. The same technique will also work with the double-push-button switch because the extended button is the one that needs to be hit. Start with a *"Paws Up!"* exercise and, using the clicker, get Tucker to extend his paws upward to hit the switch. In addition to the normal reward, Tucker is going to learn that the light going on or off is part of his reward. As you practice, keep him punching until the illumination has been changed.

An everyday toggle light switch presents more of a problem. Active movement is required to change that switch either to the up or the down position. You can add a sturdy extension to the toggle so Tucker has a greater touch and bump area, or you can order a ready-made device from North Star Canines at 1-800-BOW-WOW2. They carry an extension that runs from the light switch down to the floor for easy manipulation by even the smallest dog. (North Star also has a couple of videos on tricks.)

Two commands have to be taught if you use the standard switch: *"On!"* and *"Off!"* or *"Lights On!"* and *"Lights Off!"* If Tucker is familiar with the *"Touch!"* and *"Bump!"* commands, your job is easier. The same command is used for either the wall switch or the North Star extension, but while similar, the training method will vary somewhat.

For the wall switch, give Tucker a *"Paws Up!"* and, using click and treat, get him to push the switch up with his nose. Start out using the *"Bump!"* command, which you will change to *"Lights On!"* Teach this command first, and flip down the switch after it has been put up. (This assumes that throwing the switch up turns the light on, and down turns it off.) Teach this trick in a room with subdued lighting so the light going on will act as a secondary reinforcer along with the clicker. As the training progresses, you'll find that if the light doesn't go on the first time, Tucker will take another shot at bumping the switch up without you telling him. After he learns to turn the lights on, you can work on lights off.

Start with the *"Paws Up!"* command and the *"Touch!"* command to get him to paw downward at the switch. Once he is working successfully on the *"Touch!"* command, change it to *"Lights Off!"* Again, the light going on and off acts as a secondary reinforcer.

ALTERNATE APPROACH: Using an extender makes the job much easier for both you and Tucker because he can work at a lower level. The same type of motion is required: bumping up with the nose for ON, and pawing down for OFF. The object bumped and pawed is a small boxlike item, with a ON/OFF toggle switch, and the clicker is used in the normal manner to get approximations of the desired actions.

PRESENTATION: Remember that even when working well in your house, your dog may not do as well in someone else's house because of a different light-switch configuration.

Here are a variety of tricks that you can have a lot of fun teaching and performing.

Lean Left/Lean Right

Our goal here is to have the dog lean the top of his body to the left or to the right on command. Have the dog stand close to the edge of a grooming table, facing toward you. As you face your dog, the edge of the table will be to your left (and the dog's right). Facing him, say, *"Lean Left!"* and, with the heel of your right hand, gently push on the top of his back toward the edge of the table. You do not want to push him off the table but you want him to feel that is what you are threatening to do. It is a very gradual application of pressure. Think about this a bit. It may sound a bit confusing, but what you are doing is pushing the dog to your left, and the dog, to resist you and avoid falling off the table, is leaning back to *his* left.

PUSH PRESSURE

The key to success in this trick is the slight amount of pressure that is exchanged back and forth between you and your dog. It is pleasurable and pleasant, not offensive. I would equate it with the pressure exerted between you and your significant other when standing and leaning into one another. It's application is neither rapid, hard nor swift.

The exchange of pressure is a reward all by itself, but I want you to introduce additional rewards as the training progresses.

The first three sessions will last about six minutes each. In the fourth session, work on the *"Lean Right!"* Face the dog in the opposite direction on the same end of the table. Now your right hand is on the end side of the table, and using your left hand, you'll push the top of the dog's back to your right as you tell him *"Lean Right!"* In subsequent training sessions alternate the right and left.

After the initial sessions of pushing back and forth, the clicker can be introduced to wean the dog off the hand pressure. The motion of the hand toward the dog's back is the hand signal for this exercise. Your right hand signals "lean left" and your left hand signals "lean right." As you give the hand and voice signal, click and treat at the slightest move in the correct direction. You may not get as much movement in the shifting from left to right as you did before with the modeling technique, but the clicker is ideally suited for augmenting this exercise while speeding up leaning.

PRESENTATION: Simply having the dog shift from left to right on command is worth at least a small chuckle from the meanest of people. Convert this to another trick by introducing mambo music or playing "How Dry I Am."

Cross Legs in the Down, Sitting and Standing Positions

"LEFT CROSS!" "UNCROSS!" "RIGHT CROSS!"

Here are nine different tricks all wrapped into one. An alternate training method will be taught for each one of these tricks: nine tricks, eighteen methods—that's double! Well, not really, but there is a great deal of information to be obtained from reading this short section. These tricks should be taught in stages;

you can stop at any point you like. I would suggest you do these as side tricks while you are teaching other tricks of a greater variety. The purpose of this series of tricks is to have your dog cross and uncross his legs in three different positions: down, sitting and standing. It is not as boring as it sounds.

Puddleduck the Shetland Sheepdog in the normal down position, waiting for her first command.

Start with your dog in the down position and hunker down in front of him, clicker and treats in your left hand. It is important that the treat be in the same hand as the clicker. Although difficult to manage, the dog's attention should be focused on one hand rather than be diffused, by looking at both hands. (A quick reminder of the mirror image of the dog in relation to you, which "reverses" left and right: The dog's left is not your left.) Extend your left hand slightly to the left of your dog's left forepaw, and as he extends the left paw toward your outstretched hand, click and treat. Gradually move your hand farther and farther toward and finally over the dog's right paw, forcing the dog to reach over it with his left paw. Click and treat each improved approximation. We are looking for that paw to come down on top of the other one. If perchance the dog crosses his legs and then immediately uncrosses them, give him the signal to recross back to the way they were. Do not reward the uncrossing at this point. We want to reinforce crossing left over right leg. Each session should last six or seven minutes.

Trainer Susan Zaretsky tells Puddleduck *"Left Cross!"*

During the second session, introduce the command *"Left Cross!"* and use it continually at this point. The dog should hold the legs crossed for a period of time. You will never need him to hold the leg cross for one minute, but work up to that length of time. Once you have a degree of steadiness (twenty seconds) you are ready to work on the uncrossing. Switch the treats and clicker to your other (right) hand. Move your right hand into view at about the location of the dog's left paw before he crossed it. Offer that hand and say, *"Uncross!"* with a slight emphasis on the "un." Any motion toward uncrossing will be clicked and treated. What we are looking for is having the dog plant his left leg where it started. It will not take as long to teach as the initial crossing.

Make sure the left cross and the uncross are working successfully before working on the right cross. With your right hand chock full of treats and a clicker, hunker down again and repeat as above. At this point we want to work on the uncross at the same time. This is accomplished by moving that right hand over the crossed paws to your left and saying, *"Uncross!"* Results will be much quicker than when you originally started out.

Now Puddleduck is told *"Right Cross!"*

**Once the dog is taught to Cross Legs in the down position,
it is easy to train it to do the same thing in the sit position.**

Fine! You are finished! There is a set of *three* different tricks that you can use and present. Don't even think about moving on to the sit position yet. Forget about the future exercises. Just keep playing with the crossing and uncrossing for about a week, and introduce another trick or two. You're moving right along.

Now you are going to cash in on the previous work you did. With your dog *sitting* and facing you, start off as before when getting him to do a right cross. As soon as he does a completed right cross (not merely the starting motion), tell him, *"Uncross!"* Three left crosses and uncrosses in succession are followed by a right cross and uncross.

Now, with Puddleduck in the stand position, we have built the first trick—merely crossing the legs—into six different tricks (Cross/Uncross, in down, sit and stand positions). It is easy to build on tricks.

And you thought your dog wasn't smart! He has a better understanding of right and left than most of the people out there. He's up to six tricks in a relatively short period of time. Hey, there are a lot of other tricks in this book. Let's move forward with a couple or three of those tricks before working on leg crossing from the standing position. You don't need those additional three leg-crossing tricks right now, but you will come back to them, because they will be easy to teach at this point. When working with your dog in the standing position, you may find that he, for reasons of balance, does not plant his paw as firmly as he did in crossing while in the down position. Don't worry about it! You have the effective crosses.

AN ALTERNATE APPROACH: If you do not want to use the clicker, I still want you to consider the previous material because it will give you an understanding of what we are doing. The following approach is closer and more interactive than the clicker is. We will use treats, but not as frequently as with the clicker method.

Our starting position is in front of the sitting dog rather than the down dog. This is a modeling approach to the training. Gently grasp the side of the dog's collar in your left hand and pull out ever so slightly to the left. Say, *"Left Cross!"* as you reach for his left paw with your right hand and cross it over his other foot. The purpose of pulling the collar with your left hand is to get the dog to react to the fact that he is being put off balance. He does this by starting to elevate the opposite foot. At the first cross, you will vigorously rub and praise him. After the rubbing, he will settle down with his two feet in the starting position. Work on this for about four minutes, giving a lot of rubbing and praise. Give him a treat or two during this session. A couple of short sessions during the day are fine.

By the second day you can start using the *"Uncross!"* command the minute your rubbing causes the dog to uncross his feet. The fourth day will have him crossing left over right and uncrossing on command. Do not stop the petting and praise.

It is now time to start on the right cross. Change hands and follow the above directions for the right cross and uncross. The next step is to work with your dog in the standing position. You do things pretty much the same as when the dog was sitting. The vigorous petting on completion of the first completed cross will immediately put the dog into the uncross position. Deliver the *"Uncross!"* command the split second it occurs. Be aware that the collar pressure will have a greater effect on the dog attempting to maintain his balance in the standing position. That is why we started this trick with the dog in the sitting position. It is at this point that we are going to eliminate the collar pressure. The dog has the idea and doesn't need this additional cue and assist. The dog will be quickly trained, and you can start working with him in the down position. That collar pressure would be worthless in the down position, so it is well that we phased it out. The physical placement of the paw is the way we start out. Use more food at this point. The dog has an idea as to what you want. He's been there and done that. You can still pet him, but now is the time to slip treats to him too.

PRESENTATION: Simply having your dog cross and uncross his legs in three different positions becomes boring. Liven it up by interspersing other tricks and figuring out commands that will make these nine tricks new and different tricks. Let your imagination run wild. An example of a command that will make the *"Left Cross!"* a new trick is *"Be Elegant!"* or *"How Elegant!"*

Open Your Mouth/Catching Water

"OPEN!" "CATCH!"

Is it cruel to work a dog eight or ten hours a day? Certainly not! Dogs enjoy working, and if you want to expose your dog to this sort of regimen, go right ahead. Your dog will be willing to work far in excess of anything you are willing to do. Be aware of a number of things:

1. Your dog's enjoyment.
2. Your dog's boredom level.
3. Your dog's comfort.
4. Your dog's well being.

The first two items mean that you have to pay attention to your dog's moods. Simply changing the trick you are working on will keep his interest high. Comfort and well-being cover many aspects. Be aware of the sun and the weather. Use shady areas to full advantage. Make sure your dog is not overexerting himself. And carry plenty of spare water. This is where we use invisible training. Carry that water in a spray bottle. A spray bottle is different from a spritz bottle. A spray bottle sprays the water in a mist or fog and a spritz bottle produces a steady stream of water, much as a water pistol would do. If your dog is involved in an energetic workout, and you feel that he needs some water, spray it into his mouth. If he wants more water, he will lick the top of the spray bottle. Tell him, "*Open!*" and spray his mouth. We haven't started formally training him yet. We are merely giving him water and throwing in a little invisible training.

Now for the formal training. You have your dog opening his mouth on command because he wants some water. Now we are going to make "*Open!*" into a trick. Give the command, wait three seconds and spray. Give the command, wait six seconds and spray. Command, ten seconds, spray. Keep increasing the time period as long as the dog is interested in the water. Now, not only do we want to increase the period of time the mouth is held open, we also want to increase your distance from the dog. The water will be spraying on the dog's face as well as in his mouth as you move away. If the bottle has an adjustable nozzle, change the spray to a steadier stream. At a foot away we are going to change to a spritz bottle. If you had started with the spritz bottle and accidentally hit the dog in the face with the stream of water, the training would be over. The dog wouldn't work. Under this plan, we have desensitized the dog to any extra water that gets sprayed on his face. Only an Otterhound or an Irish Water Spaniel would tolerate indiscriminate face spraying. The desensitizing occurred in the invisible training phase, before the formal training started.

PRESENTATION: A super-soaker can add much to the presentation of this trick. You want to spritz, not spray, and you want to do it from a distance. The super-soaker will give you that distance. A spritz bottle will give you lightweight mobility. *"Catch!"* is a gratuitous command that adds to the trick. What else is the dog going to do with the water? Spit it out?

Paint

"PAINT!" "PALETTE!"

I like this trick because we actually train the dog to use tools. That is what is supposed to separate man from animal. We're closing the gap! Take into consideration the dog's size in relationship to the size of the brush. Start off with the cheapest artist's brush you can find. There is no need for camel-hair brushes at this point. Wait until your dog becomes an accomplished, skilled artist before taking that giant step. Another tool requirement is a piece of heavy-duty cardboard for "Rembrandt" to paint on. Don't worry about the paint at this point, and don't worry about the cardboard's color.

Rembrandt should be a good, reliable retriever. Have him hold the brush sideways in his mouth. You'll hold the cardboard alongside his mouth on the brush side. You'll have the clicker handy to click as he moves the brush toward the cardboard. No treats at this point. The click is to be used as the reward. Click as he gets closer to the cardboard. The first time he hits the cardboard, click and gently lay down the cardboard; praise vigorously. Be careful not to frighten Rembrandt with the cardboard in your enthusiasm over his success. At this point you are controlling the cardboard. Once he starts hitting the cardboard it is time to *brace* it. That bracing has to be rigid so that the dog does not knock the cardboard over.

Now we want to start Rembrandt moving the brush. This is

done with the clicker. As Rembrandt starts to increase the brush motion, click. Click on minor improvements in his brush motion. Only treat occasionally. Giving Rembrandt a treat will cause him to drop the brush. Augment the click with verbal praise. Verbal praise works beautifully, so don't sell it short. Introduce the *"Paint!"* command as those brushstrokes get broader and wilder.

Up to this point we haven't introduced the paint. Start with watercolors because they are less expensive and easier to clean up. We now want to expand what Rembrandt is doing to putting paint on the brush. Start with a genuine palette even if you are using watercolors. The palette's characteristic shape will be part of Rembrandt's cue. Start with the palette as you did with the cardboard, but introduce the *"Palette!"* command at the initial phase of the training. Rembrandt "sort of" has the idea at this point and will start touching the palette with the brush almost immediately. Here is an excellent example of building on tricks. Is this a "new" trick? Certainly! You have already taught the same behavior previously but a slight change in the context (palette) makes it a new trick. You are not giving him a choice when you hold out and offer the palette to him. Your job is to mix the paint and tell Rembrandt when to touch the palette and when to touch the canvas. The palette must be braced at an angle so that you no longer have to hold it. As we said previously, "Get away from your dog." We have Karla Clinch and Danny Thomson to thank for this wonderful trick.

PRESENTATION: Now we're talking business. Convince the general public that your dog is a celebrity, which should be easy to do when you have him perform his act. After Rembrandt bowls people over with his tricks and infectious personality, you can sell his works of art for outrageous prices. Replace that cardboard with canvas board and switch to oil paint. Your act shouldn't consist of having Rembrandt painting for two hours straight. Three minutes' painting is about average for an audience. If you feel you need to get more paint on the canvas during your act, keep sending him back for thirty seconds' more painting. Come up with some comic routine for sending him back. Use that canvas board over and over again until it is a masterpiece. You are the one who will determine if it is a masterpiece—unless someone rushes up and thrusts a ridiculous amount of money in your hand for Rembrandt's latest effort. Smear the entire palette with oil paint so that Rembrandt can't help but get paint on the brush when you tell him *"Palette!"* Oh, I forgot to tell you, Rembrandt is producing *abstract* art.

Stationary Zigzag or Shine My Shoes

"SHINE MY SHOES!" "ZIGZAG!"

The purpose of this trick is to have the dog weave in and out between your feet. Another way of describing it is that the dog does a continuous figure eight between your legs. This is especially cute when done by Dachshunds or Basset Hounds. If you really want your shoes shined, for brown shoes I would suggest a Pekingese or Pomeranian (just the brown ones, please), and for black shoes I'd say go with a Silky Terrier or Yorkshire Terrier. For white shoes I'd suggest—oh, forget about it.

The training method used is a combination of modeling and lure and reward. Small dogs were mentioned for shining your shoes, but this trick isn't confined to small dogs. Just be aware that if you are five feet tall and have a mature Great Dane, you will have zero chance of pulling this off. (There is a solution, however. Go to chapter 10 and see how to teach the crawl.)

Stand in front of your seated dog with your legs spread wide apart. Attach a leash to the dog's nonslip collar (not a choke collar: a flat collar). With the leash in your left hand, pass the leash to your right hand, which is behind your right leg, and start pulling the dog through your legs and to your right. As you bring your right hand around with the dog following, pass the leash to your left hand, which is behind your left leg. Three minutes is enough for the first session. We are going to increase it by a minute a session until we reach seven minutes.

Introduce the command *("Shine My Shoes!"* or *"Zigzag!")* on the second session and start using a treat to lure the dog through your legs. You still have the dog on the leash, but you will not be pulling. The dog will be following the treat. Pop an occasional tidbit in his mouth.

The handling and manipulation of the treat requires a certain skill and practice. This is why we had you spend the first session passing the leash around your legs: to teach you to handle the leash. Now it is time to handle the food. You will hold the leash with your middle, fourth and pinky fingers as you hold the lure (tidbit) between your thumb and index finger. When it is time to change hands, you should already have another treat between the other thumb and forefinger so you can simply pass the leash to the other hand. Two minutes into the third session you can eliminate the leash and use the lure alone. You will phase out the treat slowly. If you jolly your dog up when he does this successfully for about twenty seconds, you'll find you will be able to phase out the lure much sooner. (For an explanation of how to do the Moving Zigzag, see *Dog Tricks,* by Haggerty and Benjamin.)

PRESENTATION: Should you own a small and a large dog, teach both of them the trick. In your presentation you will show the smaller dog walking between your legs. Then immediately bring out, say, a Great Pyrenees and ask if the audience feels he could do the Zigzag. The smaller you are, the funnier the question. The punch line is the taller dog *crawling* between your legs in a zigzag fashion.

Front Legs Prancing

"PRANCE!"

Some dogs, when excited, lift their right and left front paws alternately off the ground. Catch that behavior! This expenditure of nervous energy is especially likely to occur when your dog is waiting to be told what to do next and can be put on command. Simply click and treat while saying *"Prance!"* You should be able to recognize when your dog is getting into that mood. Anticipation will get the two of you working in harmony with one another.

ALTERNATE APPROACH: Place your dog in the stand position on a grooming table. Tell him *"Right Paw!" "Left Paw!"* and *"Other Paw!"* in quick succession. If you get movement on both paws, click and treat. The goal is to get continuous prancing of the front feet.

PRESENTATION: You'll find that this trick aids in teaching many others—such as Cross Legs and Patty-Cake. Also, if you'd like your dog to play the piano or operate the computer, this trick is a good place to begin.

THE BREEDS INDEED AND
THE TRICKS THEY NEED

AFFENPINSCHERS, with their cute monkey faces, are great for the Three Monkeys trick—especially if you have three of them.

AFGHAN HOUNDS, a most elegant breed, look even more upscale doing the Be Elegant trick. They can then look over their minions as Serene Royalty.

AIREDALE TERRIERS, as terriers go, are laid back. This is a plus as well as a minus. They would enjoy working on the Seek Back trick.

AKITAS, with their inscrutable expression, look particularly cute doing the Beg trick. If you feel that is too demeaning for your macho Akita, why not teach him the Ride a Motorcycle trick? The question here is, do you want him to ride a Harley or a "rice burner"?

ALAPAHA BLUEBLOOD BULLDOGS are great dogs to teach the Giggle Gaggle trick. They have such a tough image that you may not want to teach them such a cute trick. Maybe you should teach the Cover trick (chapter 10) instead.

ALASKAN MALAMUTES, if you live in the colder sections of the country, are great candidates for the Post the Mail trick. They'll enjoy working in the cold you are trying to avoid.

AMERICAN BULLDOGS are a great deal more agile than

their English cousins. Take advantage of that agility with jumping and scaling tricks.

AMERICAN COCKER SPANIELS are beautiful dogs that deserve a beautiful and helpful trick or two. Pick Up the Room will help you assemble the kid's clothes and give the dog some things to do.

AMERICAN ESKIMO DOGS are so white and pure in color you do not want to teach them those down-and-dirty commands, so forget about On Your Back and Crawl tricks. Switch to some of the more elegant tricks, such as the Cross Legs trick or the cute Beg trick.

AMERICAN PIT BULL TERRIERS are unjustly maligned by many. They are a bit hard-headed but extremely bright and affectionate dogs. They can be taught just about anything. Start with Tug, Digging, Scratch and Jumping tricks.

AMERICAN STAFFORDSHIRE TERRIERS are ideally suited for the Comedy Dead-Dog trick. They have the broad back and keen mind to learn this trick, if you are patient enough in training. Their hard-charging, fun-loving, high activity level makes them a great breed for an array of tricks.

AMERICAN WATER SPANIELS have bright, quick minds that leave them open for all tricks, especially the retrieving ones. Not only is Zigzag a great trick for this breed, but you'll have your shoes shined at the same time.

ANATOLIAN SHEPHERD DOGS have an undeserved fierce reputation as livestock-guarding dogs. Their large size makes cute tricks a real gas, so teach your Anatolian Take a Bow, Balance and Catch and Shake Your Head No.

ARGENTINE DOGOS are big, macho dogs. Walk Tall is an impressive trick with a dog of this size, though it may take a little more time and strength to teach than to a smaller dog.

AUSTRALIAN CATTLE DOGS need a job. Teach them as many of the tricks in the book as possible. You'll both be happier for it.

AUSTRALIAN KELPIES are herding dogs and can be taught Come By, Way to Me, That'll Do and Come to Me.

AUSTRALIAN SHEPHERDS are working fools. Teach them the most difficult tricks and combinations, such as the Post the Mail trick.

AUSTRALIAN TERRIERS will do remarkably well with the Pull Cover and Wake Lucy Up tricks. The kids will love it, and you have one less distasteful task.

BASENJIS are *not* the breed you want to try to teach to vocalize. They are incapable of barking (although I taught one to do it). They "chortle" rather than bark, which makes for some interesting vocal sounds. Lean Left and Lean Right are two tricks that will interest your Basenji and also let you relate to each other better.

BASSET HOUNDS have a penchant for using their noses. Any type of scent discrimination is right up their alley as long as they don't have to stretch out their short little legs. If you want a dog to find drugs in a phone booth, the Basset is your dog.

BEAGLES also enjoy using their noses. They would enjoy finding explosives or drugs in tight little places, such as in the interiors of planes. But you want to leave that to the pros. Better they should find the kids.

BEARDED COLLIES require more grooming than your average dog. You'll want to put them to work. If you are on a farm and have sheep, you have a ready job for them. If you have no sheep, have them do the Collect the Eggs trick. Stick Jumping is good for the city-bound Bearded Collie.

BEDLINGTON TERRIERS look like sheep. They are not as gentle as they look, though, and were used as ratters at one time. Teach them the Bunny Hop trick and you'll keep both your Bedlington and your children busy.

BELGIAN MALINOIS are hyperactive dogs that need a lot of control exercises to slow them down. Balancing tricks will help do this. Try the Balance the Teacup and Saucer trick.

BELGIAN SHEEPDOGS are related to the Malinois, but have a calmer nature. They'd seem to be best suited to the Balance the Teacup and Saucer trick, but they would much prefer herding sheep.

BELGIAN TERVURENS have a sense of humor. I'd suggest teaching some fresh tricks, such as Knock Over the Glass or Kiss My Ass.

BERNESE MOUNTAIN DOGS are so sharp, regal and businesslike that they should all be taught to Play the Piano. Make sure it is a white grand piano. They deserve nothing less than the best.

BICHONS FRISÉS are pristine in grooming and appearance, and they need a suitable trick. No Crawl or Shake, Rattle 'n' Roll tricks here. Teach them the Tour the Mall trick. They'll draw a crowd. Make sure you give them your credit card.

BLACK-AND-TAN COONHOUNDS have great noses and love to use them. While they were bred to hunt raccoons, they'd love to find your misplaced car keys. Teach them the Seek Back trick. They love to vocalize and harmonize with "mountain music."

BLOODHOUNDS are also extremely fond of using their noses. Why not teach them to find lost dogs or, better still, lost children? Trailing lost children is the way they will find them. Bloodhounds will be good at the "OW" sound.

BLUETICK COONHOUNDS generally run in packs, so if you have one, you'll have to make up for his loneliness and desire to hunt hard by inundating him with tricks. Try any of the tricks in chapter 17, followed by the energy-burning chapter 14 tricks.

BORDER COLLIES *must* be taught tricks unless they have a full-time job herding sheep. They can be taught every trick in this book and will love you like crazy if you teach them. If not, you are like the parent of a gifted child who doesn't give the child the advantages of an education.

BORDER TERRIERS have the cutest faces in the world. I would go for cute tricks, such as the Peek trick.

BORZOIS, or RUSSIAN WOLFHOUNDS, certainly look like royalty, and I would suggest royal tricks. Play the Harp would be a great trick, but it isn't in this book, so you'll have to settle for a grand piano. The How Elegant trick and Retrieve the Vodka Bottle should also be taught.

BOUVIER DES FLANDRES, with that tousled coat, may not look impressive, but behind that bushy brow lies the mind of a genius—a placid genius, but a genius nonetheless. They don't *have to* have a job, but they enjoy working. Patty-Cake is a great trick for them.

BOXERS are dynamos, and they enjoy pulling, jumping and

roughhouse tricks. Try the I'm Gonna Catch Ya, Tug and Pull Cover tricks.

BRIARDS are also known as Shepherds of Brie, so if you are a cheese aficionado, this may be the breed for you. Let me give you a trick that isn't in this book. Teach your dog to locate and retrieve cheese by name. Make sure that the cheese is well wrapped and protected. Start off with Brie, then graduate to blue cheese. Before you know it you will be able to impress the American Society of Gourmets.

BRITTANYS are very popular in France, their country of origin, and not without good cause. They are naturals to teach to find lost children via scouting.

BRUSSELS GRIFFONS are as cute as a bug's ear and deserve to do cute tricks. Their pocket size makes them easy to transport. Go for tricks that the dog can do in your arms, such as barking math answers. These tricks are normally taught as you face the dog. After teaching the dog that way, hold him in your arms, still facing you. You will eventually teach the dog to face the audience and give him touch cues to stop the barking.

BULLDOGS are the perfect breed for Shake, Rattle 'n' Roll, Giggle Gaggle and vocalizing the sound *g*. Get Up on the Chair and Paws Up are great for your sourmug.

BULLMASTIFFS should be taught to Pull Cover. As far as vocalizing goes, work on the letters *g* and *o*. The letter *o* can be developed into the "ow" sound by this impressive-looking breed.

BULL TERRIERS are a wonderful breed and loaded with laughs. They have a fabulous sense of humor, and I'd stick with funny stuff. Chase Your Tail and Comedy Dead Dog are but two examples.

BULL TERRIERS (MINIATURE) can learn anything the standard Bull Terrier can—just on a smaller scale. I would rather teach the miniature Back Flips because these take so much strength on your part to teach a larger dog. Always be especially careful with back flips.

CAIRN TERRIERS are another of those cute breeds that revel in the humorous. Do the Hokey-Pokey and On Your Back are two examples.

CANAAN DOGS are a versatile breed from Israel that can be taught Way to Me, Come By, Come in Here and Jumping tricks.

A little Jewish boy, at a dog show, said to his father, "There are English Setters, Australian Shepherds and Irish Terriers, aren't there any Jewish dogs?" His father wisely replied, "Look at the names of the owners."

CANE CORSOS have the size and appearance to frighten anyone. The Watch 'Em and Guard tricks are right up their alley.

CAVALIER KING CHARLES SPANIELS are sweet, cuddly and cute—just like the type of tricks they should be taught. Peek, Say Your Prayers and Take a Bow are a good starting point.

CHESAPEAKE BAY RETRIEVERS will retrieve anything. In honor of their origins, I would have them retrieve crab cakes or other shellfish. It isn't hard to teach them. Read the section on retrieving a steak before starting on the crab cakes. Clams are easy.

CHIHUAHUAS are as small and cute as they come. Most things that you would want them to retrieve are bigger than they are. Make a miniature dumbbell that is just the right size for the Chihuahua.

CHINESE CRESTED DOGS, especially the hairless ones, are truly unique. The tuft of hair makes them look comical. A cute trick would be Get a Tissue. A funny trick for a dog this small would be Guard.

CHINESE SHAR-PEIS have faces that look like unmade beds. Follow that bed theme with an orderly Tuck the Kids (Lucy) In trick. Vocalizing the *w, g* and *o* are easiest for this breed.

CHINOOKS are an obscure sled dog breed that doesn't look like the standard sled pullers. Food Refusal is easy to teach. They look soooo cute, serenely sitting there and turning their heads away from the offered food.

CHOW CHOWS are the breed so great they named it twice. I'd stay away from the Guard trick because the Chow has a reputation for being on the tough side. For Chow public relations, I'd suggest the cute and friendly tricks, such as Sit High and Shake.

CLUMBER SPANIELS are cute in their massiveness. This combination lends itself to body balancing, with tricks such as Sit High and Walk Tall.

COLLIES are another classically beautiful breed. When the Collie's quietly lying down, have him Cross Legs, left over right, then right over left. As the audience applauds, have the Collie get up and Take a Bow.

CURLY-COATED RETRIEVERS, as the name implies, are great retrievers. They'll enjoy any retrieving tricks, but use a bit of imagination. The curly coat on this breed can be brought into the mix if you have an old wig he can retrieve.

DACHSHUNDS, surprisingly enough, can do a great job of sitting high. It looks great because of their long backs. Some of them will put a bit of a curve in their backs to maintain balance.

DALMATIANS are on the cover of this book, and we don't want a spotty trick. With all those spots they lend themselves to the multiple-dog tricks, such as the Three Monkeys or dogs leaping over and crawling under one another. Talk about spots before your eyes!

DANDIE DINMONT TERRIERS are cute to the nth degree. Sneeze and have the Dandie bring you a tissue. Have the phone ring and have it brought to you. Cute and handy makes a great Dandie!

DOBERMAN PINSCHERS undeservedly have that killer reputation. The Doberman's mere presence will protect your property, so you do not have to teach him to Guard. Have your Dobe wake up the children in the morning and tuck them in at night.

DOGUE DE BORDEAUX appear to have the problems of the world on their withers. To capitalize on that expression, give them any of the Three Monkeys commands. You can also have a Dogue do the Back Up Trick, but change the command to "Did you pass gas?" as you shoo him away. The Dogue's expression makes the trick.

ENGLISH COCKER SPANIELS are slightly bigger and require a lot less grooming than their American cousins. Both Cockers do a creditable job of retrieving, and these tricks work well. Vary the objects retrieved to add interest to the performance.

ENGLISH SETTERS are elegant if you have the show type. The really good working, higher-energy dog is the more functional field dog. These great Setters do an excellent job of bringing in the birds, but that trick has not been explained in this book. Let's just have them bring in the newspaper.

ENGLISH SPRINGER SPANIELS are excellent retrievers and

highly animated. Teach them the names of a half-dozen toys. After the dog brings them to you, toss them out and start over again. Boring? Maybe for you, but not him! *Caution!* Some Springers have an aggression problem, so be cautious as to teaching them guarding tricks.

ENGLISH TOY SPANIELS can be carried on your arm and still do many tricks. Vocalizing and verbalizing such words and sentences as "I love you" and "Momma" are a great place to start.

FIELD SPANIELS are few and far between. If you have one, simply teach it to Shake and you'll have the best-trained Field Spaniel on the block.

FILA BRASILEIROS are big dogs with still bigger hearts. A tough dog, in looks and temperament, the Fila doesn't need to be taught the Watch 'Em trick. Instead teach him to Balance an Egg or Balance a Book on his head.

FINNISH SPITZES are as sharp as they look. Once you start teaching jumping it becomes easier and easier. Try Stick Jumping and Arm Jumping after you have taught the dog to jump.

FLAT-COATED RETRIEVERS love to carry things. For laughs, have your dog retrieve intimate undergarments or an egg.

FOXHOUNDS (AMERICAN AND ENGLISH) are two similar breeds that love using their noses. Fox hunting is not included in this book. Although I have taught dogs to hunt *other* animals, on philosophical grounds I no longer will do this. Now, I'm not saying that this hunting is wrong, I just no longer teach it. Why, then, do I teach dogs to find lost people and dogs? Well, I could say that I do it to give the dog some fun. This is certainly fun for Foxhounds, and these are good tricks for your Foxhound. I will train dogs to *hunt* people—especially bad guys. And, as you can see in this book, I will train a dog to *find* not hunt other dogs.

FOX TERRIERS (BOTH SMOOTH-HAIRED AND WIRE-HAIRED) make wonderful trick dogs. While now considered two different breeds, they are identical in temperament. Crazy! A very high activity level makes for a dog that you can teach all sorts of agility and activity tricks, the more difficult the better. Fox Terriers will make their own moves. Teach them to soar through the air and add their own twists and turns.

FRENCH BULLDOGS are the breed designed to do Giggle Gaggle. They're good at vocalizing, particularly the letters *g*, *w* and *o*. I'm Gonna Catch Ya is another trick they love to play.

GERMAN PINSCHERS are Pinschers between the Doberman and Miniature Pinschers in size. The Hold the Dustpan trick will have your German Pinscher helping you. If you want a cute trick, have him imitate a Dobe and tell him *"Watch 'Em!"* If I were to decide to buy three dogs just to do tricks, I'd think about getting one of this breed, a Miniature Pinscher and a Doberman. What fun I'd have with my small, medium and large dogs. I could pretend to shrink them and teach them the Three Monkeys trick. Remember, there is a whole chapter on multiple-dog tricks.

GERMAN SHEPHERDS are the ultimate working breed. They have the versatility to do all sorts of tricks, but because of their reputation as working dogs, some people think that tricks are undignified. If you are of this mind-set, then teach them herding tricks.

GERMAN SHORTHAIRED POINTERS are great versatile bird dogs that are natural retrievers. Since there are no hunting tricks in this book, I recommend going for the retrieving tricks. Retrieving eggs and dimes are a couple of impressive tricks.

GERMAN WIREHAIRED POINTERS are the wirehaired version of the combination hunting dog. They make good combination trick dogs too, if you start them in a variety of tricks. Retrieving, jumping, scent discrimination and guarding tricks are a good start.

GIANT SCHNAUZERS are great working and agility dogs. The more complex and athletic the movement, the better. Here is a larger breed that will help you "invent" new moves.

GLEN OF IMAAL TERRIERS are an obscure, cute, feisty breed that make wonderful trick dogs. Should you be lucky enough to own one, go for variety with such tricks as bringing toys by name and waking the kids up.

GOLDEN RETRIEVERS require no particular tricks. Wonderful, wonderful pets that love children and work, Goldens can do everything. Lean toward tricks with kids (chapter 24). Do the Hokeypokey, Wake the Kids (Lucy) Up, Pick Up the Room and the Bunny Hop are good starting tricks.

GORDON SETTERS are the calmest of the three setter breeds, which is both a plus and a minus. The more placid dog is less likely to get into trouble. The more active dog will learn more tricks than you may ever want. Calm tricks, such as Close Your Eyes and Stick Out Your Tongue, will work.

GREAT DANES are the Apollos among dogs and this makes their fanciers reluctant to teach them tricks. This big breed requires big, impressive tricks, so I'd suggest those tricks that require props, such as Ride a Skateboard, Get on the Internet and Ride a Motorcycle. Danes can vocalize *o, w* and *g*.

GREAT PYRENEES are great! While not great at jumping because of their weight-to-height ratio, when they do jump they are impressive. Hoop jumping is an interesting against-type trick. The March trick is another good one.

GREATER SWISS MOUNTAIN DOGS are another big breed that can be taught to jump despite their size. Start with the simple jumping in and out of a car. Why should you have to wrestle the dog into the car?

GREYHOUNDS love to run, but there are few running tricks. Try Voraus and Right Spin and Left Spin to let your Greyhound run off energy.

HARRIERS, sizewise, are between the Beagle and the Foxhound. Harriers enjoy using their noses, and if you own one, take advantage of this. Teach him to find by name different family members who are hiding throughout the house. To really show off with nonfamily members, teach your Harrier to find the source of the odor that you will label "Stranger." Finding a completely strange person who is hiding is not too difficult. It can be done the first time if your dog is squared away on the names of people in your household.

HAVANESE are cute and cuddly. Shine My Shoes, Wake the Kids (Lucy) Up and 90-Degree Turns are good tricks for this breed.

IBIZAN HOUNDS claim a long history. I first saw them in the late fifties, as stray dogs lounging under carts, hiding from the hot Spanish sun. Their lounging time is over. Put them to work using their noses. See chapter 17.

IRISH SETTERS are a combination of beauty, brains and energy. High energy is always a good quality for trick dogs. It makes them a little tougher to live with, but broadens the range of tricks they can learn quickly. There are Field Irish Setters, as well as the more active Red-and-White Irish Setters. The Retrieving a Steak and Balance an Egg tricks will show off the style of your jaunty Irishman.

IRISH TERRIERS are even wilder Irishmen than the Setters. Sit High on Your Back, Back Flips and retrieve the Irish flag are good starting points for these great trick dogs.

IRISH WATER SPANIELS are the clowns of the spaniel family. Let's try some silly tricks for your dog. Sneeze and have him get you a tissue. Have him do the Bunny Hop, followed by Chase a Light Beam. Then let him Ride a Tricycle.

IRISH WOLFHOUNDS are among the calmer Irishmen. No retrieving steaks, back flips and sitting high on your back. These gentle giants would break your back. The calm, but elegant, Cross Legs would work well here. Lean Left, Lean Right looks great with a towering giant.

ITALIAN GREYHOUNDS love to lounge around. They are great pets, but be careful with the tricks you teach them. If you look at them cross-eyed, they'll break a leg. Close Your Eyes and Be Elegant will not endanger them.

JACK RUSSELL TERRIERS are the ultimate trick dogs: cute, high energy, quick moving, agile and always looking to get into trouble. Harness that energy into doing difficult, active tricks such as Back Flips, flying through hoops and walking on hindquarters.

JAPANESE CHINS are another small breed that you should teach on the table rather than the ground. Later, you will want to graduate to the tricks being done in your arms. Talking tricks are great for this breed. The Chin does a great job vocalizing the *w, o,* and *g*. Make sure you teach your Chin the Giggle Gaggle.

KEESHONDEN (the Dutch plural adds an *en* rather than an *s*) take the cake when it comes to a good, normal pet. You can change all that by teaching your Keeshond any of the tricks in this book. Here is a special trick: Tell your dog to bark once for yes and twice for no. The first question you will ask is, "Are you a Keyes-hound?" to which he'll bark twice for no. The next question: "Are you a Case-hoont?" to which he'll bark once for yes.

Even your dog knows the correct pronunciation of his breed; don't ask him the plural of his breed name unless he can spell.

KERRY BLUE TERRIERS are typical Irishmen and great trick dogs. They have boundless energy and just won't quit when challenged with tough tricks. Give them the toughest, such as leaping buildings in a single bound, Sit High on Your Back, and scaling walls. They'll do it all!

KOMONDOROK is the Hungarian plural of Komondor. The dog's corded coat looks like dreadlocks, so why not have him dance to some Jamaican music? Dance steps you have taught him can become Jamaican simply by changing the music. You'll also change the tune to limbo music. At first he'll walk under the limbo bar, and as it's lowered, you'll give him a *"Crawl!"* command.

KUVASZOK (singular Kuvasz). Another Hungarian breed. This is a singularly great breed. Kavaszok are natural guardians, so you do not have to teach your dog to Watch 'Em. Instead, have him Get the Cellular Phone or Retrieve the TV Remote.

LABRADOR RETRIEVERS are extremely popular because of their versatility as duck dogs and wonderful household pets. Their high activity level and a natural retrieving ability make them outstanding trick dogs. Have your lab bring you everything you need. If you drop your wallet, have him put it in your hand. If you lose your keys, he'd love to find them. Help him enjoy working off that excess energy.

LAKELAND TERRIERS are quick witted, fast and bright. Load them up with tricks, and they'll love you for it. If he gets in your way, use the Excuse Me trick, and move him into a different position with the Get Up on the Chair. After he succeeds, give him a High Five.

LEONBERGERS are a huge breed ideally suited to finding lost people. Now, you don't find too many people disappearing, so you will have to find some other interesting work for your dog to do. Have him use his nose to find lost items if you want useful tricks. Less useful but cute is the Sit-High trick. You can change the name of the trick to Imitate a Bear, if you like.

LHASA APSOS are another great breed to carry around. After you start them on their table work, switch them to the other exercises in your arms. Talking tricks are optimal. On the ground, have them do Shake, Rattle 'n' Roll.

LOEWCHENS are very dear to me. The first one into the United States shared a plane with me in the mid-sixties. They are cute and deserve cute tricks, such as Tell Me a Secret, Peek and Read a Book.

LOUISIANA CATAHOULA (LEOPARD) DOGS are unique in appearance and temperament. I owned them more than forty years ago. Teach them to herd livestock. They are a little too rough to work on sheep. In Texas, they are used to herd horses and beef cattle—not the easiest of livestock. In Louisiana, they hunt the feral hogs, driving them out of the underbrush in the swamps.

MALTESE are pure white bundles of fur well suited for table work before performing in your arms. Math tricks and Tell Me a Secret are good in-your-arms tricks.

MANCHESTER TERRIERS (STANDARD) are really tough terriers that love to be trained and work. Digging is a good trick to teach your Manchester. Then I'd go for jumping and scaling tricks. Dance steps such as the Conga, Bunny Hop and a fast waltz can be added to his repertoire.

MANCHESTER TERRIERS (TOY) are not as rough and tough as their larger brothers, so I would start them on table work, with barking tricks high up on the list. Toy Mans are best at the following: *a, e, x* and *z*. You can develop an entire act with the little dog in your arms. Ask math questions and get answers.

MASTIFFS are huge dogs that appear to be always worried. Cheer your Mastiff up with some fun tricks. A large dog doing cute tricks always causes laughter. Try Raus, Patty-Cake and Peek.

MINIATURE PINSCHERS are as tough as nails, even if they are as small as gnats. I would suggest starting with table work, but this tiny breed is so much tougher than the other toys that they can be trained much as larger dogs. Back Flips, and Ride a Skateboard are right up the Min Pin's alley.

MINIATURE SCHNAUZERS are one of the three different—completely unrelated—Schnauzer sizes. They can be pretty tough and do more derring-do tricks than similar dogs of the same size. Tug, Shine My Shoes and jumping over larger dogs will get your Schnauzer started.

NEOPOLITAN MASTIFFS are a sad-looking breed. Just hearing about their reputation for power and toughness should cheer them up. Now, I think retrieving is a great place to start with all dog tricks. The Neopolitan Mastiff has such a sloppy, wet mouth, with enormous flews, that I am tempted to use that old Italian expression "fogeddaboutit." I'd have one retrieve my rubber boots or rain slicker, but I can't think of anything else. Catch, Head Down, Head Up and Shake Your Head No will produce some wild expressions.

NEWFOUNDLANDS have a reputation for water-rescue work, but that's not covered in this book. We do have a bit on water retrieving, a good area in which to train a Newf. Get him to Retrieve a Fish.

NORFOLK TERRIERS are typical terriers, with a high energy level and a devil-may-care attitude. Digging is a good starting trick, followed by Pirouette, Spin, Right Turn and Left Turn.

NORWEGIAN ELKHOUNDS have great noses. Despite their name, they are not hounds, and you should teach them to scout rather than trail or track. Watch 'Em is also a handy trick.

NORWICH TERRIERS are, like their close relatives the Norfolk Terriers, typical terriers. Teach them the same tricks. Digging, Spin, Pirouette, Right Turn and Left Turn.

NOVA SCOTIA DUCK TOLLING RETRIEVERS are great little dogs and great speakers. Teach Speak and any of the talk tricks. These dogs have been bred for this.

OLD ENGLISH BULLDOGS do well with the letters *g, o,* and *u.* Teach the Giggle Gaggle, Shake Rattle 'n' Roll and Comedy Dead-Dog tricks.

OLD ENGLISH SHEEPDOGS can do a great job of sheep herding. Teach your Old English to respond to Way to Me, Come By, Come In Here, That'll Do, Take Time and Stay.

OTTER HOUNDS don't have too many otters to hunt anymore, so you are better off teaching them to hunt for lost people or lost dogs. This is a breed that should track or trail what they are hunting, rather than scouting.

PAPILLONS are cute, alert, bright toy dogs that can learn a wide range of tricks. As with most toy breeds, start with table work, bearing in mind that your dog can perform many of these tricks in your arms. Talking tricks, Tell Me a Secret and asking your dog Who Do You Love? are good for starters.

PEKINGESE are a massive toy breed that do well vocalizing the letters *g, u* and *w*. Stay away from the really active tricks. The Sit High, Stand High and Stretch tricks work well.

PETITS BASSETS GRIFFONS VENDÉENS have a French pluralization of their name, with an *s* added to each of its four parts. They love using their noses, and if I owned one, I would teach him to do Drug Detection or find lost objects, such as the TV remote and the cordless phone.

PHARAOH HOUNDS are as swift as the wind, and would rather hunt by sight than scent. That doesn't mean that they cannot learn to use their noses. The worst dog in the world has 100,000 times the olfactory acuity of his owner. Teach Be Elegant, Lean Right, Lean Left and—for the heck of it and to prove they have a nose—to find the car keys.

PLOTT HOUNDS have great noses for trailing, but you can use the Plott Hound for more than nose work. Teach your dog to Tuck the Kids (Lucy) In, touch different objects and flop over for a Flea Check.

POINTERS are great bird dogs, with energy and drive. If you are not actively hunting with your Pointer, you can work off that energy with tricks such as Voraus, I'm Gonna Catch Ya, Chase Your Tail and Chase a Light Beam.

POMERANIANS are spunky, perky dogs with handsome coats, and they love to work. Teach retrieving tricks, and find cute little miniatures for them to retrieve. A miniature dumbbell is easy to find. Go the extra step and find or make "standard" items, such as little teeny newspapers and slippers.

POODLES (MINIATURE) are actually the middle-sized Poodle. Although all these varieties of Poodle come from the same breed, you will find temperament differences among them, and thus you should teach them different tricks. Work the Miniature Poodle on retrieving with élan. These tricks can be used to show off to delivery people ("Go get him a tip") or to guests ("Go get him an ash tray").

POODLES (STANDARD) are the greatest. They may look

foppish, particularly in show clips, but they are real dogs that can be taught *anything,* the more difficult the better. Try jumping tricks, scenting tricks, guarding tricks—anything and everything!

POODLES (TOY) This breed's tiny size means that your approach to training should be different. Start with table work. With your dog on the table, you can teach Lean Right and Lean Left. Speaking and talking tricks are great for when your Poodle is in your arms.

PORTUGUESE WATER DOGS are wonderful retrievers. Teach your dog the names of different objects. As a play on names, have your dog retrieve a bucket of water. Water is very heavy, so take this into consideration when training. Miniature buckets can be found at hardware or paint stores, or try a child's sand pail.

PUGS are big dogs in a little package. Talking tricks should be worked on; the Pug vocalizes *o, u, g* and *w.* Giggle Gaggle followed by I'm Gonna Catch Ya are a good starting routine.

PULIK is the plural of Puli. (Pulik are Hungarian.) If your Puli has a corded coat, I would suggest teaching Crawl and Shine My Shoes to start. Use the Crawl exercise to have your dreadlocked dog go under the limbo bar as it is lowered (to the appropriate music).

RAT TERRIERS have that high energy level desired in trick dogs. Soaring, leaping and jumping tricks are great. Walk on Your Forequarters is a difficult but fun trick that can be found in *Dog Tricks,* by Captain A. Haggerty and Carol Benjamin.

REDBONE COONHOUNDS have a wonderful nose and it is only fair to let them use it. Teach them to find something or someone. The breed loves to vocalize, and with diligent work, you can teach them to say words.

RHODESIAN RIDGEBACKS were bred to hunt lions, but they are not as fierce as that occupation implies. They love to use their noses, and you can start off working and entertaining your dog by having him find and retrieve by name toys hidden around the house. Behind the couch cushions is a good hiding place, but insist he retrieve the toy you have named, because you will be hiding more and more toys as he gets the idea.

ROTTWEILERS are real tough guys. Because of their reputation and appearance, it isn't necessary to teach them guarding tricks. Just have them stay by an object and *no one* will attempt to steal it. For public-relations purposes, teach your Rottweiler cute tricks, such as Sit High and Balance and Catch.

SAINT BERNARDS are known as gentle giants that have rescued countless snow-stranded travelers. Thus, you know that your Saint will be ideally suited to find lost people. Do you know the brandy cask they carry on their collars? Well, buy one of those casks and have your Saint retrieve it.

SALUKIS are an elegant sight hound breed. Give them a chance to run and move fast with the Send-Away or Voraus trick and retrieving tricks. Send your Saluki on long-distance retrieves.

SAMOYEDS are spiffy white longhaired dogs that have that needed high energy. Owners are so busy trying to slow their dogs down they don't have time to teach them tricks. Actually, some good control tricks, such as Stretch, Dead Dog and Comedy Dead Dog, will slow your Sammy down considerably.

SCHIPPERKES are great vocalizers. The type of barking they do is best for counting and math tricks. But once you have that control over the individual barks, it is time to change them into words. Schipperkes are better at *y, x, r* and short *a* than most breeds.

SCOTTISH DEERHOUNDS are a regal giant greyhound breed that enjoys doing two contradictory things: running and lounging. Train your Deerhound to do what the breed enjoys most: Be elegant, Close Your Eyes, Stick Out Your Tongue and long-distance retrieves. You'll both be happy for it.

SCOTTISH TERRIERS are often pugnacious around other dogs. If you are going to add another dog to your household, might I suggest the West Highland White Terrier. That way you will have a living ad for Black and White Scotch. These two breeds in a multidog household can produce funny tricks. Try tricks such as Crawl Under, Jump Over and Clean Ears.

SEALYHAM TERRIERS are short-legged terriers with a lot of energy. How do you control your Sealy's energy? It's all in the book. Tire him out with the tricks in chapter 14. Teach him control tricks, such as Honoring, and increase your control by teaching additional tricks.

SHETLAND SHEEPDOGS aren't as close to being used for actual herding as the Border Collie. The Sheltie's herding background does lend itself to herding tricks though. You can always tell your Sheltie to do a Lassie imitation.

SHIBA INU are independent little devils, and they can be controlled by teaching some of the easier tricks. Their foxlike appearance lends itself to a great trick based on a Yiddish expression for something impossible: "Like a fox would carry a rifle?" (said with a rising intonation). Have your Shiba carry a toy rifle and you have the fox incarnate.

SHIH TZUS are cute, willful and feisty, all of which, surprisingly enough, make for a good trick dog. If you are fortunate enough to own one (or be owned by one), trick training will enable you to gain control while giving the little dog pleasure. Try Tug, Beg, Pirouette and I'm Gonna Catch Ya. In talking, concentrate on the *g, u* and *o.*

SIBERIAN HUSKIES are sled dogs. Should you own one, teach the tricks that will give your dog a maximum amount of exercise with a minimum amount of effort on your part. You'll have no trouble teaching him the Digging trick. He'd rather tug than retrieve.

SILKY TERRIERS are wonderful dogs with a lot of personality. That personality will shine through if you pick the right tricks. Peek, Flea Check, See No Evil and Get Up on the Chair are but a few.

SLOUGHIS love to run, and for this reason, if I owned one, I'd do a lot of Send-Aways and long-distance retrieves. Once your Sloughi is working well on the long retrieves, start having him retrieve by name.

SOFT-COATED WHEATEN TERRIERS are the perfect trick and show-business dogs. Cute and fluffy, they can change appearance with their flexible hairdos. Their teddy-bear look is great for the Beg trick. Their color is excellent for photographic work, and on top of all that, they have the crazy, high energy, terrier personality that lends itself to the widest variety of tricks. Try Do the Hokeypokey, retrieving an egg, Say Your Prayers and, yes, even Climb Mount Everest.

SPANISH MASTIFFS are natural guardians, and their size may terrorize some people. Cute tricks can offset people's fear. Speak No Evil, High Five, Peek, Lean Left and Lean Right can make them seem friendlier.

SPINONI ITALIANIS are Italian hunting dogs, so why not add a little Italian flavor to this goombah's repertoire. You are preparing dinner for some houseguests who have agreed to help you. Your dog "Vito" is a good retriever and has learned the names of many different items. As the water is boiling, why not tell Vito to get the pasta? When he brings out the box, non-chalantly pop the pasta into the pot and say nothing. Now, you are not a gourmet chef, so when the pasta is nearly ready, tell Vito to get the tomato sauce. He'll go to the pantry and bring out the jar of ready-made sauce. As your guests sit down, go to the refrigerator and bring out the prepared salad. As you serve the salad to your guests, say, "Vito tossed it earlier today."

STAFFORDSHIRE BULL TERRIERS are truly a great breed. They are both tough and cute at the same time. Don't let their stocky shape fool you. They are very agile. I'd suggest teaching your dog to Jump Rope and Retrieve an Irretrievable Object. He'll enjoy the challenge.

STANDARD SCHNAUZERS are bright, active and they enjoy learning, although they may show some resistance to training initially. Hide-and-Seek with your children, Retrieve a Fish and Hold the Dustpan are good tricks.

SUSSEX SPANIELS with their long bodies are ideal to teach the Stationary Zigzag, followed by the Moving Zigzag (see *Dog Tricks,* by Haggerty and Benjamin). If you teach your Sussex to sit high, he may also have a zigzag in his spine.

SWINFORD BAN DOGS were developed by my good friend the late Dr. John Swinford. He developed an absolutely ferocious guard dog, and if you own one, it is up to you to make this breed more acceptable. Go for the cute and friendly tricks. Shake—Right Paw, Left Paw, The Other Paw; Sit High and Peek. You get the idea.

TIBETAN MASTIFFS were never as large as Youatt described them 150 years ago. Chase Your Tail, Retrieve from Underwater and Tell Me a Secret will work with this breed.

TIBETAN SPANIELS are as cute as buttons, so for laughs I would teach Object Guarding and Watch 'Em.

TIBETAN TERRIERS are quick, bright dogs that will pick up tricks rapidly. Teach them to Back Up, Scratch and Chase Your Tail.

TOSAS are another breed that needs some positive publicity with cute-trick training. Wipe Your Mouth, Say Your Prayers and Balance and Catch Blindfolded will help the breed's reputation.

TOY FOX TERRIERS have all the feistiness and high energy of the full-sized Fox Terrier. You can do great tricks with this breed. If you are willing to put in the work, try Back Flips. You need tricks that will run off your AmerToy's energy. Spin and Reverse Spin will help.

TREEING WALKERS are wonderful coonhounds, and there are those who claim they shouldn't be house pets. If you are enough of an individualist to get one of these dogs, the naysayers will not discourage you. These hounds can be taught anything any other breed can be taught, and if you want them to talk, try using the letters *o, w* and *u.*

VIZSLAS are the only Hungarian breed that doesn't take the Hungarian plural in this country. This is probably because simply adding a *k* is not sufficient. An accent mark must then be added to the *a.* This is the sweetest breed. The best trick for them, the one they enjoy the most, is sit on the couch and be petted. Teach your Vizsla tricks where you can do a lot of petting. On Your Back, Ear Check and Tooth Check are good.

WEIMARANERS are a very active breed, and teaching a good repertoire of tricks will make life more enjoyable for both you and your dog.

WELSH CORGIS (CARDIGAN) are little in height, but they can play with the big dogs. You can teach them the herding tricks, but they are more drovers than herders. In other words they are best for driving stock to market. They are referred to as the Corgi with the tail.

WELSH CORGIS (PEMBROKE) are cute, bright, agile trick dogs. In addition to teaching them herding tricks, have your Corgi Get a Cold One and Beg.

WELSH SPRINGER SPANIELS are nice, solid pets that will be overjoyed if you show them some tricks. Have your Welsh Springer tuck the kids in at night and then wake them up in the morning.

WELSH TERRIERS are referred to as Miniature Airedales,

and they can do everything that breed can do, particularly the jumping tricks.

WEST HIGHLAND WHITE TERRIERS are a great match for the previously mentioned Scottish Terriers. Why not take your Westie for a walk in the woods and teach him to retrieve? Start him off retrieving a fish out of the pond.

WHIPPETS love to race around the house, so start with I'm Gonna Catch Ya trick. They love to chase moving objects. You can use this to motivate your dog to retrieve.

WIREHAIRED POINTING GRIFFONS aren't common, but they are fun. Retrieving tricks are on the top of the list. Using your imagination as to what to retrieve will add a great deal to the trick. Ultimately you'll have him retrieving a dime or a steak.

YORKSHIRE TERRIERS are cute and tough little guys. You can teach your Yorkie to Watch 'Em with ease, because he'll probably want to attack every big dog that comes down the street. Start your Yorkie with table work and graduate him to working in your arms. Your Yorkie will gravitate toward the *a*, *o* and *u* sounds.

XOLOITZCUINTLIS, or Mexican Hairlesses, deserve a place here because everyone knows what they are but no one has seen one. If you have a Xolo, his rarity deserves a rare trick, the Back Flip. It is easier to teach this trick to the Miniature rather than the Standard Xolo.

A closing word: Don't restrict your dog's enjoyment to the tricks suggested for the individual breed. Go wild!

An extended index of this book will be on www.Haggerty-Dog.com.

Would you like a picture of your dog doing one of these tricks on the Web site?

INDEX

Commands are indexed in *italics* with exclamation marks.

Index

Index